LONG WALKS WITH LITTLE PEOPLE

LONG WALKS with LITTLE PEOPLE
A GAME- FISHING FAMILY
BRUCE SANDISON

Illustrations by Ann Rhodes

MAINSTREAM
PUBLISHING

Edinburgh and London

First published in Great Britain 1991, by
MAINSTREAM PUBLISHING COMPANY (EDINBURGH) LTD
7 Albany Street
Edinburgh EH1 3UG

British Library Cataloguing in Publication Data
Sandison, Bruce
 Long Walks with Little People : A Game-Fishing Family.
 1. Angling
 I. Title
 799.12
 ISBN 1–85158–460–9

Illustrations by Ann Rhodes

OTHER BOOKS BY BRUCE SANDISON

The Trout Lochs of Scotland
The Sporting Gentleman's Gentleman
The Hill Walkers Guide to Scotland
Game Fishing in Scotland
Tales of the Loch
The Heather Isles

Typeset in Linotron Plantin 11/12pt by
Input Typesetting Ltd, London
Printed in Great Britain by Butler and Tanner, Frome, Somerset

This book is for
ANN
with all my love,
and for the members of the
Sandison Family Fishing Association –
Blair and Barbara
Brodie Telford and Fearn Elizabeth
Lewis-Ann and Michael
Charles and Eilidh
and Jean

Your Angling Horoscope

The future is all in our stars! Your personal angling horoscope will be found by locating the appropriate zodiac sign at the beginning of each chapter – starting with Aries, 21 March to 20 April, and ending with Pisces, 20 February to March 20.

These horoscopes are an historical, piscatorial *first*, specially prepared for game fishermen and cast by the world famous angler/astrologer, Ecurbykon Nosidnasopolous. Sit back, relax with a comforting dram and discover what next season has in store for you! Get ready to be surprised, astonished, terrified, uplifted, fascinated, delighted, intrigued, mystified, baffled, bewitched, bothered and bewildered. Learn the hidden secrets of your angling future in this exclusive, individual forecast for fishermen.

Important Publisher's Note

The Publisher takes no responsibility for either the content or the accuracy of these so-called 'Horrorscopes'. You have only yourself to blame if you believe a single word of them. You have been warned!

Contents

The expert in action

Introduction

Few tasks in life are more rewarding and satisfying than bringing up a family – at least, that's what my wife, Ann, keeps telling me; and although our eldest three children have now left, our youngest daughter, Jean, is still with us. No doubt in due course, she too will leave home to pursue her own life in her own way, and an era will end.

My family have given me more pleasure and happiness than I can ever hope to repay, and this book is my way of saying thank you. *Long Walks with Little People* recounts some of the trials and tribulations of our growing up together over the past three decades – not only during our many fishing expeditions, but recounting many other incidents along the way as well.

The book is loosely based upon articles that have appeared in a number of angling magazines and I would like to thank my friends Roy Eaton, David Goodchild, Mark Bowler and Sandy Leventon, for their support in these publications. May all their trout be huge. And I would also like to thank the other friends mentioned throughout the text for their company on loch and river.

I would particularly like to thank my wife for agreeing to provide the illustrations for this book, which is as much hers as it is mine. Without her constant support and encouragement *Long Walks with Little People* could never have been written. Her delightful drawings say far more than my words ever can.

And I hope that the members of the Sandison Family Fishing Association enjoy this account of our experiences, and if I have got one or two things slightly wrong I trust that they will forgive me. The next time we go fishing I promise to let them catch more fish than I do. And if they believe that, then they will believe anything!

Ruther House
December 1990

Teach Them Fly-Fishing
and Stay Sane

ARIES
21 MARCH TO 20 APRIL

This year marks a major turning point for the good in your thirty-year fishing career, and you can look forward to a happy season ahead. You will have several opportunities to branch out in new directions and to intensify your fishing activities. No longer will you have to survive as an angler on the memories of a single triumph – the 2lb trout you foul-hooked when you were ten years old. This season, you will catch another fish. Although you may not have the Walton touch, you can now stop worrying about being called the world's greatest duffer.

April will be the month when you learn to cast for at least ten minutes without getting fankled; when you will develop important new techniques, such as pulling on waders without falling over; acquire new skills in untangling leaders and retrieving flies from the back of your neck.

Your movements will be less restricted now that you have completely recovered from that little accident on the moor, and learning to map-read should ensure that you will not require the services of a mountain rescue team to get safely back to the car. Make the most of these opportunities, but maintain your private medical insurance policy.

Long familiar relationships could come to an end and everything to do with domestic and personal matters looks extremely promising. But be careful not to go to extremes in seeking to find the solution to a personal problem. Remember that not everyone enjoys fishing and that wives have a right to a life of their own. Divorce proceedings can be costly and it is far better to part friends than enemies.

Perhaps it is time to enter into a new, loving relationship. However, beware of your little foibles. You already have more than enough and many people consider large families to be anti-social and environmentally unfriendly. Try to make sure that your new partner is an angler, mechanically minded, a good orienteerer and fly-tier, medically qualified and possibly SAS trained. Above all, understanding.

Think confidently about boats, oars, and outboard motors. They do not always have to run aground, slip from rollocks, or fall over the stern. This season you will remember to tie the drogue line to a thwart before throwing the drogue overboard. Write to your insurance company and tell them their worries are over. You are a new, inspired, self-assured man.

This could also be the year when you master the art of fishing with more than one fly on the leader. Start with two, then progress confidently until you can manage three. Do not be afraid to take risks. The future looks bright, providing you remember that you should still wear your glasses.

Lively influences surround you. You will quickly notice that earlier aggravations are disappearing fast, along with much of your prized fishing tackle. Take firm action to protect your interests. Banish the family from the rod room and double-lock the door. Relationships with others appear to be on a much sounder footing, and this happy state will continue as long as you refrain from giving them spurious, unwelcome advice. Failure to attract a new fishing partner should not depress you. Given time, you will learn to accept the fact that fishing alone can be just as rewarding as fishing with so-called friends.

MOST OF US have at least one little quirk or foible. The mistake I made was having not one, but four. Still, nobody forced them upon me, so I only have myself to blame. And Ann. She had quite a lot to do with it.

We have been blessed with a huge son, Blair, now married, aged twenty-nine, Lewis-Ann, a devastatingly beautiful daughter, also married and aged twenty-seven, mad-cap, garrulous Charles, twenty-one, engaged, and a student at Glasgow School of Art, and last, but not least, Jean, a sixteen-year-old whirlwind catering student. For the best part of three decades we have been hard at work keeping them fit, healthy, happy and amused.

The last item, 'amused', could have been the most difficult had it not been for the fact that game fishing has always been one of my principal pastimes, and that I had the good sense to marry a girl similarly afflicted. Ann and I both started fishing when we were fourteen years old. We discovered this fact within minutes of our first meeting. Fisherpersons are like that. It takes one to know one. I had recently returned from the army, and a friend with whom I had served invited me to make up a foursome with himself, his girl friend and her friend – both unknown quantities.

I knocked on Ann's front door for the first time in May 1960, somewhat nervous and wondering what she would be like, and was greeted by a bright smile and a happy hello. We had a super evening at the old Maybury Hotel at Corstorphine, and arranged to meet again. That was thirty years ago, during which time we have acquired our foibles.

Ann was a student then, studying dentistry at Edinburgh University and, as important exams loomed, we used to pack the car and head for the Tweed; she to study by the murmuring banks of Manor Water whilst I caught supper – or not, as was most often the case.

13

Some days, if the books were proving difficult, Ann would grab a rod and show me how to do it.

'Come on, Bruce, move over and watch an expert at work.'

She invariably caught a fish or two and then retired to her texts, leaving me feeling rather foolish. But I generally managed to even the score, by fair means or foul.

'Did you notice the beavers have been busy, Ann?' I asked her one evening.

'Beavers?' she replied, suspiciously. 'You don't get beavers in Scotland, Bruce. Perhaps in the Macaroon Mountains, but definitely not Scotland.'

'Oh yes you do. They introduced them to Manor Water a few years ago and they are doing splendidly. Come and I'll show you.' I had noticed earlier that a number of saplings had been felled and, for some reason, the stumps of the slender trees had been left looking like badly sharpened pencils. 'There you are, see,' I announced triumphantly, 'they're building a dam further upstream. Why don't you go and have a look whilst I have a last cast or two. It's about five hundred yards, but be careful not to frighten them.'

Ann disappeared up the river bank, intent upon discovering the beavers hard at work on their dam. An hour later she returned, furious and red-faced – and has never forgiven me. Still, it has been useful. Whenever Ann claims to have seen a rare bird or animal I respond: 'Are you sure, dear? Perhaps it might have been a beaver.'

There seemed to be more time in those days; time to listen to music, talk and, most important of all, time to fish. Serious disagreements centred around fishing methods. Should one use worms? Ann was an all-round angler, ready to try different methods. I was a bigoted purist who would only countenance fly-fishing, and was equally bigoted about music. I was besotted with Beethoven: she valued Mozart, and hated comparisons.

Edinburgh is an excellent angling centre, and we spent many happy hours fishing Lyne Water, the Tweed, Portmore Loch and Gladhouse, with sorties to Loch Leven and the glorious Tay. Holidays were generally spent somewhere north, fishing Speyside, Sutherland or Orkney.

We both loved angling and the opportunity it provided to escape from the realities of life, even if only briefly. There are some things that can only be said, or understood, waist-deep in water, or halfway up a mountainside. Catching fish is a bonus, but not really important. Consequently, from an early age our

14

brood were introduced to the gentle art of fly-fishing with a thoroughness that would have elicited the highest praise from at least half the Chinese nation: who are no mean slouches when it comes to indoctrination. Nor have I any regrets. It smoothed many adolescent growing pains and gave the family a sense of unity which has stood us in good stead over the years – or 'steed', as Lewis-Ann used to say when she was little.

Lewis-Ann frequently gets the pronunciation of words hilariously wrong. Like her father. I still remember my feeling of absolute shame and embarrassment when I announced grandly to Ann and her friends, before we were married, that I had flown over the Macaroon Mountains in East Africa. They collapsed with laughter. Lewis-Ann suffers similarly. Her classic was a private recitation of the poem, 'The Burial of Sir John Moore at Corunna', now firmly embedded in Sandison family folklore. Lewis had to learn the first verse for school and, striking a suitably dramatic pose, she declaimed: 'The Burrial of Sir John Moore at Coroon. We buried him darkly, at dead of night . . .'

The rivalries engendered between our children whilst they were growing up were channelled into a useful and absorbing activity – angling – and in so doing, they developed a proper respect for wildlife and the countryside, encouraged during our frequent long walks in the hills. Therefore, the earlier you begin brainwashing – sorry, teaching – your children to fish, the better. Teaching children to fish is far more important than putting money in the bank for them. Money comes and goes, but a love of fishing gives a lifetime's pleasure.

Blair was introduced to fly-fishing on Orkney at the age of five, when we stayed in a caravan on the shores of Loch Boardhouse. Lewis-Ann first picked up a trout rod, grudgingly, in Sutherland. She said that she would show us how to do it. We stood laughing, but she caught a fish. Charles caught his first trout on Loch Sletill in East Sutherland, in the days before the Flow Country was ravaged by factory tree-farming. He was eight at the time and had enjoyed the walk out from Forsinain Farm – particularly the moment when his mother disappeared up to her waist in a peat bog. Charles rescued her.

Before the landscape was ruined by Fountain Forestry, Sletill was our favourite loch. We fished it over a period of ten years and, in all that time, never met another soul. There was always a black-throated diver waiting to greet us; golden plover and

greenshank sang to us all day; and hen harrier hunted overhead.
Sletill was one of Scotland's 'special places'.

I am sure that Charles imagined that all he had to do was to
cast his flies upon the water and, instantly, a fish would grab.
So, after two fishless hours, he was showing distinct signs of
stress – banging the boat, shouting at the water, complaining
that I had given him the wrong flies. Charles never suffers in
silence. But I could see that it was only a matter of time. He
was casting perfectly (having been taught by me) and I wondered
how he would react when the moment came. In the midst of
yet another volley of cursing, a super trout grabbed his tail fly,
a Silver Butcher, and almost wrenched the rod from his hands.
Charlie's face twisted into a grimace of unadulterated furiosity.
His glasses steamed up. He was concentrating. The fish shot
off, sending the reel screeching, and leapt spectacularly. Ann
and I kept our fingers crossed. If Charles lost the trout, there
would be a riot. He struggled on, trying to bring the fish to the
boat, but the longer the fight lasted, the more chance there was
of the fish escaping. As it sped past the boat for the tenth time,
I plunged the landing-net into the water . . . and the fish swam
straight in.

'There you are, son! Well done! Your first trout!'

Jean was only two when we first dragged her off into the hills
to Loch Eaglaise Mor, south of Melvich. Getting to the Eaglaise
is one of the hardest of our local hikes, a mile and a half over a
soggy moor, where every step sinks up to the ankles in marshy
ground.

Jean didn't mind. She was on her big brother's shoulders,
steering him by the ears, screaming with delight. The way over
the moor was marked by broken wooden posts, and I saw Blair
pause for a rest by one of the markers and ease Jean to the
ground, rubbing his aching back. The ungrateful little beast set
up an enormous roar, demanding to be hoisted aloft again,
immediately; and, silhouetted against the skyline, I saw Jean
aim a vicious kick at her brother's shins to make him obey. Jean
has always been a very determined young lady. Blair hoisted her
aloft instantly.

One of our happiest trips was to Lochs Tulachan and Sand
in Caithness, in 1975; three miles south from the road end at
Loch More. Because of the distance involved we decided to
camp out for a few days at a ruined shooting lodge close to the
shores of Tulachan. We obtained permission to do so from the
Ulbster Arms Hotel in Halkirk and set off in high spirits. Or,

16

to be truthful, Ann and Lewis-Ann did. They nobly offered to make the first trip out with some of the gear whilst Blair and I Jean-minded and fished nearby Loch Meadie. No point in wasting good fishing time, Blair and I had argued. The following day, we all walked out.

There was a good track for the first part of the way, but it quickly degenerated into a soggy stumble. However, with Jean perched proudly on Blair's shoulders and Charles asking why I couldn't provide the same service for him, we eventually made it.

The lodge stood about one hundred yards from the water's edge and was in a derelict condition, but, with a little effort, we made the main room habitable. The most difficult part was persuading the sheep that it was time for them to go. Any door the slightest bit open instantly resulted in half-a-dozen lazy-eyed ewes glaring unblinkingly at what they obviously considered to be intruders. But apart from a few semi-wild ponies, our companions were red deer, peregrine, Arctic skua, whooper swan, red-throated diver and a curious otter. Tulachan gave us super sport with brightly marked, lively little brown trout, providing breakfast fit for a king.

The day we visited Loch Sand, the sky opened and it poured with rain. And to keep the rain company the wind howled at gale force. Undaunted, we struggled across the wet moor and huddled in the shelter of an overhanging bank at the south end of the loch, close to the inlet burn. Determined to show willing, I reached for my trout rod, intent upon a few casts. I had been more than particular in selecting the flies. All guaranteed to catch fish. My prize selection. The rod had gone. At the far end of the loch, Lewis-Ann was busy catching fish, regardless of the weather.

Eventually the rain stopped and we fished on until supper-time, fighting our way back over the heather against the unrelenting force of the wind. Poor Charles was suffering, and I had to help him along over the last few hundred yards, with frequent rest stops and endless encouragement.

Sitting in the comparative shelter of the lodge, Charles quickly regained his composure and claimed that he hadn't really needed any help at all.

'I'm all right,' he said, 'a little bit of wind can't hurt me. Look!' He stepped out of the lea of the building and was almost instantly blown to the ground. I dragged him back to safety.

Charles has always been the eternal optimist, utterly fearless.

A little bit of wind can't hurt me

I can recall my first, trembling attempts to ride a two-wheeler bike, terrified that I would fall off. When we presented Charles with his, he leapt aboard and set off down the garden path like an arrow.

'Rinky dinky do!' we heard him shout with joy. Then crash, as both bike and Charlie hit the deck. He struggled to his feet.

'Rinky dinky do!' Crash.

'Rinky dinky do!' Crash. I can still hear the shouts and bangs, as they faded into the distance and Charles disappeared from sight, but he came back riding the bike like an expert.

We spent three wonderful days at Tulachan and, in the evenings, in front of a warm fire with a comforting dram, Ann and I surveyed our handiwork, lying in a neat, sleeping-bag-filled row – and thought that we hadn't done too badly after all.

Over the years I have learned to live with the fact that Ann always catches more fish than I do; or, if I catch more than her, then she invariably lands a monster. My worst moment came a couple of years ago when we were fishing Loch Seilge (pronounced 'Shallag') a few miles south from Melvich in Strath Halladale.

It was a very windy day and I had to spend most of my time rowing and holding the boat on to the drift. At least that was my excuse. In between times, I was kept busy either landing Ann's fish, or unfankling her cast. By lunch-time I was running out of patience. A particularly vicious gust had fankled Ann's cast, yet again, and as she sat happily sipping coffee in the stern of the boat, I wrestled with the flies with one hand, trying to keep the boat off the rocks with the other. Sort of.

When the cast was in order, I handed her the rod. She cast – and instantly hooked a 2lb 4oz trout. During the course of the day, in spite of the fact that we were fishing with exactly the same patterns of flies, she hooked and landed twelve fish, retaining four weighing around 6lb 8oz. I never rose a single trout.

However, as far as the children are concerned, provided I take home a heavier basket than my offspring, then all is well. Honour satisfied. My position as the ultimate arbiter of all things piscatorial secure. I know that they can now all swim further, run faster, climb higher, walk more rapidly than me. So they should. That my pupils at chess and bridge now teach me tricks I never even dreamed of; that their knowledge of art, literature, music, mathematics and all things academic is far superior to mine, I know, because they tell me so; and Blair frequently gives practical demonstrations.

I taught Blair to play chess when he was about nine years old and he found an instant affinity with the game. A constant puzzle. Blair likes puzzles. Within a few years I realised that I no longer had to worry about trying to let him win. I was losing regularly, and have been doing so ever since. No matter how hard I try, books, computer-chess programmes, when we sit down at the board, I only have to take one look at his face and I know that I am going to lose yet again. Tragically, the same applies to darts, snooker, billiards and bridge. Even when fishing, Blair occasionally gives me lessons that I should have learned long, long ago; such as returning foul-hooked fish. I generally do but, at times, particularly when it is a large fish, although the spirit may be willing the flesh is sometimes weak.

Ann, Blair and I were fishing Loch Caladail in north-west Sutherland, one of the famous Durness limestone lochs, and I had done surprisingly well, taking three nice fish before either of my companions had touched so much as a snout.

'Gets boring, you know,' I gloated, 'having to do all the work. When are you pair going to start making a contribution? Or is that beyond your abilities? Of course, this is expert's water. You really have to know what you are doing to catch fish here. No place for beginners.'

At that moment Blair hooked a beauty. It slashed at the flies and set off like an express train pulling about twenty yards of line out before Blair managed to bring it under control. Even then the fish refused to be tamed and roared off again, leaping wildly along the way.

'Gosh, Blair,' I exclaimed, 'that was lucky! It must be a monster to fight as strongly as that. For goodness sake don't lose him. Keep the rod up.'

'Shut up and mind the oars!' roared Blair, struggling with the fish which showed no sign of tiring.

By this time the boat had been blown almost on to the north shore by the high bank that overlooks the loch, so I let the boat ground gently whilst the fight raged on. At last Blair managed to bring the big trout to the net, and all became clear.

It was a big trout, and must have weighed in the order of 4lb; a typical Caladail fish, utterly perfect in every respect. Indeed, *probably one for the glass case*. But it had been foul hooked. The fly had caught the flank of the fish as it splashed at the cast and consequently it had fought like a trout of twice its weight.

Blair removed the fly and I handed him the priest:

'Go on, son, knock it on the head. It's a beauty,' I urged. Ann agreed, but Blair had other ideas. He placed the big trout in the water, cradled in his hands.

'I don't think so, Dad. Let it live to fight another day.'

The fish recovered and swam off, back into the clear waters of the loch; and I blushed.

The others are just as bad. Lewis-Ann constantly baffles me with the convoluted logic of her philosophical arguments, which I never understand or win, and Charles gives me endless lectures on the 'real meaning of art', usually ending up with him stamping off, crossly muttering that it's like trying to speak to a brick wall. Jean I have never been able to do anything with anyway, and probably never will. I simply agree with everything she says, regardless.

But from time to time I do remind them of their fallibility, generally when I suspect that it will do most damage to their egos. Such as Charles, crossing the Forth Road Bridge thrice in the space of fifteen minutes. Now that's artistic, I tell him sarcastically. He was travelling south with his betrothed, and pulled in for petrol on the Edinburgh side. Talking nineteen to the dozen, they unaccountably found themselves back on the approach road, heading north. And crossed the bridge again. Several miles up the M90, they turned south once more and crossed the bridge for the third time. One pound twenty and a very red face.

Or Lewis-Ann, driving home to Northumberland from

Caithness with Charlie as a passenger. They stopped at the Little Chef near Killiecrankie and had a meal before resuming their journey. After half an hour, Charles turned to his sister and inquired politely: 'Lewis, shouldn't we be going south, towards Edinburgh?'

'Shut up, Charlie, of course we are.'

'Well why did that signpost back there say "Inverness and the North"?'

Charles, on the other hand, can always be brought to heel by mentioning the alphabet. Not so many years ago we were sitting after supper and, as a matter of interest, I asked my son how many days there were in the year.

'You mean in every month?' he asked, hesitatingly.

'Come on Charles, everyone knows how many days there are in the year!'

Charles began trying to add them up, month by month, and eventually, after a massive burst of mathematics, arrived at the conclusion that there were 352. He tried again and got 365.

'Well done, Charles,' I exclaimed encouragingly, 'but how many are there in a leap year?'

There followed a long explanation about February and 366 days until he seemed to understand. Wickedly, I then asked: 'And how many letters are there in the alphabet, Charles?'

He paused and began reciting and counting. With the satisfied smile of one who knows that he is right, Charlie announced proudly: 'Twenty-six.'

'Well done Charlie! Now, how many letters are there in the alphabet in a leap year?'

Charlie paused, then asked, quizzically: 'Twenty-seven?'

When the chips are down and my back is against the wall, I tell these stories with relish. Just as long as I can catch fish when they don't is all I ask, but the trouble is that I seem to have done the teaching bit rather too well, and my paramount position is coming under ever-increasing pressure from the rest of the tribe. They have all developed into really skilful anglers – or, as I quickly remind them when they out-fish me, 'lucky' ones.

Charles is worst. Regardless of conditions, Charles comes home with a fish. And a wet friend. It used to be Andrew, one of the gang whom Charles had trained to wade out and land anything he caught.

I once sent them to a tiny loch in the hills to the south of Wick, the Loch of Warehouse, happy in the belief that they would at least get some exercise, if not catch fish. Charles came back with a trout weighing 1lb 8oz. Andrew was wet to the waist. Their next expedition was to Loch Stemster. Charles brought back two fish, one weighing nearly 2lb and an excellent trout for this little loch. Andrew was wet to the waist. However, Charlie's finest hour came when fishing Beat 1 on the Thurso River. He hooked a good salmon but, after several minutes and a splendid fight, he lost it. Andrew was soaked to the skin. His parents banned him from further fishing expeditions with Charles.

The only time I ever remember Charles returning fishless was when he brow-beat his gang into an all-night camping and fishing expedition to Loch Toftingall, eight miles from our home at Watten in Caithness. Ann and I readily agreed. The Loch is very shallow, averaging four feet deep, the four boys were competent swimmers and there was an excellent boathouse on the shore to provide shelter. It all seemed perfectly reasonable and safe.

The telephone rang at two the following morning: 'Dad, it's Charles. Can you come and get us, please. They want to go home.'

'Where are you calling from, Charlie?' I asked. The nearest phone box was in the village, six miles from the loch.

'The village,' he replied.

I sallied forth and collected Charles in the village, then continued on to the loch to collect three very cold, wet, miserable boys.

'What's wrong, lads?' I inquired.

'It's Charles. He's scared the living daylights out of Peter, telling him ghost stories and running about in the loch, banging on the side of the boathouse. Peter wants to go home.'

'Charles!' I said angrily.

'Honestly, Dad, I didn't mean it. Anyway, the fish weren't rising and I had to do something to keep them happy.'

Blair, when he lived and worked in the Outer Hebrides, used to telephone constantly with tales of ones that didn't get away – sea-trout, salmon and superb wild brown trout – safe in the knowledge that I could never check up on his stories; Lewis-Ann can land a fly like an expert and even Jean now wields a double-handed salmon rod with great skill. So in order to counter this threat, many years ago I decided to change my image into that of an elderly sage, rather than equal participant; more content to sit and watch others catching fish; happy to spread around words of wisdom and advice from the bank whilst they lashed away. But it doesn't fool anyone.

'Keep your elbow tucked in, Blair.'

'Yes, Father.'

'Pretend that you have a book under your arm.'

'Yes, Father.'

'There, you see, you missed that fish. You must learn to concentrate.'

'Yes, Father,' Blair responded wearily. 'And no doubt I will miss the next fish too unless you go away and stop distracting me with your maniacal bleating.'

'That's no way to talk to your father, Blair, I'm only trying to help,' I complain.

'Do me a favour, then, will you? Go and help Lewis-Ann, or that bush over there. Read a book or something, but stop interfering.'

There's gratitude, after all I have done for him, I mumble crossly as I wander over to where our youngest daughter, Jean, is thrashing away. At that time Jean was too little to answer back effectively. Or so I thought.

'Hello, Jean. How are you getting on? Look, give me the rod and Daddy will show you how to cast. Let me have the rod, Jean.'

'Ann, Ann, tell him!' Jean screamed. 'I'm fishing and he wants my rod. Make him go away.'

Such is life. Nor do I get any sympathy or support from my wife.

'I'm only trying to help, you know.'

'Yes, dear.'

'After all, how will they learn if they won't listen to what I have to say?' I argue.

'Yes, dear.'

'You should tell them to listen.'

'Yes, dear. I will.'

'Jean will never catch trout unless she learns to cast properly.'

'Yes, dear.'

'What do you mean "Yes dear"? You aren't listening to a word I am saying.'

'Yes I am. Look, Jean is into a beauty. Her casting can't be too bad after all. Why don't you go over there and have a nice chat with that sheep. I'm sure it would love to hear all your fishing stories, Bruce. I'll catch supper.'

Learning to cast is not difficult. Any reasonably well co-ordinated human being can master the basic principles in half an hour; thereafter, he will catch fish with the best of them. But there is a certain mystique about it which tends to put people off. Rather than make fools of themselves, they fall for the easy option of spinning and in so doing miss out on the real fun of angling which is fly-fishing.

During my fishing career, I have introduced many beginners to fly-fishing and have always enjoyed doing so, apart from Alf Barker, one-time town clerk of the Borough of Blyth in Northumberland.

I had taken Alf to the Tweed and we were fishing on the stretch known as the Red Yetts, a few miles downstream from Peebles. The day was warm, not too bright, and there was the promise of a good evening rise. Alf had never handled a trout-rod before but, as he gained confidence, I began talking about shooting the line, false casting and other technical matters. Out of the corner of my eye, I had noticed a particularly promising rise towards the far bank, beneath the branches of a magnificent beech tree which overhung the stream. The best fish always rise in places like that. Muttering suitable words of encouragement to Alf, I edged off down the river.

I cast sideways, rod parallel to the water. As my March Brown snaked in below the branches, I raised my wrist and drew back slightly. The fly stopped and jerked upwards and the light breeze did the rest. Floating in perfect order, the March Brown approached the trout – certainly one of the largest fish I had seen all season. I could hardly breathe . . . every muscle and nerve in my body was tense, poised, ready for action.

At that moment an ear-splitting screech rent the air. I turned to look. The fish rose. I instinctively struck. Too late. There was a brief turmoil on the surface and then the monster was gone.

I waded back to Alf and found him sitting in the middle of the river, line wrapped round his neck, clutching his rod as though his very life depended upon it. I helped him to his feet. Together we reeled in. Firmly attached to his first dropper was one of the smallest trout I had ever seen.

'My, what a beauty!' he exclaimed.

But Alf hadn't finished with me. After getting him sorted out, I sat on the bank for a while, waiting for things to settle down. Particularly, I hoped, the large trout under the trees. Half an hour later found me inching towards its lie, false casting to judge the distance. Once more my cast was perfect. Again I watched and waited as the fly floated down to where the monster lay;

once more my attention was diverted at the last minute by yet another shout from Alf.

This time he had caught himself in the eye-lid and was standing, line-draped, with a worried frown on his face. I cut the cast, helped him ashore and drove him to the doctor's in Innerleithen. The fly was speedily and painlessly removed.

'That was close, Alf,' I said. 'You must remember to wear the glasses, just in case of accidents. Do you want to call it a day and set off home?' I asked solicitously.

'Not on your life, Bruce. Come on, back to the river! There's still time for another hour's fishing.'

My most difficult beginner, Ken Thompson, was less easy to instruct. Ken, a Londoner – my boss at the time, and not noted for being one to listen – much preferred to do the talking, and the closest he had ever come to fishing was at Billingsgate Market. With typical Cockney confidence he studiously ignored my advice, thrashing away backwards and forwards, making it impossible for either Ann or myself to fish. I considered that the fish were far safer than we were in the cramped confines of the boat. I sat watching him in speechless amazement. Flies were whistling backwards, landing with an almighty splash, then hurtling forwards with demonic fury, crashing into the water about two feet in front of the boat.

As a particularly violent back-cast hit the water, astonishingly, a trout rose and grabbed the tail fly a fraction of a second before Ken lashed the line forward. Why neither cast nor rod broke I shall never know, but Ken sat there with studied indifference, facing the action.

The trout set off for the horizon, jumping spectacularly along the way. Ken started to reel in. He didn't stop until the fish was hanging, half-drowned, its snout pressed hard against the top ring of the rod:

'What do I do now, Bruce?' he asked.

I couldn't resist it, and gave him the old gillies' answer: 'Well, sir, why don't you just climb up the rod and stab it to death?'

I sorted out the mess and eventually landed the fish.

'There you are!' gloated Ken, lighting a cigar and smiling broadly. 'Nothing to it.'

Most anglers will confirm, however, that actually catching fish is only a small part of the pleasure of fishing, and our family days out have become treasured memories. I often wonder if Ann and I would have been quite so able to cope with the slings and arrows of life, and retain a sense of humour, had it not been for the magic of fishing.

Sometimes, to while away the hours whilst tramping over the hills, and to encourage the little ones, we used to play 'I-Spy'. It kept their minds off the gradient and helped them along the way.

Charles was the expert: 'I spy, with my little eye, something beginning with D.D,' he announced enigmatically one morning, as we plodded over the Caithness Flow Country.

'What did he say?' I shouted into the wind to Blair, burdened with the not-inconsiderable weight of Jean on his shoulders. She was having one of her 'I'm not walking another step' tantrums.

'He said B.B., I think.'

'I thought it was D.C.?' yelled Ann.

'D.D!' roared Charles.

Our party was spaced out along the crest of a ridge, halfway from Lochan nam Breac, a four-mile trek over the moors from Dalnawillan. Rain hurtled horizontally over the heather and the track ahead appeared and disappeared in breathtaking, knife-like squalls.

Lochan nam Breac, the Gaelic name for trout, is another of our favourite Caithness waters. It is rarely available and we always value the opportunity when given permission to fish it. There is a reasonable track most of the way and, after following it for about three miles, you turn right along the line of the outlet burn and on, up to the loch.

' "Dreadful doughnuts"?' suggested Ann.

' "Dead daisies"?' I ventured.

'What's D.D?' Jean asked hopefully from her perch.

'Ah, that's for you to find out,' replied Charlie, smugly.

'How about "daft dotterils"?' I tried again.

'More like "daft donkeys",' grunted Blair, easing the bulk of his little sister on his shoulders. Not for the first time I offered up a silent prayer of thanks for the blessing of a six-foot tall son. Jean must have weighed a ton by then.

'Now look here, Charles,' I said threateningly, 'if this is one of your fancy ones you'd better get ready to run. Are you sure it's D.D.?'

'Yes, I'm sure. And I can see some now,' came the prompt reply.

We trudged on and, as we went, I wondered how I had ended up, middle-aged and playing 'I-Spy' in a thunderstorm miles from anywhere. But it was worth it. Not just for the children, or the occasional thrill of catching the occasional fish, but as much for the wealth of pleasure that goes hand in hand with fishing: the beauty and loneliness of distant hills; the feeling of being at one with the ordered progression of the seasons; seeing a soaring golden eagle; surprising a wild cat; the sudden shock of red grouse, rising rocket-like from the heather; red-throated divers, elegantly gracing small, reed-fringed pools. We prefer to fish the more remote and inaccessible lochs and, for little people with little legs, some of the walks are hard, and, at times, just getting there can present problems: hence 'I-Spy', guaranteed peace for at least a mile and a half.

Lewis-Ann had stayed at home that day. She was at the rebellious stage and it was always a fight to get her to come along – unless the boy friend of the moment expressed even the remotest interest in fishing. Then she was off over the hill like a startled deer, tying blood knots and turle knots without missing a step, basking in her knowledge and skill as an angler. Her long-suffering husband, Mike, used to enjoy coarse fishing in the waters round his home in Norfolk. Now he is restricted to fly-fishing only and receives a constant barrage of advice and instruction upon how to conduct himself in proper fishing circles. One day, soon, I will have to have a quiet word with him about 'our little treasure's' past angling exploits.

The first time we headed for the hills as a family was in 1971, before Charles and Jean were born. Blair was ten, Lewis-Ann, eight. We stayed at Scourie with Ian Hay, who advised us on the best lochs for the children. Scourie is a wonderful place for a family fishing holiday. The hotel is one of the most comfortable and best-run angling establishments in Scotland and there are more than three hundred lochs waiting for your attention. The scenery is spectacular: grey shouldered Foinaven and Arkle; shapely Ben Stack; everything that makes Scotland the most beautiful country in the world.

We walked out to Eilenach, climbing the steep shoulder of Ben Stack, and the children managed fine. I puffed and gasped far more than they did. The ragged shore-line of the loch was a delight to fish; an endless succession of rock promontories and fishy corners. We had a super time, returning with seven nice trout.

The following day we walked out to sea-girt Loch Calva, surely one of the most lovely of all Sutherland lochs, where Blair caught his first 'proper' trout. I can still see him, bright-eyed and excited, running over the heather to show me his prize. I caught nothing. We trekked up to the Black Rock, getting lost on the way and taking far longer than we should have done. By the time we arrived we were all hot and tired. No one complained, and the fish were rising. We spent a glorious few hours amidst the splendour of the hills, exploring the four little lochs, enjoying the magnificent panorama of mountain, sea and moorland.

On our last day, Lewis-Ann decided to accompany her grandparents to a roadside loch, but Blair, by this time a committed hill-walker, came with Ann and me. Ian Hay had kindly marked on the map (OS Sheet 9) a small lochan along the Gorm track and we headed off into the hills in high spirits.

On these occasions, Ann does the 'steering'. During two years military service in Southern Arabia I was allowed to lead convoys through the rebel-infested Radfan Mountains. However, apparently this does not qualify me for map-reading in Scotland. To be honest, Ann is a far better map-reader than me, and I happily follow her directions.

We eventually arrived at the small, H-shaped water and started to fish. Young Blair walked along a high bank close to the edge, the sun casting his shadow further over the surface than he could throw his flies. Ann did likewise. There was a light breeze, but it was not strong enough to stop their casts landing on the water in a tangled, unmanageable heap.

Shaking my head in despair, I left them to it and cautiously made my way down to a reedy corner. Approaching on all fours, I crouched upright and silently waded in through the reeds, casting out into deeper water.

Ann came along to see if I was all right.

'Is your back hurting, dear?' she inquired solicitously.

'No, damn it, go away. I'm stalking the fish. Leave me in peace.'

She returned to the high bank, muttering that she had not known that Quasimodo had been an angler, and rejoined Blair, who was lashing away with all his might.

'Your father is having a fit,' I heard her announce.

'Pretend that you don't notice.'

I fished round that corner meticulously for about an hour, inch-perfect every time, demonstrating my superlative casting technique. And caught nothing. My excuse for this unhappy state of affairs was the disturbance I created, wading in and out of the water, landing fish for Ann and Blair – one of 1lb 12oz, and another of 1lb 10oz, to name but two. Eventually, fishless and suffering from a severely deflated ego, I allowed them to guide me home.

I was pondering these matters as we marched, line ahead, through the Caithness storm, Jean still perched on Blair's strong shoulders. Then I fell, with a resounding thud, straight into a black peat hag. As is their wont, the family roared with laughter.

'Do it again, Dad,' shouted Charles, 'I didn't see you the first time.'

I struggled to my feet.

'Not on your life, Charlie . . . but at least I now know what D.D. is.' I held up my hand, stained brown. ' "Deer droppings"!' I announced triumphantly.

'Curses,' yelled Charles, 'I was sure that I had you all that time!'

'Do it again, Dad,' shouted Charles, 'I didn't see you the first time'

Unhappy Landings

TAURUS
21 APRIL TO 21 MAY

The year ahead will see things happening, projects coming through, dreams realised. Take your angling life by the shoulders and shake it, do just that. If you are determined to carry on with your current, uncertain plans, then you will make progress.

In May, trends accentuating your fishing career are in the

ascendant and your need for independence may lead you to act in a selfish way. For instance, you will be tempted to buy a new landing-net for your exclusive use. Do so, unhesitatingly. Also, purchase that rod you have always been promising yourself; the new garden shed can wait. Buy the deluxe Hardy reel; decorate the spare bedroom some other time.

This will be the year when you finally master the art of tying blood knots. The patch you applied to your left wader will hold. Fish will not get away. You will not fall in. The outboard motor will always start, first pull. There will be no blank days. You will catch your first salmon.

Fishing friends are very much in the picture this month so be ready to go fishing at least twice a week. In addition, plan four week-long fishing holidays, coinciding with the new moon. Providing you make the most of this favourable phase, then your angling dreams could come true.

Beware of being too smug when you catch more fish than your companions. This could lead to a deterioration in your angling relationships and, in extreme cases, could find you swimming for your life. Be humble, particularly in April. There are indications that suggest that this could be a particularly cold month for you. Remember to wrap up well.

Follow the decisions of others and always say yes when invited to join fishing expeditions, regardless of family pressure to do otherwise. Concrete over the garden, sell the lawnmower, use an automatic car-wash and buy a dish-washer. Protecting your precious fishing time is all important.

This could also be your 'one for the glass case' year, so order it now: six feet in length, two feet high and one foot in depth. Prepare a space above the mantelpiece and contact your local taxidermist. Buy a new, large, landing-net. Always have the camera ready and loaded.

Personal affairs are well favoured to run smoothly and finances look set to show a considerable improvement. You will not need to buy waders, and your stars predict that boat fees will be minimal. Consequently, a trip abroad seems likely, possibly to Iceland, or perhaps South Island, New Zealand. Spend all your spare time reading up on both locations, and take extra care of your health, particularly as you may be feeling tired and run down at present, due to long, fishless, winter months. You need to be in top form, so cheer yourself up each evening with an extra-large night-cap. It will boost your self-confidence and help you see the opportunities ahead more clearly. Two extra-large night-caps are even nicer.

Your partner may feel you do not take your domestic responsibilities seriously enough, but do not compromise. You should find yourself better equipped to deal with difficult individuals by keeping your opinions to yourself and remaining tactful. Smile sweetly when she complains and continue sharpening your flies. Warn in-laws, relations and others that you will be busy all year. Cancel the family summer holiday in the South of France and get ready for a bumper fishing season.

I FREQUENTLY catch trout when no one else does. This habit does not help me to make friends. Indeed, some acquaintances now refuse to go fishing with me, and, on occasions, I positively pray that I will catch fewer trout than my struggling companions.

My prayer is rarely answered and, come lunch-time, I have to confess, with a small feeling of guilt, that I have caught more than the rest of the party put together. It wouldn't be so bad if I were a more humble sort of man; self-effacing, gentle and kindly. Trouble is that I secretly enjoy my success and find it very difficult to hide my feelings. Whether or not I'm first back or last, it is impossible to restrain the sense of mounting pleasure I get when the basket is counted. My self-satisfied smile quickly turns into a face-splitting grin, calculated to drive even my closest friends to distraction. Regardless of the time of year, in good weather or in bad, snow, sleet, hail, wind, sun or rain, if there are fish about, I will catch them.

Nor does my success lie in a deeply-rooted study of angling, devouring every morsel of angling wisdom ever written like some oversized cannibal trout. I am not a walking encyclopedia of piscatorial excellence. In fact, what I really *know* about angling could comfortably be inscribed on a pin-head. I'm not particularly proud of this, just incredibly lazy. Whether or not a trout views life through an angle of forty-five or 360 degrees is of absolutely no interest to me. Arguments about the relative merits of wet or dry fly-fishing leave me utterly cold and I find the perpetual squabbling over such matters to be slightly vulgar. However, I still manage to catch trout.

The truth is that I have blank days like everyone else, but I do generally manage to catch more than my fair share, and the method I use has remained the same for nearly forty years: a nine-foot built-cane rod, ancient reel and equally ancient line, and a small selection of flies which I rarely change: Ke-He, Black Pennel, Soldier Palmer, Woodcock & Hare-lug, March Brown, Greenwell's Glory, Silver Invicta, and Silver Butcher. They always catch fish.

Success in fishing is all about confidence – confidence in your own ability and confidence in the flies you use. And of course, how you dress. The cardinal error most anglers most frequently make. To be consistently successful in trout fishing, the angler must have a highly developed dress-sense. After all, it is a well-known fact that trout are extremely discriminating creatures. Show me the fisherman who has lots of blank days and I'll bet he never wears a tie whilst fishing; or the angler who always misses fish, and I'll guarantee that he wears a woollen hat with a little pom-pom. Ask yourself, what self-respecting trout is going to rise to a fly presented by a man wearing a bright-blue, turtle-necked sweat-shirt, sun-glasses and black beret?

Being properly dressed and properly equipped whilst fishing, and having supreme confidence in both clothing and tackle, are of vital importance. Failure in any one area can lead to disaster, as I have often found to my great embarrassment and discomfiture. Remember, *the habit oft proclaims the man*, and be prepared. Which is why, eventually, I cut the shirt up and used it for dusters. The buttons came undone by themselves. Slowly, I would realise that the person to whom I was speaking was not concentrating upon my words of wisdom, but looking curiously at my navel. The self-unbuttoning shirt was at it again.

This garment seemed normal but was completely untrustworthy and landed me in many embarrassing situations. Whilst giving a talk or lecture, I see my audience's attention beginning to wander. Why are they looking at my middle, rather than my face? The self-unbuttoning shirt.

I like to be able to rely upon things doing what they have been designed to do. Landing-nets, for instance. You would have thought, given a bit of luck and sufficient practice, that any reasonably well-co-ordinated human being should be able to scoop a trout out of its natural habitat into a net bag without too much difficulty. Sadly, however, I have to report this is not so. At least, not in my case, and certainly not with my landing-net. With the malicious fickleness of the self-unbuttoning shirt, my landing-net always lets me down, without warning, at all the crucial moments. More often than not, just as I am about to net 'one for the glass case', I am left, lashing about in the water, with a sodden, useless heap of string whilst the object of my desire swims serenely off to freedom; and the air above turns blue with my despairing curses.

I have lost more fish because of the capriciousness of landing-nets than have ever escaped my clutches due to errors of judgement. It should be simple. Surely a race capable of landing a man on the moon is capable of designing a fool-proof, reliable contraption for landing trout?

Our present net is a malignant horror. Once afloat, the net has to remain open all the time – constantly catching rods, flies, feet and line. Ann has a theory that if the net is neatly folded on the bottom of the boat, it goes into a trance, refusing to open, regardless of how much we shake it. She believes, from bitter experience, that the net collapses the moment it is put into water so, consequently, she resorts to all manner of antics to try to avoid getting it wet – swiping at trout as they jump near the boat, trying to catch them in mid-air. Fishing shouldn't be like that, although at times, fish do jump into the boat all by themselves.

Frank Binnie, a senior Border gillie at Tweed Mill, told me that it had happened to him, not once, but three times, whilst salmon fishing. The largest salmon weighed 17lbs and came over the stern of the boat like a rocket, knocking him clean off his seat.

In 1986, when I was fishing Loch Watten with my mother, I hooked a trout of about 1lb in weight. I asked Mother to hand me the landing-net and, as she was busy trying to unfankle it from a nail in the bottom of the boat, the trout jumped straight in, landing at my feet. Would that all fishing were as simple.

I paid a good price for the net, and it bears a well-known tackle manufacturer's name, but in spite of its pedigree it has never worked properly. The fish it has lost me would have fed a small army. I have no confidence in it. I hate it.

I cringe when I remember the number of times the net has failed. Because of this net, I lost a specimen trout when Ann and I were fishing a series of small hill lochs near Dalnawhillan in Caithness. I'm sure the monster is still there, my Black Pennel firmly embedded in its jaw.

We arrived at the lochs, and I assembled Ann's rod and made up her cast whilst she had a cup of coffee.

'There you are, dear, the finest cast in the North of Scotland.

Every fly a winner: Black Pennel, Grouse & Claret and Alexandra.'

'You know I never catch anything on a Grouse & Claret. Why have you put it on?'

'It just seemed like a good idea at the time,' I pleaded.

'Take it off. I must have a Ke-He,' Ann commanded, pouring herself another cup.

Reluctantly, I obeyed, tying on to her cast the last Ke-He in the box. Greater love . . .

'That's better. Where are you off to?'

'Oh, just over the hill to fish the last loch.'

There are three principal waters and I intended to leave Ann fishing the largest whilst I wandered over to investigate the most southerly one.

'You take the net, dear,' she had said. 'You are far more likely to catch something. I'll just have a few casts and then look for wild flowers.'

Suspicious, I asked: 'But what will happen if you hook a decent fish? Are you sure that you will be able to land it?'

'Don't worry about me,' she replied, 'I'll manage. Off you go.'

On the way, I passed a small, dark, peat-stained pool, barely half an acre in extent. Having nothing better to do, and not expecting to catch anything, I decided to have a cast. As I adjusted my fishing-bag from one shoulder to the other, my leader came loose and fell on to the water about a yard from the bank and immediately became snagged on some weeds. Good Lord! I thought, I have hardly started fishing and already I have to make up a new cast. Is there no justice?

I gave a tentative tug, hoping to pull my flies free. The surface exploded in a cascade of spray and bubbling water as the most enormous trout that I had ever seen threw itself clear. I reacted instinctively and panicked, almost strangling myself with my fishing-bag as I struggled to hold on to the rod and avoid being pulled straight into the loch.

The trout shot off like the *Mallard* breaking the railway steam locomotive speed record, reaching 125mph and still accelerating. It eventually stopped and cautiously I reeled in, the trout following, shaking its great head and splashing furiously on the surface as it came towards me. It made several, short, stomach-churning, storming runs to right and left, trying to reach the safety of the weeds. I fought to keep the monster under control, the strap of my fishing-bag biting savagely into my neck. Eventually, the trout lay at my feet in the weeds, at least 5lb, golden, deep-bodied, splendidly marked, utterly beautiful. Ready for the net. I felt behind my back for it and tried to drag it free. It stuck. The trout's tail swirled. I wrenched my fishing-bag round, almost throttling myself in the process and got the net loose. It snagged in the heather. I flicked. Nothing. Flicked again. Halfway open. I started to curse and shout. Why wasn't anyone about to lend a hand? There never was when you really needed them. Come on you brute of a net. Sort yourself out. Please, God, make the net open. If I could only lay my hands on the misbegotten son of an idiot who designed this misbegotten apology for a landing-net, I'd tear him apart with my bare hands!

By now the monster trout had begun to recover and roared off again sending waves crashing into the bank by my feet, its huge, sail-like tail clear of the water like a mocking, waving flag. Come back! Please stop! Just let me land you and I promise I will never do anything wrong again as long as I live.

Slowly, in agony, I worked the big trout back towards me, inch by breath-taking inch, until my tail fly caught in the weeds. In a torment of despair, clutching the still half-open net, I lunged for it. The tip of my rotten net barely reached. As I slipped it under the fish, the twisted arms sprang free, breaking my cast. The fish leisurely turned tail and headed for the middle of the loch. I staggered back to Ann, utterly dejected.

'Darling,' I blurted through mist-filled eyes, 'I have just lost an enormous trout. You will never believe it. The bloody net wouldn't open again.'

'Never mind, Bruce, see what I managed to catch, without one.' She had three absolutely stunning, perfectly matched trout, each weighing about 1lb 8oz. 'You really should learn to beach your fish, you know. It's far safer and only takes a little practice. And skill.'

I thought that I could never experience such disappointment again. I was wrong. Last season I hooked the largest brown trout that I have ever seen, on a loch near Tongue, in Sutherland; the fish that I have been waiting for all my life, certainly well over 5lb. The previous year, Blair, Ann and I had paid a visit to the loch but found it difficult to fish because of the soggy margins. The west shore was completely unapproachable and, due to a weed fringe, it was very difficult to fish effectively from the east bank. More as a gesture, than with serious intent, I decided to walk out again, on my own, and have another look. I discovered that if you ignored the soggy east shore margin and waded in, beyond the weeds, it was possible to wade down the bank, covering a wide area of water. And I had seen one or two fish rise as I arrived.

After an hour, fighting against a wicked, contrary wind, I decided to give up and wade ashore. Dragging my cast behind me, I turned to go. At that moment, the trout grabbed and shot off like an express train. I have never experienced such a vicious 'take' and I was confident that if I could hold on, I would have him.

The fish stripped twenty yards of line from my reel in its first mad rush, leaping spectacularly at the end of its run. I reeled in rapidly, only to find the trout making a similar run, ending in another wild leap. Already I was rehearsing the story I would tell the family, envisaged the fish, proudly above the mantelpiece with my name engraved on a modest, unassuming brass plate. The trout ran again and jumped a third time. I reeled in madly and the fish followed, tugging and splashing on the surface. Nearer. Almost there. Ready for the net. I scrabbled behind my back. The net would not come loose. I tugged and struggled, twisting and turning as the trout lay there, barely a yard from my grasp. Eventually, I managed to get hold of it. I flicked upwards, by now yelling in anger. Its folds were entangled with one of the legs. I stuffed the rod under my arm and attacked the net with maniacal fury, managing to get it half open. Would the fish fit?

I needn't have worried. By this time the trout had recovered its strength and made one final dash for freedom – not out into the middle of the loch, but straight between my legs.

In retrospect, I should have simply reeled off line and allowed the fish to run. Instead, I panicked, attempting to step over it. In an agony of despair, I saw the nylon go taut as the middle fly snagged my wader. As the cast broke, I toppled over backwards, ending chest-deep. The fish had gone.

My natural instinct is to jump up and down on the net several times and chuck it in the loch, but Calvinistic upbringing restrains me. Or someone always seems to be watching, and they think that I am daft enough already. I have tried to 'lose' the net, believe me I have, on several occasions, wandering off nonchalantly, pretending to forget it. But it never works. The best I managed was a week; then a well-meaning fellow angler appeared at the door one evening, triumphantly clutching the damned thing:

'Hello, Bruce. Look, I've found your landing-net. Bit of luck really. Just happened to stumble on it in the heather. Can't imagine how it managed to get itself so buried. Glinting it was. The hotel said that you had been out so I knew it was yours. No, no, no trouble at all. Well, if you insist, I would love a dram.'

'Glinting' he had said, I mused, as this so-called benefactor emptied my bottle of whisky. Once he had gone, I 'accidentally' dropped the net into the dustbin, but come collection day, a Thursday in our part of the world, Willie, the driver, a keen angler, knocked on the door:

'You must have plenty of money, Bruce, throwing out a perfectly good landing-net like this? Lucky one of the lads noticed it. Here you are. Take more care next time or you might lose it.'

You would have thought that the net would have been satisfied with just collapsing, or failing to open; but no, it further frustrates my skilful efforts to catch fish by becoming wickedly entangled with any fly that approaches within a mile. I am sure that it must be one of Mr Murphy's laws that the moment you manage to get one trout into the net, an even larger fish immediately rises nearby – when all your flies are entangled. The captured trout lashes about in the bilges as you struggle with an advanced model of the Gordian knot, and even at the last moment, when victory seems in sight, the tail fly will invariably dig into the last loop.

I attempted to resolve the problem by purchasing a second landing-net. To me, it seemed the proper thing to do, in spite of the expense involved. Nobody could be so unlucky twice; and I am pleased to report that the new net worked not too badly to begin with.

I explained the matter to the rest of the tribe, announcing brightly to Blair and Lewis-Ann: 'Now you will always have a net when you are fishing. Isn't that super!'

'When you say "net",' grunted Blair, 'I presume that you mean to lumber us with that self-collapsing monstrosity, whilst you use the brand new species?'

'That's just great,' joined in Lewis-Ann, outraged as usual by everything I do. 'Thanks for nothing, Dad.'

'Now look here, Blair,' I explained, 'for all the fish you catch it's not going to make that much difference anyway, is it?'

'And what about me, when he is bank-fishing and I am in the boat? I suppose that I am expected to persuade them to jump out of the water all by themselves,' complained Lewis-Ann.

39

'No, my little treasure, you will share the landing-net with your big brother,' I replied firmly.

'Ha! that's what you think. Can you imagine Blair rushing across like a knight in shining armour to land a 2lb trout for me?'

'The day you catch a 2lb trout I will eat my hat,' responded Blair.

'Yes, I can. That's what brothers are for,' I replied.

'Says who?'

'Be quiet, Blair,' I snapped.

'He's far more likely to stick cotton-wool in his ears and pretend he can't hear me.' Lewis-Ann was cross.

'Stop it!' interjected Ann. 'That's quite enough bickering. You should be grateful to your father for providing you with a landing-net, not rude.'

'But he hasn't provided us with a net!' yelled Lewis-Ann. 'He is only using it as an excuse to dump the old one.'

'Try to think of it as a challenge, children,' said my reasonable spouse, eyeing the new landing-net appreciatively. 'How do you think they used to land fish in the olden days, before landing-nets were invented?'

'I haven't the faintest idea, Mummy. Why don't you tell us? How did you land your fish in the olden days before nets were invented?' Lewis-Ann responded sweetly.

I shouldn't have worried because the problem solved itself – with help from Charles. He had decided that since he wasn't allowed to pinch (or 'borrow', as he put it) Blair's air-gun to shoot rabbits, then he was perfectly justified in misappropriating the new landing-net to try and snare them – and anything else foolish enough to come within his reach.

It was some time before I realised what was going on. Charles would disappear for long periods after supper and return red-faced, cross and out of breath.

'What on earth have you been up to?' I would ask, suspiciously.

'Oh, nothing, Dad, just out for a run. Must be able to keep up with you and Blair in the hills.'

Thoughtful, sensible child, I mused. Perhaps after all I had been misjudging him. Perhaps he really was taking an interest in physical fitness, as I had suggested.

I should have known better. All was revealed at the outset of our next fishing expedition. I loaded the car the night before, smugly anticipating the joys of using a landing-net that actually worked, but when I went to fetch it, I was confronted by a broken, one-armed object with a torn and tattered net dangling limply from the end. My pride and joy had to be consigned to the ever-increasing heap of casualties resulting from Charlie's exploits and experiments: binoculars, cameras, watches, 5,000 yards of Sellotape, old radios and an astonishing array of assorted cutlery, all inextricably locked together with Super Glue.

In order to preserve my sanity, I now give up my place in the boat to anyone who wants it and fish from the bank, as far away from the net as possible, beaching the few fish I catch. It gives me a vast amount of malicious pleasure, listening to the howls coming from the direction of the boat, as fish after fish is lost, and flies fight for a place amongst the net's ample folds.

'It's not my fault! The net just collapsed!' I hear Lewis-Ann scream.

'You did that on purpose. I know you did. I was watching. What a dirty, rotten thing to do. That fish was a monster!' cries Blair, furiously.

'Now, now children,' I call sarcastically, 'try and behave to each other in a civilised fashion. You don't want to upset the sheep with all that shouting, do you?'

'It was the only fish I've touched all day!' roars back Blair.

'Oh, what a pity! Poor little Blair,' responds Lewis-Ann.

Alarmed, I shout angrily, 'Listen, son, Lewis-Ann didn't really mean it. Put that oar down! Please?'

In spite of the fact that I no longer use the net, its malevolence pursues me with seemingly unrelenting fury. Walking home last season after a great day's sport, I was extolling the virtues of bank-fishing in general, and my skill in particular, to the rest of the clan. They had been fishing from the boat and had caught nothing. The disgusting net, which I had been fooled into carrying, slung from my fishing-bag, chose that precise moment to play a final, dastardly trick on me. Somehow or other it became entangled between my legs and neatly tripped me into one of the nastiest peat bogs I have seen in years. Covered with wet slime and peat, dripping and shaken, I staggered to my feet and glowered at my audience.

'Not a single word. Not a single word, do you hear!'

'No, Father, of course not. Not a single word,' Blair replied solemnly.

'Are you all right, Daddy?' Lewis-Ann simpered.

'I'm warning you. Not a word. You tripped me, Blair.'

41

'Would I do a thing like that to my own father?' Blair feigned shock.

'Yes,' I roared.

I wrenched the net free and, grabbing it, whirled it round and round my head like some latter-day Bedivere wielding King Arthur's sword Excalibur. I let go and the net shot off into the furthermost reaches of the bog and sank from sight. Satisfied, I squelched home.

Trouble is I have started having nightmares. I am walking over the moor, going fishing, when all of a sudden I see an arm rise from the peat, clothed in green waterproofs, slimy, horrible, clutching the net. So far I have been able to resist the temptation of walking over and taking it – but for how much longer, I ask?

Next to nets, my second pet hate are waders. Doing so much bank-fishing, no matter how far we were walking I always used to lug them along. I know that the purist will claim that the first sign of an inexperienced hill-loch angler is his feet in the water, but at least I liked to have the option of doing so. Just in case.

Now, after years of disappointment with poor-quality waders, I leave them at home. My first action upon arriving at the water's edge is to remove trousers, pants, socks and shoes. Whilst others heave on mountains of pullovers, fur-lined jackets, waterproof trousers, scarfs, gloves and waders, I, whenever possible, do the reverse. I brave the elements and simply wade in. It saves me about £50 each season.

Nor is it because I am a tight-fisted Scot. That old story is not true. We Scots are among the most generous people in the world. Most of the time. Nor, as my nearest and dearest frequently suggest, am I a complete lunatic. To me, it has become a matter of principle. I have spent a fortune on waders over the past twenty years, few of which have lasted more than a single season. I refuse to waste any more of my hard-earned cash pandering to the voracious appetite of the exponents of planned obsolescence: manufacturers of waders that spring a leak or self-destruct like something out of a Hollywood horror movie at their first glimpse of water.

It is not so bad for single, unattached anglers, but all our lot fish. If I am to maintain them in a reasonably dry and comfortable state, I can't afford a similar luxury for myself, and the cost of replacing six pairs of waders every season is beyond me. Now I encourage the family to fish from the boat whilst I stalk the bank like some overgrown, prehistoric heron. This saves me from a lot of hard rowing, and from the nightmare of sharing a boat with Lewis-Ann. Fishing with Lewis-Ann is like playing a highly dangerous game of Space Invaders: I always lose and generally end up with a Silver Butcher in my left ear.

'Why do you keep getting in the way, Daddy?' she will announce crossly. 'How do you expect me to concentrate on catching fish with you doing a Highland fling in the middle of the boat?'

'Sorry, dear.'

'Now hold still, I'll soon have it out.'

'Lewis-Ann, what are you doing with that needle?'

'It's all right, relax. I know what I'm doing. Stop being a baby. I read about this technique in *Trout and Salmon* and they say that you don't feel a thing.'

'Help, Ann! Anyone!' I scream.

Now, I wouldn't like you to think that I am making unjust accusations. I never do. Or that I am exaggerating. I never do that either, unless it concerns fish that get away, but as far as I am concerned, what I have said about waders is absolutely true, and I have years of unhappy, wet-legged experience to back my claim.

When I was a boy, I had a superb pair of waders: heavy, black and indestructible. They lasted me for years and, season after season, I would drag them out from where they had been dumped unceremoniously the previous year and don them with complete, waterproof confidence. I never managed to wear them out and only parted with those wonderful boots because I fell for a trendy, up-market advert extolling the virtues of the new breed of green wellies; as far as I could see, they guaranteed that you caught more fish – and met all the right people. They lasted a couple of weeks.

Even other people's waders always seemed to land me in trouble. I remember once, I had invited a friend for a day's fishing on the Tweed in early May, borrowing my father's waders from him – which Father agreed to lend with great misgiving (he was convinced that we were both completely untrustworthy and that something was bound to go wrong – which it did). My fishing companion, Tony Sykes, is by nature accident prone, but, I reasoned, provided I made sure that he used the gates rather than climbing barbed-wire fences, then all should be well. Unfortunately, that was the day that Sykes decided to play St George to a fellow angler's salmon-dragon, and, in doing so, both waders were filled with water as he forded the river to help.

43

Father didn't believe this story, though, and for years afterwards viewed Sykes with uninhibited suspicion, absolutely convinced that, with malice aforethought, he had deliberately filled the precious boots and that I had stood by and allowed him to do so. Nothing I said could convince him that it had all been in a good cause.

For a long time I used to pretend that getting wet didn't really matter. After all, what's a little dampness between friends? You soon dry out. But I soon began to realise that spending five or six hours in clinging, cold socks and trousers in a bitter wind was not really much fun and tended to spoil the day. It also tended to spoil the evening, if we stopped off on the way home for refreshment. 'They' all pile in and crowd round the bar while I am left shivering and dishevelled in the car. I'm lucky if they remember to send out a half-pint and a packet of nuts; and that only happens if they have caught more fish than me. It's 'Catch 22': heads they win, tails I lose.

Consequently, I gave up buying waders years ago, keeping my last pair exclusively for river-fishing, where my loch-fishing technique would be ill-advised and certainly frowned upon amongst the salmon-fishing fraternity of Tay, Tweed or Spey. I determined that if I couldn't be really dry, then I might as well be really wet; which is why you will often find me by the loch in a state of semi-undress – other than on very hot summer's days when naturist-wading is a pure delight, and takes you to places you might not otherwise reach.

And as they say, 'like father, like son'. In this case, Charles. Blair would never countenance such wayward behaviour. He always wears a tie, regardless of the weather. Charles is different. When the needs must, he wades in regardless.

The first time I noticed this was when we were fishing Loch Bhac, near Pitlochry. I ended the day, fishless yet again, but Charles had a beauty. He was also wet to the waist.

'What happened, son?' I inquired solicitously.

'What do you mean, what happened?' he replied.

'Did you fall in? You are soaking!'

'Oh, no, it's just that this fish rose a bit far out, so I waded in after it. You do, all the time. What are you complaining about?'

'But I'm properly dressed for it.'

'No you are not, you are *un*dressed for it.'

I gave up. Still, Charlie's conversion is very useful, particularly when we have children with us. He drags out the boat,

Takes you to places you might not otherwise reach

carries the little ones, never seeming to notice that he is getting wet in the process. If one of them should happen to lose an oar, for instance, I shout: 'Charlie! Would you mind retrieving that?'

'All right, Dad, no problem.' He wades in.

Daughters too. We were once fishing Loch Toftingall when Jean was about ten years old. I had stripped my lower half and put on Wellingtons and a pair of light over-trousers. Jean, also wearing Wellingtons and over-trousers, followed me round the east bank and we began fishing.

I waded in and was soon having sport with a number of trout which were rising a few yards beyond Jean's casting distance. I noticed her giving me a quick glance, then wading into the loch, casting furiously in the direction of the feeding fish. As she got to knee-depth, she stopped, and a worried look crossed her face. Quietly, she reeled in and headed back to the shore. A moment later, she was by my side, furious.

'These things don't work, Dad. They're leaking,' she announced, accusingly.

'What things, Jean?' I asked carefully.

'My over-trousers. They are just like yours, but they let the water in!' Jean still has a lot to learn.

The early months of the season are worst. Even June and July can sometimes be cold in the far north, and August and September are frequently vile. As a matter of fact, I suppose the truth of the matter is that I spend most seasons blue from the waist down and numb all over. It's that first, sudden rush of ice-cold water that is most shocking. To protect my feet, I wear thick socks and Wellington boots, covered by light-weight over-trousers, and then as much warmth as possible above the waist. As the Wellingtons fill and socks become sodden and loch water begins to refresh the parts other lagers can't reach, it is the moment of truth. Still, a sharp intake of breath, coupled with the reassuring knowledge that I am saving a fortune, steels both mind and body to the task in hand. Rising trout help. When the going gets tough, I wade ashore. A quick half-mile burst across the heather soon restores sanity and circulation. Then back to the action.

There are other benefits. You no longer have to hump two useless lumps of rubber over the moor, and, once you have adjusted mentally and physically to the situation, it becomes quite fun. It's amazing how many of those fish that rise just beyond the reach of my wader-clad neighbours, end up gasping in my bag. My theory is that fish actually understand the limitations of casting and play with the angler; like Red Indians keeping just out of rifle range, they taunt fishermen, tempting them to take that fatal, soaking, one step too far. Waderless, I sneak up behind and catch them unawares.

Unfortunately, sometimes, unsuspected rocks and holes do the same to me and many's the time I have taken a ducking. So what? Half-wet or all wet? There is not much difference. At the end of the day, when the catch is being examined, when words of wisdom are bandied about, when wit and humour fly like barbs of silver, I am the one in the corner with the blue legs. Smiling weakly, teeth chattering like out-of-control castanets, I vainly try to down a spirit-warming dram.

However, it always pays to be cautious and adjust sensibly to weather conditions at the time. A few years ago a friend invited me to spend a day with him on the River Helmsdale, my first visit to this magnificent Highland salmon stream. Dragging out my dusty waders, I fervently prayed for reasonable weather. As luck would have it, we had a fishless day, dogged by weal-raising hailstones and a forty-mile-an-hour blizzard. It was March. Nevertheless, I enjoyed myself, having gone prepared: string vest, woollen shirt, two woollen jumpers, heavy tweed sports jacket, thermal drawers, two pairs of socks, pristine, waterproof waders and over-trousers. The whole ensemble loosely rounded off with gloves and an eight-foot, hand-knitted scarf. As far as I was concerned the weather could do its worst. Safe within my cocoon I was completely impervious to it.

Of course, people react in different ways to the cold. I have farmer friends who stride about in the depths of winter clad in only dungarees. Many's the time I have come across some hardy Highland angler, hatless and snow-smothered, kilt lifting in the gale, unconcernedly fishing away. As I waddle by, rolling from side to side in the wind, I invariably receive a cheery greeting: 'Rare! Grand day for it. Any luck?'

Jimmy Oswald, who has gillied on the South Esk for several decades, has never owned a pair of trousers in his life.

'What do you do when you are landing fish, Jimmy,' I inquired, politely, with considerable interest.

'Och, I wade in and get them. The kilt just floats up around me and soon dries out afterwards.'

After my first experience on the Helmsdale, I was somewhat more cautious when Michael Wigan invited me down for another thrash, this time in April. Still, I reasoned, April should be much warmer, spring lambs gambolling, daffodils dancing, so I thanked him kindly and said yes.

The nightmare weather experienced during my first visit repeated itself and I froze all day. I could hardly cast I was so cold. Nothing daunted, John Hardy, my gillie, seemed perfectly at ease, lightly clad and cheerfully helpful throughout the storm, in spite of it being another fishless day – although on this occasion I did manage at least to hook one.

Of all our family, Ann suffers most dreadfully from the cold. During the early months of the trout season, a glance at her nose is a far more accurate temperature indicator than any thermometer and she has accumulated an astonishing array of cold-weather gear – trousers, jackets, rugs, plaids, scarves, hats, blankets and gloves – with which she positively festoons herself. I almost have to build her into the boat, layer by well-constructed layer. All that generally remains visible at the end of the process is the protruding cigarette and the faintly discernible outline of her fingers, rapidly manipulating rod and line. I wouldn't mind so much, except that she also always manages to catch the first fish of the season into the bargain.

Summer does eventually come, sometimes, up here in Caithness. The wind drops, we remove the ballast stones from our pockets, adopt an unaccustomed, upright posture and stride over the hills with the family in search of sport; clothing as light as our hearts, we haunt our beautiful hill lochs. In June it never really gets dark and at times we stay out all night, sharing some magical loch with a friendly otter or curious black-throated diver.

My introduction to naturist-wading came one splendid, blisteringly hot, Caithness August afternoon. Abandoning my leaking waders, I decided that swimming would be a far more profitable pastime than fishing. After carefully stacking my clothes, and ignoring the ribald comments of the clan, I was wallowing about in the warm shallows when a large trout rose, out towards the middle.

I scrambled ashore, grabbed my rod, and gingerly waded towards the widening rings. With loch water lapping under my armpits, I cast over the fish. It rose immediately, and I staggered backwards towards the shore, carefully maintaining tension on the line. It was a glorious trout, weighing 2lb 14oz.

'That's how it's done, folks!' I explained. 'Be properly dressed for the occasion and you will always catch fish.' I have been, on every suitable occasion, ever since.

Ladies First

GEMINI
22 MAY TO 21 JUNE

There is a strong possibility that June could bring major problems, leading to sore feet and back pains. You must bear in mind that decisions you make now might have far-reaching implications. You could get lost. Things are often not as they seem to be and could affect your judgement. It is essential that you improve your map-reading abilities. If you are propositioned, then insist upon knowing all the details, including what you are expected to carry, before setting out.

This is also particularly important for anglers considering an expensive time-share purchase. After several fishless months, it is all too easy to fall for the tempting blandishments of glossy brochures; and looking at stunning pictures of people catching fish is a lot easier than catching them yourself. Be cautious. Beware of such phrases as '. . . In recent years the beat has only been lightly fished.' Ask yourself why? The most probable answer is that there have been no fish there to catch for several decades. Or, '. . . Last September, 752 fish were taking during one week.' Upon investigation you may discover that it took two thousand anglers, prawn-fishing from dawn until dusk, to catch them.

Lack of support from those close to you will complicate your plans – not all bank managers are anglers, but you should listen carefully to their advice. Otherwise, house moves and job changes are strongly indicated. After all, £500,000 is a lot of money to pay for a week standing up to the waist in freezing water watching every fish in sight stream straight past you on their way upstream – without so much as stopping to give your flies a second glance.

Your energy level is high and, given caution, you should achieve excellent results through the season, bringing you enormous pleasure and satisfaction. Don't fall into the trap of irregular meals and late nights. Keeping an even tenor of life is the key to your well-being. The fishing could be quite good too.

Travel is highlighted this year, so Geminis planning a fishing holiday should think of the world as their oyster. Paying for the oyster should not be allowed to dampen their enthusiasm. Having avoided the time-share trap, they should be *bullish*. Book the holiday and be damned – something will turn up. If it happens to be a pale-faced man in a pin-stripe suit clutching a summons, so what? Travel again!

It is also a good idea to look further afield in your social life. After all, some females do fish. Make this the year when you exchange that grunting, complaining, unshaven, male lump of a fishing partner for a sylph-like, sophisticated, blonde-haired, Swedish female fly-fisher. Whilst you could get off to a shaky start with her – given your high energy levels – there are some splendid indications suggesting that you will be able to resolve these problems quickly and trends point in the direction of great fun for you both. A discreet, box-numbered advert in one of the

50

fishing magazines could well do the trick – perhaps something along the lines of: 'Mature, financially secure fisherman, non-smoker, teetotaller, seeks private fishing holiday tuition from female instructor. Age not important providing she is between 18–20. Must be able to row. Replies, with colour photograph, in strictest confidence.'

Come alive again this season and recapture some of your spirited youth. This is the year when you should be game for anything – before it is too late. You should also have a full medical, make your will and carefully check your pension rights, prior to getting afloat.

OUR FISHING expeditions generally begin with maps. Ann loves maps. For days, brows knitted, she pores over the Ordnance Survey Sheets and, when this happens, I simply start packing. There is no point in arguing.

Shortly afterwards, come the dreaded words: 'Bruce, I've been looking at the map . . .'

No comment.

'What do think about fishing that loch?' she asks, indicating a small blue dot, surrounded by thick, brown lines without either road or track for miles. 'Wouldn't it be fun!'

'Fun! Good grief, Ann, it would be a nightmare getting there, and by the time we arrived it would be time to come back. Are you mad?'

'We could camp out.'

'What's wrong with St John's or Watten?' My protests are always so much wasted breath, for all the notice Ann takes:

'Yes, won't it be wonderful. Come and look. See, there is a track, winding through the hills almost right to the loch.'

'Hills! Hills be damned. They're ruddy great mountains!'

The battle is brief, the outcome a foregone conclusion. There follows a short, sharp lecture on coronaries, a few discreet hints about the perils of obesity, and the beauty of nature, and good, clean fresh air. I can recite it all, word perfect, and just carry on packing.

'Oh good, you've started packing. Don't forget the camera. I think I saw Charles with it in the garage the other day.' Which comes as no surprise.

Perhaps I am being unreasonable. Ann leads a busy life, locked all day in surgery looking down people's throats or

A place to rest her back and a spot to prop her book

otherwise tending to the needs of the family. To her, a ten-mile hike across the moors is relaxation; a chance to recharge batteries and to escape from the pressures of a busy, demanding lifestyle.

Most people would find the walk and subsequent fishing more than enough. Not Ann. Every aspect of wildlife has to be examined along the way. Is that a hen harrier or a buzzard? Could this be chickweed-wintergreen? Who lives down that hole? Must get these colours right. I just carry everything: Keble Martin's *Concise British Flora*, P. A. D. Hollom's *British Birds*, map and compass, binoculars, camera, sketching-pad and water-colours. Then all the fishing-gear: rods, basket, landing-net and picnic. At times I feel like Bunyan's burdened Pilgrim and look like Sherpa Tensing attacking Everest.

Nowadays, after lunch, she has a short rest. I used to worry when, on looking round, Ann was nowhere to be seen. Perhaps she had been carried off by a golden eagle whilst trying to sketch its lair; savaged by a wildcat whilst feeding it after-lunch scraps; fallen into the loch, attempting to photograph a black-throated diver. But experience has taught me simply to look for the thin spiral of smoke from her cigarette. It marks her den; dry, sunny, sheltered from the wind, with a place to rest her back and spot to prop her book.

In spite of everything I always enjoy our days out in the hills. There have been times so silent that it was almost as though the world had stopped going round. Such grandeur, beauty and absolute serenity; and I suppose it makes the effort involved in

'What a feeble excuse to make for losing my fish'

getting there worthwhile. (I may have exaggerated a bit about what I carry.) Unless Ann encouraged me, I suppose like many men I could become a fireside sluggard, glued to the television, grasping a large dram. Instead, I trip nimbly along behind, up grey, boulder-strewn screes, over desolate, trackless moorlands, and never complain at all. Other than on the way home when, regardless of all the bird-watching, painting and sketching, she has invariably managed to catch more fish than me.

Over the years, I have run out of excuses – which for me is saying quite a lot – all the standard ones, dear to the hearts of duffers throughout the world who blame everything, other than themselves, for lack of angling success. Now, when results are being compared at the end of the day, I try to look unconcerned. Or the other way. I even elevated making excuses into an art form: 'As a gentleman, it would be rude of me to catch more fish than you'; 'I am happy to gillie whilst you fish'; 'I get more pleasure out of watching you catch trout than I do from catching fish myself'; and other such lies. But it fools no one, not even me. Today I am reconciled to the fact that if I catch two fish, then Ann will catch four; if I land a fish of 1lb 8oz, then, as surely as night follows the other thing, she will immediately hook one of 2lb. Regardless of seemingly hopeless weather conditions, Ann always catches fish. Loch Loyal in mid-summer, blisteringly hot, not a ripple to be seen. First cast, a trout of 1lb 8oz. Seven men remained fishless. Loch Watten on a late-August evening, white with midges. A trout of 2lb. I caught nothing. Little Loch Borgie, in Sutherland, during a rainstorm. A magnificent trout of nearly 4lb. Two supposedly 'expert' male companions failed miserably.

I say 'nearly' 4lb, because that particular fish was never properly weighed. When Ann hooked it, inches from the bank, I ran round and took a few gripping photographs of her playing the monster, landed it and hit it on the head. Leaving the trout in the heather I carried on fishing for about fifteen minutes. Then, because it was raining furiously, I retreated to the shelter of the boathouse, taking Ann's fish with me.

In order to keep it in good order I placed the trout in a plastic bag, impaled on a sharp stick adjacent to the building in some six inches of water. It seemed perfectly secure, and there was a strong on-shore wind blowing. If the fish did slip out, it would end up on the bank. Or so I thought.

During lunch our guest, Stanley Tuer, the famous Scourie Hotel 'Boardmaster' announced casually: 'Bruce, you know, I would almost swear there was nothing in that bag.' He waded out and had a look: 'Thought so, the fish has gone.'

'Come on, Stan, stop fooling around. Of course it's there!' I exclaimed.

Ann was watching, carefully, with growing alarm.

'Have a look, if you don't believe me,' called Stanley.

With a sinking feeling, I splashed over and examined the bag. The trout had indeed gone.

I turned helplessly to Ann:

'Darling, I'm sorry, I could have sworn that I had killed it. It must have only been stunned and the bag has acted like an oxygen tent. How can I begin to apologise?'

'You can't,' snapped Ann. 'Just say no more, Bruce, not a word,' she simmered with rage. 'That was the biggest trout that I have ever caught. The depths you men stoop to are unbelievable! What a feeble excuse to make for losing my fish.'

My excuses had worked reasonably well in the early years of our marriage, but began to wear thin as the decades advanced. I now have to resort to more desperate measures, such as making sly comments about casting techniques, insinuating that every fish for miles around has been put down by a certain person's wild splashing. But it never works. Invariably, the moment I open my mouth to complain, *she* hooks yet another.

Once, I really thought that I had finally got the better of Ann. It had been a splendid day – for me. We were fishing a remote hill loch in Caithness and I had taken twelve superb trout, each averaging just under 1lb in weight. Ann had fished hard all day and caught nothing. During lunch, with heavy-handed, pseudo sympathy, I had offered advice, reassurance and even the opportunity of fishing with my flies, giving hints on improving her

casting technique and generally being insufferable. That evening, I reeled in well content and began to walk round the loch to
collect Ann, the weight of my fishing-bag bumping comfortably
behind. The sun was dipping behind Ben Alisky, casting long
shadows across the loch. A golden eagle soared overhead. Late
larks twittered. My joy was complete.

Ann was fishing near the mouth of a small feeder stream,
standing well back from the water's edge, and, as I approached,
I saw the rod-tip bend almost double as a large trout grabbed;
and I wondered just how sorry I would really be were the fish
to escape.

I need not have worried. Ann played the trout like an expert,
neatly beaching it after a fine struggle lasting some ten minutes.
The dammed fish weighed 2lb 15oz, was in perfect condition
and had fought like a demon.

'Well done, dear,' I managed to croak, weakly.

'Thanks, Bruce, just you keep concentrating on quantity.
Leave the quality to me.'

However, my worst moment came a couple of years back,
when we were fishing an East Sutherland hill loch near Melvich,
called Seilge. This is one of our favourite lochs, as yet largely
unaffected by the mass afforestation that has so devastated other
Strath Halladale waters in recent years. Seilge has some wonderful fish and, on its day, can be one of the best lochs in Scotland.
The surroundings are magnificent, peaceful and serene, and
there is a delightful little island, full of wild flowers, loud with
bird-song and the ideal place for lunch.

I would like to pretend that due to high winds I hardly had
time to put my flies in the water, slaving away over hot oars all
day, rowing about the loch like a steam engine just in order to
put her over rising trout. Regardless of my bad back. I would
like to believe that she only caught fish because I personally
selected the three flies which were doing the damage; that with
constantly landing her trout, unfankling her flies and keeping
the boat off the rocks, I was too exhausted to fish. The truth of
the matter is that we were both fishing with the same patterns
of flies. The moment she began catching trout, my supposed
'killer' cast was back in the box quicker than a concert pianist
doing a rapid glissando. It did not a whit of good. Ann caught
twelve trout, keeping five weighing 7lb 8oz. As far as I was
concerned, two more and I would have had a brace.

On another occasion, when we were fishing Loch Sletill in
Strath Halladale, I suggested that my friend Ted Peacock shared

the boat with Ann whilst I stalked the bank. It seemed the polite thing to do, and ensured that I would have the semblance of a reasonable excuse if, at the end of the day, I remained fishless. Bank-fishing can be hard work.

Fortunately, the fates were kind to me, which was more than can be said for Mr Peacock. That evening, when they came ashore, Ann had taken four lovely fish, including one fine specimen of over 2lb; poor Ted hadn't risen a thing.

'It's not bloody fair,' he complained bitterly. 'She only casts where the fish are!'

I knew the feeling, all too well. Once, when fishing Eaglaise Beg in East Sutherland, I was in the stern of the boat, Ann at the sharp end with Blair in the middle, looking after the oars. When fishing three in a boat, we have a rule that everyone takes turns on the oars, half an hour each, then one hour fishing.

Eaglaise Beg is a small, circular loch, reputed to contain excellent quality wild brown trout. There is a large patch of weeds towards the southern shore, and I had directed Blair to arrange the drift in order that we should skirt the edges. As we passed the main body of weed, Ann hooked a beauty and, encouraged by Blair, commenced playing the fish. Meanwhile, several other large trout began rising, just to my right. In such a situation, rather than reel in and wait for Ann to land her fish, I cast urgently over my right shoulder, straining to try and land the flies over the brutes. Ann's fish was making a wild run, and Blair, kind soul, pulled the boat after it, making it impossible for me to reach the rise.

'Hang on, Blair!' I yelled. 'Give me a chance!'

As soon as Ann's fish was safely in the boat, she hooked another, then a third, both expertly landed by our gillie, grunting with delight. I reeled in and sat watching, despondently. In the space of a glorious fifteen minutes, Ann had landed four trout weighing approximately 8lb and lost two more. Then everything went quiet. The rise was over.

'Have fun, did you? Great sport?' I moaned.

'Stop being a baby and get on with your fishing. You will never catch fish unless your flies are in the water. Isn't that what you are always telling us?' she replied.

'Not just now, he won't,' said Blair, indicating his watch. 'My half-hour on the oars is up. Come on, Dad, into the middle. What about trying another drift past the weeds, Mum? What do you think?'

'Not a bad idea,' she answered promptly.

Ann's casting technique is minimal. From the bank, she invariably remains on terra firma, rarely wading, and always keeps well back. At times there is barely the cast to be seen dangling in the shallows, but she seems to persuade them to grab nevertheless.

Strong winds play havoc with Ann's flies and she spends much of the day reconstructing casts. One moment she is there, the next, the landscape is bare. Ann is crouched behind a boulder, out of the wind, wrestling with blood knots.

I have learned not to offer to help, other than at the start of operations, when I am kindly allowed to put up her rod and tie the first cast – whilst she has a cup of coffee and a cigarette. Her attitude is born not out of any great sense of independence, although Ann has that aplenty, rather out of a sense of self-preservation. The last time I offered to help was when we were fishing on the Don:

'Come on, dear, let me carry your rod for you.'

'No, I'm perfectly capable of carrying my own rod.'

'Give me it!'

'No.'

I grabbed Ann's rod and as I did so a size 14 Grouse & Claret dug deeply into the tip of the forefinger of her left hand. She looked at me, eyes watering:

'Thank you, darling.'

Without another word, Ann disappeared behind a large beech tree. I stood, foolishly, and waited. She reappeared, holding the fly.

'Now, give me my rod, please,' she demanded.

From the boat, Ann confines herself to fishing with about two yards of line, moving the flies rapidly across the surface, right to the side of the boat, or simply dancing them over the water, allowing the wind to move the flies and giving the rod the odd jerk from time to time, presumably to encourage the trout. Which it does, mightily. I had first seen this method employed with devastating results on Loch Leven in 1953, whilst fishing with Mr and Mrs Tom Kelly. Tom sat in the stern of the boat, casting at the horizon. Mrs Kelly lay in the bow, flicking the flies across the surface. By the end of the day she had caught more fish to her own rod than the whole of the Perth Angling Club had caught put together. Ann is a natural disciple of Mrs Kelly, who is now casting over that great trout loch in the sky, no doubt regularly out-fishing the rest of the celestial host; and my two daughters, Lewis-Ann and Jean, follow suit. Three of them at it together is an almost unstoppable angling force and very bad news for trout. I believe that there are two instantly recognisable signs of inexperience when it comes to loch fishing north of Mr Hadrian's Wall: one is the angler standing up in the boat, and the other is the long-distance casting battalion. The first is in serious danger of losing his life, quite apart from scaring every fish in the immediate vicinity of the boat, and by the time the second reacts to a rise, the trout has usually long since gone.

A few years ago I was invited to spend a day fishing with a friend who was a well-known and expert angler. Ann came with me and when we arrived at the loch it was apparent that he had not expected that she would be joining us. Like many of our tribe, he obviously considered that a woman's place was in the home, not in a boat with him. Nevertheless, with great courtesy and typical Scottish hospitality, he ushered her afloat and, to smooth matters over, I persuaded them that I should take first stint on the oars.

I arranged the drift and watched as my friend began stripping off miles of line, whisking it expertly out into the far distance.

'Aren't you going to have a cast, Ann?' he asked politely. She had been fishing away for five minutes with her usual short line. He simply hadn't noticed. I could see my companion shaking his head in disbelief.

When Ann hooked and landed the first trout, he was gallant, congratulating her profusely, obviously putting it down to luck. The second fish she caught was greeted with somewhat less enthusiasm and, by the time Ann had a third trout in the boat, he was asking serious, probing questions about her flies and technique.

Me? I sighed wearily. Here we go again, I thought. I only hoped that our friendship would stand the test. I am pleased to say that it did and we all had a wonderful day, some more so than others. Ann caught the fish. We men swapped stories about the ones that had got away. Within the 'Brotherhood of the Angle', men can laugh off their failures. After all, we males naturally make allowances for each other's little foibles – knowing instinctively just how far to go, when enough is enough; sharing angling trials and tribulations in good humour, pals together over post-fishing pints.

It is the 'Sisterhood of the Angle' that bothers me, and the sad fact of life that any one lady angler is far more skilful and successful than any ten men. Bitter though the pill may be to swallow it's true, and there is ample evidence to prove this beyond reasonable doubt.

Georgina Ballantine, on 7 October 1922, landed her famous 64lb Tay salmon below Caputh Bridge, a quarter-of-a-mile from where she hooked it. One can almost hear the grinding of teeth as the Duke of Portland describes the event in his book *Fifty Years and More of Sport in Scotland*:

'I understand that her father was rowing home in the evening with a large spinning bait trailing behind the boat. The bait was suddenly seized and Ballantine told his daugther (who was in the boat) to catch the rod. She did so and kept the point up.'

Clearly, the Duke regarded Ms Ballantine's role in the matter as little other than that of a bystander, lucky to have been in the right place at the right time but by no means to be considered an *angler*. The only reason the fish had been hooked and safely landed was because there was a man in the boat.

Less equivocal is the second-largest salmon ever landed in Scotland, from the Mountblairy Beat on the Deveron, where Mrs Morrison caught a fish weighing 61lb; Mrs Huntingdon, on the River Awe in 1927, taking a 55lb fish, followed three years later by one of 51lb; and more recently, a stream of fish over 20lb in weight, all taken by ladies from our major Scottish streams.

In 1986 Ann and I were hosts to a party of friends fishing the River Forss in Caithness. The group consisted of father, a very experienced salmon angler who had fished all over the world, his two sons, both keen anglers, and their sister, Clare, happy to tag along and have a cast or two when allowed to do so by the *real* fishermen.

During dinner, the night before they were to fish the Forss, I propounded my theory about the excellence of female anglers, and found myself being savagely attacked by what may only be described as rampant male chauvinism.

'Utter rubbish, Bruce. The odd woman may catch the odd fish, but by and large they only do so by luck. They have neither the temperament nor the technique to make good anglers,' said Clare's father, with the air of a man who really knew the facts.

'What about Georgina Ballantine?'

'Exactly. The fish hooked itself. It would have grabbed regardless of who was on the other end of the rod. Pure luck. Nothing else.'

'I suppose that if you had been on the other end of the rod it would have been skill?' I responded.

'Far be it for me to state the obvious, but yes. Men are far more efficient anglers.'

Half an hour later I retired, bloody but unbowed, and the next morning they set off for the river, light of battle glinting in their eyes.

'Coming, Clare?' asked Father.

'Well, only if you don't think I'll be in the way,' she replied.

Although conditions were far from perfect, during the course of the following two days six salmon were landed. By Clare. Her companions never so much as touched a fish, in spite of their best endeavours.

As I laid the salmon out to be photographed, Clare smiling happily in the foreground, I grinned wickedly at her disconsolate companions. Click!

'I rest my case,' was all I said.

Whilst there is nothing certain about fishing, there is perhaps one, unimpeachable rule: *you will not catch fish unless your flies are in the water*, and I think this gives us a clue to the secret of the ladies' success. Determination. A man will stop for a yarn, dram or smoke. Not so the ladies. They fish relentlessly on, ruthlessly inch by inch, meticulously yard by yard, never wasting a moment in idle chatter. When we males are sitting idly in the fishing-hut, swapping stories about the ones that got away, the ladies are still on the water busily catching them. As we watch the hands of the clock creeping ever closer to opening time, the ladies are calculating exactly how many more casts they can get in before close of play.

Jimmy Wallace, a senior gillie at Tillmouth on the River Tweed, used to work with Lady Burnett, the laird's wife, and an expert salmon fisher.

'What time is it, Jimmy?' Lady Burnett would inquire.

'Two minutes to go, Madam.'

'Good! Time for another few casts.'

More often than not, Jimmy told me, during these last few casts, Lady Burnett would hook a fish, including one of the largest Tweed salmon caught in recent years – a magnificent fish weighing 43lb, taken from Pot Pool. In the face of this awesome display of unadulterated dedication to duty, is it any wonder that ladies catch more fish than men? Or is there, perhaps, something else, above and beyond male understanding, more powerful than fine technique or fine casting? I think that there is, but I am equally certain that the ladies are never going to let us in on their secret, no matter how much we may beg, plead or promise. And that's another fact of life.

Sometimes, however, long-held secrets have a nasty habit of resurfacing, much to the embarrassment of the individual concerned. Which only goes to show that truth will out – regardless, I am glad to say, although Ann was less than pleased. It all centred upon worming.

When I started fishing on the River Lyne, at the age of fourteen, I didn't know that my future wife was doing the same, a few miles upstream. If we had met, we probably wouldn't have spoken, both of us being rather shy creatures. In any case, if fish were not rising to the fly, Ann would resort to worms – sheer heresy in my opinion. I didn't speak to people fishing with worms, so you can imagine exactly what sort of a young prig I was; and, I am afraid, when it comes to worming I'm not much better now.

Ann and I look back down the years to these first stumbling, tree-catching, boot-filling days with lasting affection, and I often speculate about what might have happened if we had got to know each other then. I bet I could have persuaded her to abhor worming but, by the time we met and married, it was too late. She had become fixed in her evil ways.

One evening, shortly after we had started going out together, I must have been boasting about how clever I was at catching fish because, with a sigh of exasperation, Ann stopped me in mid-flow and began scrabbling about in her handbag.

'There,' she announced, proudly handing me a photograph, 'that's what I call a trout.'

Lying on the heather was a superb, wild brown trout, weighing approximately 2lb 8oz. There could be no dispute: she had taken the precaution of placing a ruler above the fish.

'You never told me about this,' I said, suspiciously.

'Oh yes I did, but you were too busy blowing your trumpet about all the tiddlers you murder to pay any attention.'

'Where did you catch it?'

'Up the Lairig Ghru.'

'A fish of that size in one of these small burns? You must be joking. Are you sure?'

'Yes, Bruce. You see it's all a matter of skill. Not that I expect you to understand that, being a chuck-it-and-chance-it wet-fly man.'

Suddenly I saw the answer: 'Worms! You were worming. You caught it on a worm.'

'How I caught it doesn't matter. What matters is that it is a far bigger fish than anything you have even lost, let alone caught.'

'But that's not fishing! That's murder. Where on earth is there any skill in dangling a half-drowned worm in front of a hunger-crazed trout ten miles above the snow line? I wouldn't be seen dead doing such a thing.'

'You couldn't,' replied Ann.

'What do you mean, couldn't? Any fool can catch fish like that,' I snapped, witheringly.

'Not if they are dead, my precious,' she announced sweetly.

There the matter rested, and I don't know if it was just out of deference to my feelings or because of an incipient complex, but ever afterwards Ann always waited until I was out of sight before starting to dig. In all our time together, I have only once actually caught her at it.

We were on holiday at Nethybridge, fishing the River Spey during a week of almost continual rain. The cottage was warm and well furnished so we managed to make frequent sorties into the wilds, but fishing was virtually impossible. The Spey was living up to its reputation as the fastest-flowing river in Britain, hurtling by at an amazing speed, bank-high and brown.

One afternoon, in the midst of a particularly vicious thunderstorm, Ann announced that she was going for a walk by the river. I quickly said that I would look after the children and she agreed. This was suspicious because normally, if Ann goes for a walk, everyone goes. To keep us fit. Stop us getting bored. For our own good.

The moment the door closed, I made up the fire and settled comfortably with a good book, but not for long. The children wanted to play games. Blair always wanted to play games. Still does, in fact. Out came the Snakes-and-Ladders, Ludo and Happy Families and I soon regretted avoiding going for a walk.

After an hour or so I began to worry. Ann should have been back, and by then she had to be soaked to the skin. Thinking of the swirling Spey, I panicked and rushed Blair and Lewis-Ann into wellies and waterproofs. We set off at the double, in the gathering darkness, to search for the missing mother.

Blair was wearing a kilt, one I used to wear as a child, and complained bitterly as I almost dragged him through the undergrowth. Lewis-Ann was perched upon my shoulders, hands firmly gripping my nose and ears. I urged the children on, encouraging them to keep a good look-out for Ann.

We found her, standing by the banks of the Allt Mor Burn, close to where it meets the Spey after its long, cold journey from the grey corries of the Cairngorms.

'Are you all right, dear?' I asked. Clearly upset, Ann was crouched in the long grass by the river, tears mingling with raindrops. I noticed the trout-rod by her side. That's why she had suddenly decided to go fishing. She had been worming the burn. 'What on earth is the matter?'

The pool she had been fishing was perfect for her purpose: deep, with a strong central current, calm eddies, overhanging branches, steep banks. I imagined Ann crouching in the storm, expertly casting her worm into the stream, working it through all the likely lies. The evidence of her effort lay at her feet: a beautiful trout of about 1lb 12oz.

'Gosh, that's terrific! But what's the problem?'

'I can't get the hook out of its mouth.'

'Hold on a moment, I'll do it. Look, children, see what Mummy's caught. Trout for tea!'

'You mustn't kill it,' Ann cried.

'Why ever not? Why did you catch it in the first place?'

'Take the hook out and put it back. Now.'

'Are you sure?'

'Now!'

There are times when I know that it is pointless to argue with Ann. Instant obedience is all that is required. I removed the hook, carefully held the trout in calm water, head upstream, and waited until it swam off into the depths. I don't know a lot about fishing, and I most certainly know even less about women. Strange creatures.

Our battle regarding fishing with worms has raged on and off throughout our married life, and it is only since we moved to the far north that Ann has given up worming. Nowadays we mostly fish lochs and even she would never consider fishing them with anything other than flies. However, as we cross some small, rushing Highland stream, streaking the moorland white, tumbling urgently seawards, I sometimes notice that look in her eyes. She will stop and watch the current sweeping round a large rock, leaving circular, frothing eddies. And I know that she is thinking of the Lairig Ghru trout.

That damned fish plagued me for nearly thirty years. The wretched photograph, dog-eared and fading, would miraculously appear the moment I began to bleat disparagingly about the worming brigade. Ann would raise a quizzical eyebrow and counter-attack: 'Well, if you haven't done it, how can you say that there is no skill in worming?'

'That's not the point. Worming is immoral.'

'Do you want to argue about morals or fishing, dear? Make up your mind.'

'Can't you see that fishing with worms is too easy. It is not sporting. The fish don't stand a chance.'

'I'm only trying to point out, Bruce, that in certain conditions, such as when fishing a tiny, narrow, Highland stream in spate, then worming is the obvious method to use. Do you understand? Or would you like me to give you an example?'

I suffered in silence. Until 1989. Then, one afternoon, whilst I was working away at the deathless prose, the telephone rang. It was my elder brother, Ian, calling to have a blether, and to impart world-shattering information. Apparently, he had just returned from an Edinburgh business-lunch, during the course of which his neighbour had asked: 'Are you related to Bruce Sandison, the writer?'

'Yes,' Ian had replied.

He has learned over the years that honesty is the best policy. Trying to deny any relationship generally only leads to greater confusion. He owned up bravely, wondering which of my lies his unfortunate lunch-time companion had fallen for.

I am made of sterner stuff. Once, whilst waiting for Blair to come ashore from Loch Watten, I was accosted by a fellow angler who had laboured mightily all day and caught nothing. The substance of his complaint seemed to be that he had only come north to fish the loch after reading my glowing reports about the quality of the sport.

He turned on me: 'If I could lay my hands on that blighter Sandison, I'd tell him a thing or six. The greatest writer of angling fiction in Scotland, that's what he is. Do you know him?'

'Not really,' I replied, 'although I think he lives somewhere round here.'

Ian braced himself, expecting the worst.

'Well,' came the reply, 'I don't know him, but I do know his wife, Ann.'

Ian was immediately interested.

'Oh?' he responded, casually, trying not to sound too eager.

'Yes, I taught her to fish.'

I interrupted Ian: 'Just a minute, Ian, this didn't happen to be in the Lairig Ghru, by any chance, in about 1958?'

'Yes!' Ian said. 'How on earth did you know?'

'And did this chap just happen to catch a 2lb 8oz trout, on a worm, when Ann was there?'

'Amazing! You are absolutely right. He told me that they had taken a photograph of the fish, but that he had lost it, years ago.'

A great weight lifted from my mind:

'Thank you, Ian. How very kind. However, the next time you meet him, tell him that he didn't teach Ann to fish, it was Charles Rhodes, her father.'

I returned to my words, pondering this informative gem of purest ray serene, relishing the hours ahead, before Ann returned home from her surgery. How would I approach the question? Surely a gentleman would say nothing? Let sleeping dogs lie?

'Hello, Ann, had a busy day?' I asked, solicitously, when she returned. 'Ready for a transfusion?' After work, Ann sometimes enjoys a glass of red wine, and friends of ours, Ron and Mary Morris from St Andrews, with whom we fish each year at Altnaharra, had christened the event 'Ann's transfusion'. The moment she appeared in the bar before dinner, Ron rang the bell for Ann's refreshment.

I poured the glowing red fluid and handed her the glass. Unnerved by such a dutiful, unusually warm reception, Ann glanced at me, wondering what was coming next.

'Do you remember that big trout you caught in 1958, up the Lairig Ghru, dear?'

'For goodness sake, Bruce, surely you are not going to start lecturing me about worming again? I've had a terrible day. At least let me sit down.'

'Do, do, by all means, darling,' I replied, courteously.

'Of course I remember it.'

'Well, all I want to know is who caught the fish? Was it really you, as you have been claiming for damn near thirty years, or could it have been someone else?'

Ann gulped into her wineglass and blushed brightly. Slowly, she sat down and peered up at me.

'How can you possibly know that, after all these years? Can't I get away with even a tiny white lie? I knew that I would live to regret it.'

'And it's regretting time now, dear!' I exclaimed triumphantly.

'Listen, Bruce, the moment I told you about that fish I knew that you would instantly leap to the wrong conclusion and imagine that I had caught it.'

'Rubbish! You told me that you had caught that trout.'

'All I ever said was that the fish had been caught, on a worm, up the Lairig Ghru. Never once did I say that I caught it. You only assumed that I had.'

'Well, you certainly did nothing to correct my error, and I have suffered nearly thirty years' torment because of that damned fish.'

I told Ann about Ian's phone call and poured her another transfusion to steady her nerves.

'Fancy splitting on me like that. You would have thought that after all these years he could have kept quiet about it. Telling your brother. I ask you.'

'Me? I'm delighted, dear. I think Ian is a public benefactor. I am forever in his debt.'

'Anyway, he is no better than me, pretending that he taught me to fish. Father taught me to fish, long before I met *him*.' Ann was angry and clutching at straws.

'As I have always suspected, amongst fishers, honour there is not. At least I'm off the hook, if you will pardon the expression.'

'That's what you think,' she responded, ominously.

'What do you mean? There is no way that you will ever be able to cut me down to size again by threatening to produce that photograph. I'm free.'

Ann paused, and then, with a wicked grin, said: 'Tell you what I'll do, Bruce. If you promise not to mention the Lairig Ghru trout, I'll promise to forget about that huge fish I caught when we were out with Stan Tuer. You remember. The one you *accidentally* lost? The plastic bag in the loch?'

I gulped, stunned, stuttering for words.

'That's really below the belt.'

'Do you, or don't you, agree?'

'What about the photograph?' I protested.

'Easy,' replied Ann. 'Give me the photograph of the Borgie trout, and I promise that you will never see the Lairig Ghru trout again.'

'But what will you do with the Borgie photograph?' I inquired weakly.

'That, my darling, will be entirely up to you.'

I capitulated, meekly, gasping like a well-played trout.

66

Test Your Angling IQ

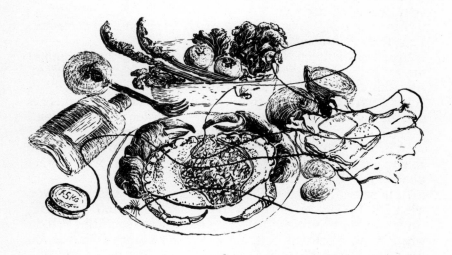

CANCER
22 JUNE TO 23 JULY

You should have a pleasant year as your finances improve and you might be tempted to look for a project that will become a second source of income. However attractive these options might seem, caution and care are advisable.

An opportunity to increase your earning capacity will arise in

July, but if you grasp it you will undoubtedly end up spending the greater part of this year, and the next three years, as a guest of Her Majesty. Therefore, beware of tall dark strangers in pubs, bearing nets and maps of Scottish salmon streams.

You are coping well enough with the rising cost of angling. Concentrate upon saving for that month's salmon fishing you have booked on the Spey, and try not to over-react to the problems that arise in personal relationships. Just keep the wife and kids working – providing this does not interfere with the provision of packed lunches, or getting you to the river on time.

This is a good year to seek favours, so you might suggest that the family take on evening jobs as well. Every penny counts when it comes to funding the important things in life – such as your fishing – and the omens suggest that they will be understanding and supportive, at least for the time being. Use this good fortune to consolidate your angling privileges.

You appear to be surrounded by helpful people, in itself helping to create the atmosphere in which you thrive, whether on a river, or out in a boat on a loch. Use their helpfulness ruthlessly to your own advantage, and accept every fishing invitation that comes your way.

A change of scene is also a possibility, so be ready for the unexpected. Make sure that your passport is valid for British Columbia, and that your bag is packed, so that you can respond instantly when the call comes.

It will be obvious early in the year that your affairs promise to show some rapid progress. The double Spey cast will become second nature and you will land every fish that you hook. At the moment the outlook is ideal for anything which involves long-term commitment. Buy the beat on the Tweed. Raise the cash by any means, fair or foul. If you are prepared to make a determined effort during this phase, there is every likelihood that you will end up on a winning streak, but you will need to be alert in order to reap the benefits of these remarkable trends. Concentrate constantly when salmon fishing. You could catch a fish of over 40lb in weight.

Whatever your plans or undertakings you can count on successful results. Meanwhile, spend every moment of your time either fishing, or getting your tackle into really tip-top condition for your assault on the Spey. Get your mind into tip-top condition as well by studying angling techniques and tactics. Are you really as well informed as you think you are? Read everything you can find about your chosen beat. You will have a wonderful month,

, with wonderful sport, and return to your family refreshed and invigorated, ready to support them in their endeavours to provide sufficient funds for your future fishing expeditions.

DO YOU REALLY enjoy fishing? Which would you least like to lose: your wife or a 56lb salmon? How often do you talk about anything other than angling? Would your best friend tell you if you did? Have you a best friend? Indeed, have you any friends at all, other than fishing companions? Answer these and all the other angling questions hidden deep in your subconscious by completing the test below. Discover the real angling YOU!

This IQ test has been specially designed to reveal your true attitude towards fishing. It is the result of nearly forty years intensive study into psychosomatic angling attitudes arising from accumulated self-induced physiological fishing disturbances. Or, to put it in layman's terms, how otherwise intelligent humans become fishing daft.

The test has been compiled by Bruce Sandison, one of Scotland's most expert and knowledgeable anglers – at least, that's what he keeps telling everyone. Mr Sandison began fishing on the Tweed in 1954 where he caught his first trout on the backcast, somewhere near Lyne Station. He caught another one recently.

The marking process has been statistically designed to ensure that account is taken of your natural instinct to hide from the truth – and the fisherman's natural instinct to make small things seem much bigger than they in fact are. Higher marks may not necessarily denote higher excellence, or greater sanity. Be truthful. If you can.

Answer the questions carefully to see how far along the road to complete fishing madness you have progressed. Who knows, perhaps you may find that you are one of the lucky ones for whom there is some hope. There may still be enough time, with proper treatment, to effect a cure. Read on to find the truth about YOU!

SECTION ONE

This section tests your attitude and adaptability to certain common angling situations. Each question has three possible answers. Tick the one closest to your reaction to the problem described.

(1) You have been told of a magnificent loch, four miles out into the hills, unfished for twenty years, and full of monster trout. Would you:

    a) share the secret with your regular fishing companion
    and invite him to join you?   (8)
    b) pretend that you had to paint the garage and sneak
    off alone?   (6)
    c) think that your informant was talking nonsense,
    having heard that one before?   (4)

(2) Having decided to have a look, just to make sure, you hike out into the hills and arrive at the loch only to find that you have forgotten to bring nylon to make up casts. Would you:

    a) unravel your nylon socks and plait the strands
    together?   (8)
    b) pull the longest hairs from your head, and other
    parts of your body, and use them?   (6)
    c) walk back to the car for the nylon?   (4)

(3) Having walked back to the car for the nylon and then back to the loch, you fish all day in the pouring rain and catch nothing. You do not even see a fish rise. Having arrived back at the car, you discover that you have dropped your landing-net somewhere along the way. It is getting dark. Would you:

    a) pin a note to the fence, with your name and address,
    asking the next angler passing that way to return your
    net to you?   (8)
    b) walk back along the track in the unlikely chance that
    you might find it?   (6)
    c) go home and buy a new one?   (4)

(4) You have decided to abandon the net and go home. The car will not start. It is now completely dark and raining heavily. Would you:

    a) walk ten miles to the nearest phone and call a garage? (8)
    b) try to effect a temporary repair using binder-twine
    and anything else that comes to hand?   (6)
    c) scream loudly and kick the wheels?   (4)

(5) You phone the garage and eventually arrive home at 4 a.m. Your wife

does not speak to you. Recovery and repairs to your car cost £500. Neverthe-less, you decide to return to the loch the following Saturday. When you arrive at the loch, an ill-considered cast entangles your 'killer flies' beyond reach in a tree. Would you:

    a) gather large boulders and build a mound to help you
climb the tree?   (8)
    b) reverse the rod and attempt to 'hack' the branch
down to your level?   (6)
    c) make up a new cast?   (4)

(6) You reverse the rod and 'hack'. In the process, you discover the butt section of your rod has come loose and is now firmly entangled in the tree along with your cast. The line has snapped, due to ill-considered, fierce tugging. Would you:

    a) attempt to cut the tree down with your trusty fishing
knife?   (8)
    b) pray for a thunder storm and a bolt of lightning?   (6)
    c) walk back to the car for the roof-rack so that you
can use it as a ladder?   (4)

(7) Having humped the roof-rack to the tree, you manage to climb up and retrieve both rod and flies. Ten hours later you have caught nothing. You have not seen a fish rise. You are tired, hungry and dispirited. Would you:

    a) slaughter a passing sheep for sustenance, spend the
night in the boathouse and try again come dawn?   (8)
    b) end it all by throwing yourself in the loch?   (6)
    c) stagger home with the roof-rack but decide to return
again the following week?   (4)

(8) Your wife is seeing a lawyer about divorce but, nevertheless, the next Saturday you set off for the loch. The car has been serviced and you have carefully double-checked your fishing-tackle; and you have booked the boat. Upon arrival, you find that the boat is beached, upside down, a hundred yards from the water's edge. Would you:

    a) round up six deer and persuade them to help you
tow the boat to the water?   (8)
    b) risk a heart attack and attempt to man-handle the
boat to the loch by yourself?   (6)
    c) walk back to the phone and invite your fishing friend
out for a day's sport?   (4)

(9) You and your fishing friend, after a great struggle, manage to heave the

boat to the water's edge. After your exertions, you have a rest. When you awaken, you find that the boat has sunk and that one oar is missing. Would you:

a) drag the boat to the boathouse and set fire to them
both? (8)
b) return home and have yourself committed to a lunatic
asylum? (6)
c) bank-fish? (4)

(10) Having bank-fished all morning without catching anything, you find a two-inch Devon spinning minnow lying in the heather. Would you:

a) confiscate it and report the matter to the appropriate
authorities at a later date? (8)
b) throw it in the loch in order that other anglers should
not be tempted to use it? (6)
c) attach it to the end of your line, for safe keeping and
'accidentally' fish with it? (4)

(11) You have fished with the minnow for three hours and still caught nothing. You rejoin your fishing friend. He has been fly-fishing and has caught forty-six trout weighing 86lb. Would you:

a) foam at the mouth and accuse him of spinning? (8)
b) smile politely and compliment him on his ability? (6)
c) offer to help him carry his catch back to the car? (4)

(12) Once back at the car, your friend offers you part of his catch as a reward for helping him carry the fish, and also for introducing him to such a splendid loch. He gives you three trout. You arrive home. Your wife is packing. Would you:

a) apologise to your wife for catching so few fish? (8)
b) say that you gave most of your catch to the local old
folks' home? (6)
c) tell the truth and hope for sympathy? (4)

SECTION TWO

This section of the test will give you the opportunity to demonstrate your grasp of angling phraseology. The listed sentences are all common, oft-used expressions, in daily use by anglers throughout the world. Three alternative meanings are given for each. You should select the alternative nearest to your understanding of the true meaning of the expression involved.

(1) Casting aspersions

    a) accusing someone of spinning   (6)
    b) high-heeled waders   (4)
    c) new kind of fly-line   (2)

(2) A dry boat

    a) a boat with no water in it   (6)
    b) a boat with no fish in it   (4)
    c) a boat with no whisky   (2)

(3) Free-rising fish

    a) you do not have to pay to make them rise   (6)
    b) a single trout rises once, at dawn   (4)
    c) a single trout rises once, at midday   (2)

(4) Well over the 2lb mark

    a) 1lb 15oz   (6)
    b) 1lb   (4)
    c) 15oz   (2)

(5) A fair walk

    a) walking when it is not raining   (6)
    b) at the top of a mountain, after a four-hour hike   (4)
    c) walking for three days   (2)

(6) Safe wading

    a) eight-feet deep underwater pot-holes   (6)
    b) glutinous peat   (4)
    c) it is guaranteed that you will fall in   (2)

(7) Wife

    a) a person who cooks trout   (6)
    b) someone who looks after the children when you go fishing   (4)
    c) a woman capable of rowing a boat in force eight gales   (2)

Gather large boulders and build a mound

(8) Fishing friend

a) a young lady with the same abilities as your wife   (6)
b) a companion who catches fewer fish than you do   (4)
c) a casual acquaintance with a good salmon beat   (2)

(9) Casting technique

a) casting for three minutes without getting fankled   (6)
b) something everyone else seems to have   (4)
c) a fishing method which ensures that flies avoid trees, rocks, ears, hands, and fish.   (2)

(10) Local knowledge

a) advice about the worst places to fish   (6)
b) a thirsty local angler   (4)
c) down-right lies   (2)

(11) Fishing Hotel

a) a place where you spend a vast amount of money not
catching fish (6)
b) an establishment that locks the front door at 9 p.m.
each night (4)
c) a charitable institution supported by anglers for the
benefit of the owner. (2)

(12) Expert angler

a) an angler who has caught a fish (6)
b) an angler who claims to have caught a fish (4)
c) everyone else other than you (2)

HOW DID YOU DO?

Well, how did you get on? To find out, add up your score and
consult the tables below to see how you rate. If your result is
not all that you expected, don't worry – there isn't much that
you can do about it anyway. If you are really concerned, then I
suggest that you do what I do when things don't go as planned:
go fishing! It's amazing just how quickly troubles fade and a
proper sense of perspective returns. Regardless of your score,
carry on fishing, and Tight Lines in all your efforts!

0 – 40 You are letting things get you down. Stop worrying. We
can't all be experts. Relax. Learn to live with your limitations.
Enjoy your fishing in whatever way you can. Remember, success
in fishing is largely a matter of luck. You might just get lucky,
who knows? I should also learn to swim.

40 – 100 You are a normal, healthy angler with no hang-ups
and have nothing to worry about. Your attitude towards fishing
is well-balanced and realistic. You would never do anything
unsporting; you always return undersized fish to the water. You
are considerate and courteous to your fellow anglers at all times.
In fact, just like me.

100 – 168 Sorry, but it has gone too far. You are only interested
in catching fish and completely oblivious to anything else around
you. You measure success only in terms of numbers and size of
fish caught. You also invariably catch more fish than the rest of
us. Your only hope is to give up fishing, immediately, thereby
leaving a lot more fish for the likes of me.

Full Fathom Five

Leo
24 JULY TO 23 AUGUST

Travel and changes on the home front are highlighted in July, although upsets within the family circle are also likely. Take great care that you do not expose yourself unwittingly to family ridicule by ill-considered actions. Lack of communication may be one cause, but it is difficult to communicate with them if you spend most of your time halfway up a mountain, fishing. Something they never seem to be able to understand. More important, however, is the fact that each member seems to be pulling in a different direction, and this could seriously damage your fishing opportunities.

From the summer solstice onwards, your affairs are likely to meet complications. Beware of accidents, particularly to tackle and equipment, but the real crunch could come in the Central Court of the Old Bailey, around the time of the New Moon, when you realise that business colleagues and others have been taking advantage of you; dipping substantial fingers into the till and forging your signature whilst you were otherwise engaged, fishing.

This is the time for clear thinking and a good lawyer, and recognising the need to wield your authority whilst you have any left to wield. Be prepared to experiment, particularly with creative accounting, and break new ground – which, if your plans fail, you could find yourself doing, on the end of a pickaxe.

Take comfort in the fact that, in spite of what it may seem, the planets are working to your advantage and to the ultimate benefit of your fishing career, if not for your business interests; but prepare for action when the Sun enters Cancer, when there will be moments when you feel isolated and rather alone – particularly whilst on remand. It would be a good idea not to contemplate any new business ventures at this time.

However, circumstances should change for the better and your unselfish handling of a friend's medical problem should bring you just reward – in the shape of a very large trout – and you will soon be able to concentrate upon your own plans, rather than upon those of others. The family will survive, somehow. Your angling future looks bright and there are marvellous opportunities for full-time fishing. Now that you have sold the Rolls-Royce, the yacht, the villa in the Bahamas and the country mansion, settled the alimony, and provided for the children, you can at last afford to take that job as a gillie in Wester Ross.

Be confident that the outcome of the court case was the best thing that has ever happened to you. Be delighted that you escaped a long prison sentence, which would have seriously interfered with your fishing. City scandals are soon forgotten. Fishing is forever.

With an end to your present money problems, having none, your job will be more than adequate to provide for all your needs. Accommodation is usually included, along with all necessary fishing-tackle, three meals a day, and unlimited quantities of whisky from grateful gentlemen. From now on your fishing will be constant and entirely free of charge.

Practise a grunting, slurred, Scottish accent and seek financial assistance from the Department of Social Security for the purchase of a kilt and a deer-stalker. Send regular, scenic, Scottish postcards to your late business associates, c/o HM Prison, Parkhurst, Isle of Wight.

Be happy. You deserve it.

I F MEMBERS of my family do anything really utterly careless or stupid, I count up to ten – then have apoplexy, and tell them what I think . . . if I get the chance . . . which is rare. In our household, there seems to be a built-in 'Father's-about-to-have-a-fit' warning system. It's called Charles. For years he has been able to forecast my imminent outbursts accurately to the second, and by the time I get going there isn't a single Sandison to be seen. Other than me, left foaming at the mouth, uttering dire threats, spluttering at departing backs, listening to their derisive hoots of laughter.

Of course, Charles has had more practice than the rest of the clan, since nine times out of ten it is his blood that I am after. I ask you, what would you think of an angler who knocked his rod over the side of the boat into the deepest part of the loch? Nor was it windy at the time – the reverse was true, an almost dead flat calm. Can you imagine it? Two hundred pounds' worth of custom-built cane disappearing into the depths. 'Good grief!' I hear you utter, 'how could anyone be so stupid?'

I can provide you with a detailed account because, unfortunately, I was the one that did it, and when I returned home that evening, rodless, they loved it. Of sympathy there was none. After the first momentary expressions of sorrow and barely concealed mirth came their wickedly barbed shafts, faster than English arrows at Agincourt.

'Say that again, Dad, exactly what happened?' crowed Blair, by now glowing with pleasure. 'You knocked the rod out of the boat with which part of your anatomy?'

'My behind. You heard me the first time and it's no laughing matter.'

'Well you only have yourself to blame, Father. If you had

stuck to the diet mother gave you your behind wouldn't be
so . . ..'

'Lewis-Ann, that's quite enough,' said Ann.

'Like Dad's behind?' quipped Charles, joyfully.

'It was a stupid thing to do though, Bruce. How did it
happen?' added Ann, unkindly.

'It was an accident . . ..'

'Accident!' exclaimed Charles, delighted, 'I thought you
didn't believe in accidents, Dad?'

I had been out that day with a farmer friend, Sandy Bremner,
fishing on Loch Watten, when Sandy had hooked a rather nice
trout. Being a decent sort of fishing companion, I reached for
the net and landed the fish:

'. . . and as I turned round to hand him the trout, I knocked
the rod over the side. Believe me, that's how it must have
happened.'

'Believe that and you'll believe anything,' grunted Blair. 'It's
far more likely that he threw his rod into the loch in a rage
because Sandy had caught a fish.'

'I can't imagine Dad helping anyone land a fish. He always
makes me land my own. Says it's character forming,' complained
Lewis-Ann. 'Are you sure that's what happened, Father?'

Once Sandy's trout had been placed safely in the bag, I turned
round to continue fishing; it took me a moment or two before I
realised that the rod was missing. Puzzled, I even peered under
the thwarts, wondering where it could be.

My partner fished on, unaware of my plight, then looked
curiously at me.

'Not giving up, are you Bruce? Come on, look, there's a fish
rising in front of you.' It was difficult to respond, but eventually
Sandy noticed my deliberate mistake: 'Hey, where's your rod,
then? No, it hasn't! You didn't!'

I must have had a premonition that day because, for the
only time in my life, I had taken a second rod. A last-minute,
inspirational gesture. But my heart wasn't in it and I knew that
when I got back to camp that night I would have to face the
music. A major orchestra in full cry. The rod was a particular
favourite, specially built to my personal specification, a trusted
old friend – now residing at the bottom of Loch Watten. It
would be impossible to replace.

I seemed to have had bad luck all season. On our first outing,
I had broken the tip of the rod. Another *accident*. Ann and I
were fishing a hill loch in Strath Halladale and the wind was

'My behind. You heard me the first time'

blowing hard. As usual, I was minding the oars whilst my better half caught the fish.

'Well done, dear, that must be your fourth fish this morning. What does it feel like, catching trout?'

Ann turned to glower at me and her cast fankled in the strengthening breeze. Whilst I was busy sorting out the mess, I left my flies where they had been for most of the morning, trailing behind the boat. Ann lit a cigarette and waited patiently. Meanwhile, my own flies became snagged on some underwater obstruction, unfortunately finless, and, whilst my reel screamed in protest, I wrestled with the oars, trying to keep the boat off the rocks, with the fankle, Ann's rod and my own.

'Can you manage, dear?' asked my considerate fishing partner.

All the backing ran out and a sudden gust of wind swung the boat viciously round. There was a snap, and the tip of my rod slid down the line into the water.

'Oh look, Bruce, your rod's broken.'

'Yes, dear,' I replied, 'I had noticed.'

I managed to effect a temporary repair and fished on for the rest of the day. I caught nothing. She caught another three.

Friends joined us on our next expedition, nice people, reasonably competent anglers, good fun to be with – except in a boat on a North of Scotland trout loch when fish are rising. There being only one boat on the loch, I knew exactly what was going to happen the moment we arrived:

'Now, Bruce, don't you worry about me, I'll just bank-fish. There's only room for three in the boat and I'll be fine. Look on the bright side. If you break your rod again, you will only have yourself to blame; I'll be miles away,' Ann announced

81

cruelly. 'After all, you are far better at telling people what to do than I am.' She was off down the bank like a rabbit, disappearing over a small hill, then reappearing again, several hundred yards along the shore on a narrow promontory, lashing away almost before she had come to a proper standstill.

I launched the boat and, resigned, took the oars. Three hours later, with trout jumping all round, we were still fishless. I noticed Ann, inching down the far bank, stopping every so often to land yet another fish. Not that nothing was being caught in the boat, you appreciate, except for the fact that it was mostly me:

'No, no, it's all right! Really. The hook wasn't very far in anyway, and I do have another ear, just in case!' ha, ha. 'Just lower the point of the rod and I'll sort it out. Oh, now you've caught John's rod. Never mind, let me have them both. This wind is making things very difficult for you both. . . . Another dram? Certainly. Hold on a minute whilst I get the boat out a bit . . . there you are.' Crash. 'Not to worry, often happens in a boat, that. You put the glass down and suddenly the wind changes. Mind the broken glass. No, you fish on, I'll clear it up and pour you another. Have my glass. More water? Or is that enough? . . . Cast to your left . . . a bit further. It was a beauty. Stop! Hang on! I think your tail fly is in the back of my neck.' All part and parcel of the joys of angling. At least I didn't damage my rod. It was never out of its case.

Perhaps I'm accident prone and deserve to be punished for lack of care, for being too impatient. I would never admit this to the rest of the family but, in my heart of hearts, I have to confess that more often than not I really only have myself to blame for most of my mishaps. Sadly, however, this sometimes affects others, as poor Ann has found out to her cost all too frequently.

It would be silly of me to try and single out one supremely embarrassing moment, there have been so many, but a memory that makes me shudder particularly, is the time when I broke not my rod, but Ann's – motivated by nothing other than the best of intentions; only trying to help.

We had walked out with Stanley Tuer, southwards from Scourie towards Ben Stack, past the Gorm Loch and on to a series of excellent little waters – Pound, Aeroplane, Boot and Otter – many of which contain large trout. When we arrived at the first, we assembled our rods. Or at least Stanley and I did. Ann was struggling to join the middle and top sections of hers

82

together. They refused to fit for some unknown reason. If I had left Ann to it, no doubt in time she would have resolved the problem. Instead, I grabbed the rod, irritated: 'Let me have it, dear, I'll soon sort it out.'

Ann gave me that look she reserves for occasions when she senses disaster approaching, but handed the two sections over. Two minutes later I had succeeded in breaking off the ferrule from the top section.

'Ann, I'm sorry, I was only trying to help,' I whined, mortified. We were miles from base and there was no possibility of going back for another rod.

She took the broken bits and delved in her fishing-bag, producing bandages, splints and binding tape. A few moments' work produced a reasonable repair.

'Now,' Ann announced firmly, 'I want your garter tabs.' These were bright yellow and my pride and joy. I had acquired them in Aden, whilst serving Queen and Country, and they were part of my life. Meekly I removed them and handed them over. They were unceremoniously wrapped round the repair to hold everything together.

We fished on for the rest of the day, with Ann making adjustments to her rod as we went. The top section tended to fall over at forty-five degrees to the main section but, in spite of that small difficulty, Ann still managed to catch trout.

As we tramped homewards, Stan turned to me and muttered: 'You know, Bruce, Ann is an amazingly tolerant person. If you had done that to my rod I think that I would have chucked you straight into the loch.'

The loss of my trout-rod in Loch Watten seemed to confirm my suspicion that I was not as perfect as I thought and, consequently, I tried to keep calm as the family waded in.

'I'll lend you my goggles and flippers if you want, Dad,' offered Charles.

I was just about to buffet him when I realised that he had probably hit upon the only possible solution. Ann meets all kinds of people in her surgery and I remembered her talking about a keen sub-aqua man. At the time I had made caustic comments about thick-skinned idiots incapable of feeling the cold and only intent upon scaring fish. Now I positively grovelled at her feet begging this paragon's name and address; and veritable paragon he proved to be, the very pinnacle of underwater efficiency, listening carefully to my tale of woe, agreeing to help.

Two weeks after the 'accident', which I insisted upon calling the event, we launched the Watten Lodge boat and set off in search of the missing rod. I had marked the location in my mind, as accurately as I could, and as we approached, my companion donned his gear and toppled backwards into the loch. The plan was simple. We would plough the area, with me on the oars rowing and up and down in as near parallel lines as possible, the diver following behind, coming up frequently to check directions. Watten is not a deep loch and only averages eight feet, but there are one or two deeper spots, and my rod had gone down close to one such hole.

I rowed around for forty-five minutes. The diver surfaced to change cylinders. We ploughed on, in spite of my suggestion that we abandon the search:

'Look, it's very good of you, but I think this is hopeless.'

'I've half an hour left in this bottle, Bruce, we'll give it until then,' he replied kindly.

Minutes before time ran out I saw my rod break the surface, clutched in his hand, the reel screaming because the flies were still intact but snagged on the bottom. I will never forget the feeling of relief and gratitude, and supreme joy, at seeing my old friend once more. I was sure that the rod had gone forever. We returned home triumphantly and the family gathered round to inspect the damage.

'Come on, Dad,' said Lewis-Ann. 'Let's have it. You are now going to tell us that there was a 6lb trout attached to the tail fly but that you put it back.'

'No, my little precious, would I invent such a story?' I asked.

'Yes,' came the reply. But for weeks afterwards, there were some very strange stories circulating amongst the Caithness fishing fraternity, concerning sightings of a huge trout in Loch Watten – so big, that one angler claimed to have seen the splash it made from a distance of at least half a mile when it rose! I didn't disillusion them. Nothing like stories of big fish to encourage the rest.

The rod was refurbished and is as good as new but my credibility and dignity suffered an almost mortal blow. Now, no matter what goes wrong, whatever disaster occurs, they always trot out the same old excuse: 'It was an accident, Dad. You know, just like when you dropped your rod into Loch Watten. Remember?' Remember! I will never be allowed to forget. But later that same year I did manage to regain a certain degree of dignity, by catching a really super Watten trout; and I believe that in doing so my fishing God was rewarding me for coping so nobly with the season's trials and tribulations.

I had gone to the Hebrides with my friend, Roy Eaton, then editor of the fishing magazine *Trout and Salmon*. Our plan was to fish a few of the machair lochs on South Uist and then write an article about our experiences. Blair and Barbara had kindly agreed to accommodate us, and John Kennedy, Fishery Manager of the South Uist Estate, had reserved fishing and boats.

The trip was a complete disaster, ending up with Roy being rushed down to Daliburgh Hospital and strongly advised to get home as quickly as possible. I was travelling with Roy and faced the problem of somehow getting back to Caithness from Kyle of Lochalsh at two o'clock in the morning. Ann, driving north from visiting her parents, eventually picked me up and we got back to Ruther House, tired and exhausted, at about dawn. We slumped into bed and instantly fell asleep.

I was woken the following morning at about nine o'clock by Sandy Bremner:

'Hello, Bruce? Pattie and I are going fishing. Do you want to come? I'll be along in ten minutes.'

The last place I wanted to go was fishing, but it would have seemed churlish to refuse, so I dragged myself upright, grabbed a cup of tea, and was ready and waiting when they arrived. Happily, they allowed me to attend to the oars and I managed to nod off in between landing their fish.

'Come on, Bruce, you have a cast,' offered Sandy, solicitously.

'No, no, Sandy,' I replied, stifling a Gargantuan yawn, 'honestly, I'm fine.' I was half-asleep and worried about how Roy had survived the journey south.

'That's not fair,' said Pattie, abandoning his place in the stern. 'I'll have a go on the oars, you fish,' he insisted.

I picked up my rod, loosed the flies and flicked them out over the stern. Instantly, the big trout grabbed, and after a few, intense minutes, was lying safely in the boat – a fish of just over 3lb and one of the biggest trout to come from the loch for several years. My reward.

That evening I made the most of my triumph, telling the family that it was all a matter of skill and perseverance; that, in spite of being so tired, I had fished relentlessly on, regardless of personal discomfort; how I saw the trout rise, the accurate, thistledown landing of my fly above its nose; the skill I displayed playing it. I had them, cold, the irrefutable evidence of my ability gloriously overlapping the kitchen scales.

I suppose that we all have somewhat inflated ideas about our own angling abilities. My friend Robert Burns certainly knew a thing or six about that – 'Oh, would some power . . . ' – but then, to the best of my knowledge, Burns wasn't an angler and part of the great charm of fishing is dreaming – about ones that don't get away and about filling the glass case.

My favourite dream concerns the dawn rise, when first birds sing and fox and badger seek the safety of their lairs. A light breeze ruffles the water as I crawl on all fours, green-clad, towards the bank of the river. A late owl blinks and flaps off, ghost-like into the gloom of the surrounding forest. I grasp my fishing rod and, in one easy, expert motion, cast over the nose of a rising trout. The moment of truth. There is a sudden tug as a huge trout grabs. I leap to my feet, reel screaming, every muscle aching in anticipation. The trout runs for the weeds. I skilfully turn it. It leaps spectacularly. I drop the point of the rod. Then, triumphantly, I bring the monster towards the net . . . which is generally when the alarm-clock rings.

It's a pity it's just a dream, all make-believe, but that is how I like to think of myself; up at the crack of whatsit and down to the river before first larks stir, let alone ascend. Reality is very different. I could no more get out of bed in time for the morning rise than fly to the moon. I know. I've tried. Even as a child the advent of morning used to fill me with such horror that it could take the combined efforts of the whole family to get my feet on the deck; and at weekends, they didn't even bother to try. In an agony of despair, my mother took me along to see Doctor Henderson, in Brunswick Place, Edinburgh, to make sure that I was 'all there', but the assurances she received did nothing to alter my habits.

Service in the army should have cured me, but I managed to take it all in my stride. I simply altered my sleeping habits: what I lost in the morning, I made sure that I recouped in the evening. But I did fall foul of authority once, though, being late for morning parade. A cardinal crime. The battalion was all lined up, ready for inspection, with one noticeable absentee: me. My OC was outraged and I anticipated a firing squad at the very least. So, determined not to commit the same error again, the very next morning I set the alarm for 6 a.m. and the moment it sounded, leapt from bed, washed, shaved, dressed and dashed off to the parade ground. Glowing with inner pride, I discovered that I was first there. I lurked behind a building, smoking a cigarette, waiting to strut smartly on at the appropriate time.

An hour later, when still nobody had appeared, I realised that it was Sunday morning. Shamefaced, I slunk back to my room.

My OC, whose name I am glad to say I have forgotten, did all that he could to help me. Having discovered that I was a keen and not incompetent swimmer, he volunteered me as captain of the battalion team:

'Just the thing for you, Sandison. Collect the team at the guard house at 0600hrs, and you will all be in the water by 0630hrs at the latest. That will give you an hour's training and still have you on parade by 0830hrs. Don't be late.' For me, an absolute nightmare. Poised in the half-light on the edge of the freezing pool, surrounded by unwilling water-babies, five days a week. For this I had joined the army?

Salvation arrived one night when I was Orderly Officer, in the form of a signal marked TOP SECRET. I dug out the Adjutant from the Mess and together we opened the envelope:

URGENT. OP IMMEDIATE. SUPPLY TWO OFFICERS,
A CAPTAIN AND A 2/nd LIEUTENANT FOR SERVICE
IN ADEN. CONFIRM NAMES BY RETURN.

'My God!' exclaimed the Adjutant. 'Who on earth am I going to find to send to that damn-awful, desolate place?'

'Excuse me, sir, but I rather think that would suit me,' I offered, thinking of the swimming team.

'Are you sure, Bruce?'

'Absolutely.'

Two weeks later I was winging my way across Africa, with stop-overs at Kano in Nigeria and Entebbe on Lake Victoria, then north to Aden where, at last, I was in my element. We worked from 7a.m. until 12.30p.m., and then stopped, leaving me to indulge in a positive orgy of mind-bending, relaxing, undisturbed slumber all afternoon. In fact, it was not until I had the good sense to marry Ann that I began to find sufficient energy to rise at a reasonable hour; and to achieve that took her nearly twenty years' prodding. As far as I was concerned, the spirit was willing but, alas, the flesh was always very, very weak.

Ann used to talk glowingly about fishing the dawn rise and, eventually, I succumbed to her powers of persuasion. But the nearest we came to actually achieving it was in 1966, when we arrived early one morning to fish Derwent Reservoir on the borders of Durham and Northumberland. Trouble was that we caught ten fish, the limit, within moments of arriving and were back home again well before breakfast. If I remember correctly, that was opening day on the reservoir and the fish were giving themselves up, no matter what was chucked in their general direction.

As much to improve our dawn rise fishing opportunities as anything else, in 1968 we moved to a fine old house close to the banks of the River South Tyne, near Bardon Mill in Northumberland. The Tyne was only a ten-minute walk from the house. Five if you ran. Which I frequently did. Nevertheless, somehow, in spite of being so close to the river, in the six years we lived there I never once managed to get out before dawn, to catch them at it. There was a large garden to tend, painting, decorating, pointing, visitors and a hundred and one other things that required urgent attention – petty details of life that always seem to stop a man going fishing. Work is the curse of the fishing classes. By the end of most days we were so tired that the thought of springing brightly from bed and dancing through the cornfields to the riverside had no appeal whatsoever. More often than not, my fishing was confined to quick, pre-dinner-party bursts:

'Bruce, dash down to the river and catch half a dozen trout, would you? They will make a perfect starter for dinner.'

Much to everyone's astonishment, including my own, more often than not I generally managed to comply with Ann's instructions. The South Tyne was one of the finest trout streams that I had ever fished and in those days, far superior to even my beloved Tweed.

For the past sixteen years we have lived in the far north of Scotland, in Caithness, surrounded by some of the finest trout lochs in the land. Our house overlooks Loch Watten, and dozens of other excellent waters are but a short drive away. We have had one attempt at the dawn rise but, like so often before, it was a total disaster.

The loch in question is one of our favourites, Ruard, a short walk west from the A895 Latheron/Thurso road, 'the way Across the Bog' as we call it. In days gone by, travellers used to strap bundles of branches to their saddles, laying them over the dampest parts to allow them and their animals to cross safely. From leaving home, we could be fishing on Ruard in approximately one hour. I say approximately, in order to allow for stops along the way. There is a good track from the road, out to an old farm building at Acharaskill. From there, a sheep path follows the banks of the outlet burn up to the loch and this route is a naturalist's delight; myriad wild flowers, bog asphodel, tormentil, bugle, eyebright, primrose, wonderful clumps of yellow flag, and many more. The surrounding moorlands host golden plover, dunlin, greenshank, meadow pipit, lark, curlew, hen harrier and the occasional golden eagle. Otter fish both stream and loch, and wildcat hunt amidst the heather. The time it took, walking up to the loch, depended entirely upon how often and for how long we stopped and stared.

Ruard is a stunning setting, surrounded by glorious moorlands, including magnificent Blar nam Faoileag, 'the sparkling place', a Site of Special Scientific Interest and a growing, living peat bog, red-sphagnum decked, summer white with cotton grass and alive with the hum of insects. Ann and I have spent many happy hours around there, sometimes hardly bothering to fish for the perfectly marked, red-spotted trout it contains in vast quantities – although in all the years we have fished Ruard, we have never returned empty-handed.

Another of Ruard's attractions is the fact that there is an excellent boathouse close to the water's edge, and it seemed to be the perfect place to spend a night, prior to attacking the dawn rise.

It was mid-May when we decided to have another crack at dawn fishing, and we set off on a Friday evening full of hope and good intentions. Ann had packed a small portable cooker. I packed the hip-flasks.

'Don't worry about taking too much food, Ann,' I announced grandly. 'We will eat the trout we catch.'

'Are you sure, Bruce?'

'Oh Ye of Little Faith!' I responded.

Spring in the Highlands. What memories! The first blink of the warm sun, soft, zephyr-like breezes, curlew calling romantically down the hill. Everything went well, at first. The walk out was wonderful and, by early evening, four trout were gently cooking on the stove. Content, we unrolled the sleeping-bags and settled in for the night, full of anticipation of the coming dawn's delights.

It started snowing at about 9.30p.m. The wind had reached gale force by ten. Waves, blown from the loch, lashed the side of the boathouse with unremitting fury. We huddled in our sleeping-bags, numb with cold, shivering miserably, like twin Calibans locked in riven oaks. Frequent resort to hip flasks did little or nothing to bring back feeling, but through sheer exhaustion, we finally managed to fall asleep. And slept soundly until 8.30 the following morning. Dawn rise? What dawn rise? I don't believe that it ever happens.

All that has ever happened to me, following the elusive trail of early-morning fishing, has been the discovery that the longer one waits out in the hills, the more likely it is that you will be eaten alive by midges: the largest species of animal on planet Earth; and, in my opinion, the most furiously voracious. Ask any angler which animal has existed since pre-Cambrian times, and has lance-like jaws capable of drawing blood, and he will instantly answer, midges.

We fishermen are a curious breed and some become so engrossed with Diptera that fishing sinks to a secondary position on their horizon. Others, particularly in the far north, think of arthropods more in terms of their lance-like jaws. I certainly do, and so does my daughter Jean. Since the age of two-and-a-half, at the first sign of Aptera, Diptera or Hymenoptera she runs a mile. Which proves the potent power of past experience. Once bitten, never forgotten; and as a baby, Jean had suffered a dreadful attack which became ineradicably fixed in her mind.

One hot afternoon in August 1977, Ann and I had taken Jean and Charles out to the Flow Country, intent on a picnic/fishing day. I was more intent on fishing, Jean and Charles on the picnic. It was a blazing summer in Caithness, one of the hottest on record. Our two beaches, Reiss and Dunnet, were crowded with locals and visitors, many swimming in the normally ice-cold waters of the North Sea.

We crossed the bridge at Westerdale and drove out past Loch Dubh, which was then still functioning as an hotel; the gaunt, grey building dominates the moorlands, and for some years was a popular venue with stalkers, shooters and anglers. The last time Ann and I had dinner there, we were the only British guests, and it is tragic to see how sad the old house looks today. Turning north at Altnabreac Station, we followed the railway line and parked overlooking little Loch Caise. There can be few more lovely settings. The heather was brilliantly purple, its scent held in the gentle breeze of a haze-filled summer day. Well, it was then. Now, the moorlands have been ripped up and the whole area devastated by mindless blanket forestry. More than one hundred thousand acres of tax-avoidance conifers have been planted: miles of regimented rows of lodge-pole pine and Sitka spruce cover the landscape. And recently, not content with smothering the Flows with conifers, local 'entrepreneurs' have started to rip out the peat itself: to sell as barbecue charcoal, for southern and continental supper parties.

I intended to fish Loch Garbh, a mile away over the moor, so I quickly unloaded the car and carried everything down to Caise: fishing-tackle, rugs, picnic-basket, binoculars, books, toys, papers, paints – just the essentials for a day out with Charles and Jean. With the family comfortably ensconced, Ann larding out the sun-tan lotion and Charlie's first cast scaring every trout for several acres, I left them to it and set off over the moor.

Loch Garbh used to be one of my 'special' places, not only because of the utter beauty of its surroundings, but also because of the fact that it held some really excellent wild brown trout. The average weight of fish now is in the order of 8oz, but there are still some monsters, and trout of over 4lb have been caught.

One morning, whilst fishing with Blair and a friend, Harry Officer from Castletown, I hooked one of these big trout. It was a nasty day, raining heavily, and Harry and Blair had retired hurt to the shelter of the old, tin boathouse by a small, sandy bay at the north end. This structure provided only a minimum degree of shelter, being largely open to the elements through age and general infirmity. Nevertheless, it gave at least a sense of protection and I saw them dourly watching me as I inched along the bank in search of sport.

'Fair weather fishermen!' I yelled in derision. The wind was blowing hard, straight down the loch, and my waders were full of water. I had got overexcited, trying to cover a particularly promising rise, just too far out in the north-east corner, but I was concentrating hard. There are times when you just know that something large is about to take.

When the trout grabbed, the force almost wrenched the rod from my hands and I let out a roar of delight: 'Got him!'

Harry and Blair jumped up and started towards me across the heather, landing-net poised, as the reel screamed in anger. There was a momentary glimpse of a huge, sail-like tail above the surface . . . and then the cast broke.

'What did you say, Dad?' called Blair.

Harry Officer also has urgent memories of Loch Garbh, apart from the fifteen fish he caught that day. Ann and I had persuaded him and his wife Connie to join us for a day out in the hills, and we chose Garbh as the venue. Connie Officer is never first over the fence in the pursuit of nature, and remained by the car whilst we fished, venturing out into what she described as 'the wilds' for brief walks.

After a super day, we three proudly returned to the parking place to display the results of our efforts. Loading the car, we set off down the track homewards.

'Step on it, Bruce,' commanded Harry, 'and we will be back in time for a nightcap.'

Two miles further, the car broke down.

'Good grief, can't you fix it?' asked Connie.

Harry and I tried, but to no avail. It was a seriously broken car, probably due to the hammering it had taken crossing the rutted track out to Altnabreac.

'Don't worry, dear,' Harry assured his wife, 'Bruce and I will walk into Westerdale and collect our car, then come back and pick you up.'

'Harry,' I complained, 'that's an eleven-mile hike!'

'Have you any better suggestions?' he responded.

In the gathering gloom, Harry and I set off down the track, leaving the ladies surrounded by hooting owls and hunting hen harrier. Fortified with the remains of our hip-flask. To keep out the cold night chill.

Four hours later, we returned in Harry's car to find them safe and well, but less than pleased with their adventure. Worse was to follow. The following morning, Harry telephoned.

'Bruce, you will never guess what has happened.'

'No, I will never guess. Tell me.'

'Whilst we were busy fishing Garbh, someone was busy acquiring two new tyres. Mine. I've just noticed. He took off the new ones I bought last week and replaced them with two bald beasts! These trout have cost me a fortune and Connie says she never wants to see another hill as long as she lives.'

I fished Garbh hard all day, but it was far too bright and far too hot for sport. However, apart from some very active clegs and the infamous Garbh punt, my afternoon was splendid. I swam (and bailed out the punt), ate (and bailed out the punt), and finally decided to fish from the bank.

Unless you had seen these lochs before mass-afforestation – Caise and Garbh, and Caol and Skyline to the west of the railway – it would be hard to appreciate fully the enormous damage tree-planting has done. They lay like silver gems amidst the heather, virtually untouched by the hand of man for thousands of years. Now, the moorlands have gone, ripped up by deep, forestry ploughing. New roads scar the wilderness, deer fences and locked gates bar the way. Greenshank and golden plover have left, their traditional nesting sites destroyed. The lochs are thick with silt and coloured muddy brown. In my opinion, a monstrous act of wanton environmental vandalism has been perpetrated, in the name of spurious progress.

At about 5 p.m. I packed up and walked back. Coming over the brow of the hill I paused to survey Loch Caise lying unruffled before me – absolutely peaceful – and I knew instantly that something was wrong. Nothing looks absolutely peaceful with Charlie around, but there was no sign of the family.

A movement at the far end of the loch caught my eye. I saw them. Their boat was beached. Ann was lifting Jean out. Charlie was jumping up and down in the shallows, apparently doing some kind of war dance. Then they formed into a line and set off across the heather at a brisk trot, stumbling and falling as they went.

As they came closer, arms waving furiously, I heard Jean yelling: 'Mummy! Mummy! Flies eat me!'

I ran down the hill and as I neared the water's edge, I instantly became aware of the reason for their panic. We were in the midst of what seemed to be millions of midges, all possessing lance-like jaws and all drawing blood by the gallon. We had become tea-time for at least half the midge population of the Highlands. Retreat was the only possible solution.

I grabbed Jean from Ann and we rushed for the car. Once safely inside I examined the damage. Jean was covered with bites on every exposed part of her body, Charles was just as bad and Ann was rubbing furiously.

When calm was restored, Ann announced: 'You will have to get the boat.'

My heart sank but I knew she was right.

'Why on earth did you take it out in the first place?' I asked crossly.

'I'll get the picnic gear.'

'What's that got to do with taking the boat out!'

'Well, we were sitting peacefully when suddenly Jean began to yell. I didn't know what was wrong until Charlie started. Then they got to me. I just thought that it would be safer out in the middle of the loch. Have you any idea how heavy that boat is? Charlie and I almost broke our backs getting it afloat,' she exclaimed.

'But why is it at the far end of the loch? There is no wind.'

'There was then, that's why we left it there.'

I had no answer to that and, feeling like a warm-weather Titus Oates, I took my courage in both hands and leapt from the car.

The next hour was one of the most uncomfortable I have ever experienced, heaving away on the oars, flapping my hands in despair as the midges winged in on my unprotected body. Interviews with the bank manager, fifteen-mile, full-service-marching-order route-marches, travelling British Rail, the after-dinner lounge of a Highland fishing hotel, all pale into insignificance compared to the havoc determined Diptera can wreak. I dragged the boat ashore, secured it with the quickest round-turns and half-hitches that I had ever tied and hurtled back to the car. Regardless of the rutted track, we shot off at a speed that would have left Jackie Stewart speechless.

For years afterwards, Jean had a great fear of flying insects. When *Libellula quadramacuala*, *Locusta uirdissima* and their ilk appear, Jean disappears. Me too. However, what does puzzle me is why Loch Garbh, barely a mile away, is virtually midge-free, whilst Caise is like a Roman amphitheatre where unsuspecting anglers play the part of Christians to ravenous, lion-like midges. This sort of local knowledge is invaluable and the lack of it can turn an otherwise pleasurable day into a nightmare. In the North of Scotland, insect repellent is as essential a part of your fishing gear as rod and line. If you don't believe me, ask Jean. She knows, all too well. Be warned. Beware of the flies!

Look Before You Leap

VIRGO
24 AUGUST TO 23 SEPTEMBER

Changes at work will give you a fresh outlook on life. You will also realise that, contrary to what you imagined, you are not indispensable – and that taking five weeks' holiday each year, along with the maximum entitlement of sick leave and compassionate leave of absence to attend funerals, can strain even the happiest of business relationships.

Do not let this worry you unduly. Few of us are indispensable. Look on the bright side. Social Security is wonderful these days and, with careful husbandry and sending the wife out to work, you should now be able to spend the greater part of your time fishing.

You should also be able to provide a large part of the family food by the skilful use of your rod; and if, in the course of your ramblings, you should happen to stumble upon the odd unwanted deer, grouse, pheasant, cow or sheep, then so much the better. Point this out, frequently, should anyone suggest that you obtain regular employment.

Forget financial problems. The State will provide. Free your mind for some serious fishing. Do the things you really enjoy, especially if your interests express your vivid imagination. Design a new range of historic flies: the Heseltine, with wide, staring eyes and rotating wings; Maggie, fireball-red and black-bristled; or Howe's Fancy, bright yellow, on a tiny, barbless hook. You have endless opportunities for occupying your time, without the need of working.

This could be a particularly carefree phase in your life and, to enjoy it fully, you must check your natural tendency to wear dark suits and carry a rolled up copy of the *Financial Times*. Burn your briefcase. Shred your commuter season-ticket. Put these things behind you. Think like an angler.

Due to your present situation, it would be unwise ever to consider seeking employment, since this would seriously interfere with your fishing. Therefore, in order to avoid temptation, make it a strict rule to leave all mail unopened and spend as much time as possible away from home, with your fishing-rod.

September storms could irretrievably damage some of your social relationships. Make sure that any beginners you offer to take fishing can swim. Insist that they wear a life-jacket. Water plays an important part in your stars this autumn and you can expect to spend much of it soaked to the skin.

Romance is well aspected this year, and at last you and your partner, if she can spare the time off work, will be able to have glorious days alone in the hills far more often than it was possible in previous years – without you having to bother about the boring necessity of making a living.

Sadly, conditions will begin to deteriorate towards the end of the fishing season, with dark clouds gathering after the tenth month, when you will be offered suitable employment which you may not be able to refuse. However, with a little effort on your part, developing a strident, offensive, bullying nature, particularly during job interviews – which you should attend dressed in waders and fishing-jacket – you should be able to avert disaster and spend the following year, at least, fishing.

Otherwise, your future looks bleak, crowded once more with offices, meetings, telephone calls, earnest financial discussions and long lists of figures. Make the most of your present, happy situation, for as long as you can.

'I THINK WE'LL have to swim for it,' announced Ann.
'Now look, dear, don't worry. Just keep bailing,' I replied, encouragingly.
'I can't bail any faster. If I move an inch we'll capsize.'
'How about a song then?'
'What do you suggest: "Abide With Me"?' said Ann.
'Very funny.'
We were sitting at either end of a flimsy, plywood, water-logged punt, about one hundred yards from the nearest shore of a remote Caithness loch. Water was lapping both inside and out and things were beginning to look desperate. Fortunately, we could swim, but the year was creeping onwards and the imminent prospect of a sub-zero ducking did not fill us with joy. We did our best to creep slowly shorewards, Ann bailing furiously, me gently manoeuvring the unmatched, mis-shapen oars.
We made it, but only just. Exhausted, we hauled the useless, sopping hulk ashore and retrieved our saturated belongings.
'There, I told you it would be all right,' I tried to console my better half.
'All right?' she yelled. 'What do you mean, all right! I'm soaking, frozen and you tell me that it's all right. Why didn't you examine the wretched thing before we set out?'
'I'm sorry, darling, I just didn't think.'
'You jolly well should have thought. We might have drowned.'
I am pleased to report that the next time we visited this loch, the punt had been replaced by a serviceable, proper, fibre-glass boat. Not, I suspect, out of consideration for fishing guests, but rather because the punt had simply blown away and been completely destroyed by spring gales. Bits of it were littered all round the shore, and I was not sorry.
But there's the rub. How often do we simply jump in and

push off without properly inspecting the craft to which we are entrusting our lives? Not often. We take it for granted that the boat we eagerly launch will be comparatively water-tight and remain afloat all day. The sun is shining, fish rising, conditions perfect and spirits high. Why waste good fishing time looking for problems?

I've committed this error more times than I care to admit, and, in consequence, have often come pretty close to paying for my indolence with my life. If a boat is beached, upside down, fifty yards from the water's edge – as they frequently are in the far north – then, in the blood-vessel-bursting struggle to heave it to aqua, you sometimes notice faults. The trouble is that you have had the exercise by the time you spot the holes and loose planks, and then have to forgo the benefits, watching helplessly as the damned thing sinks before your very eyes. All you can usefully do is curse.

Ann and I once fished a Caithness hill loch near Altnabreac, and it took an hour's pulling and shoving to get the boat into the water – where we discovered that just as fast as we bailed it out, the water flooded in again. Closer inspection revealed that the planks were held together with little other than faith, hope and tar. By the time we had finished trying to staunch the holes we were virtually stark naked. Handkerchief, vest, pants and various other items of clothing were all pressed into service, plugging leaks, but to no avail. We spent the day bank-fishing instead.

Such experiences do nothing to endear the proprietor to the overworked hearts of piscators. If only they would come clean and tell anglers the state of the boat prior to setting out. At least then one would know what to expect. Few do so. They either don't care or, more likely, don't know.

Fortunately, most of our northern waters are best fished from the bank; indeed, some of our most memorable days out have been whilst bank-fishing. Particularly in the evening, when large fish cruise up from the depths to feed in the shallows. But for the visitor, or the disabled angler, finding that he can't get afloat must be very annoying indeed.

However, whilst I'm sure that punts of all descriptions are very bad news for anglers, quite sound boats can be just as dangerous. Not so long ago I booked a boat on one of our principal Caithness lochs, famous for the quality of its trout and the fierceness of its sudden storms. Three of us arrived at the water's edge, where we were confronted by one of the smallest boats I have ever seen. I'm over six feet tall and my companions were no midgets. With three in the boat it would have sunk like a stone instantly; with two it might have stayed afloat for about as long as it takes Leighton Rees to get double-top on a dart board. Even with one, the boat was downright dangerous in anything other than a dead-flat calm. Astonishingly, the farmer who hired us the boat had said nothing. We all spoke to him, full-frontal, passed over the money, and followed his directions to the mooring-bay. He must have known that he could have been sending us to our doom. We bank-fished and remained alive to tell the tale.

I once made the mistake of buying a small boat for a loch I rented, without first trying it out in situ. The farmer who was selling the boat took me round to the back of his yard to inspect the vessel, which was perched on a trailer, in pristine condition and newly painted. It seemed perfect: clinker-built, broad beamed, deep keeled, sharp at both ends and very Shetland-looking. We agreed a price, including delivery to the loch, and, although I offered to help with the removal, he assured me that there was no need: 'No, no, Bruce, just leave it to me. I'll put it in the water for you. Don't worry.'

I should have been suspicious, but foolishly said nothing. All was revealed the next time I went fishing. Yes, the boat was sound and water-tight, but it rocked from side to side, alarmingly, the moment you twitched a muscle. Furthermore, the keel was so deep that it required Herculean effort to get the wretched thing afloat. The children would wait by the mooring-bay whilst I dragged the boat out into the loch, returning for each embryonic angler and carrying them on my back, one at a time, out to the malicious, tilting craft.

In the slightest wind, the boat couped dangerously in unison with our casting. That season, we invented a new Olympic sport: synchronised fishing. Casting by numbers. It was essential that we all moved at the same time, and changing places was a death-defying nightmare.

My worst moment came when we had friends staying, Mavis and Peter Greaves, from Esher in Surrey. Peter was an experienced angler, but had never managed to persuade his wife to join him in the delights of fly-fishing.

They were charming company, easy to entertain and delightful guests and, although Mavis was clearly not very interested in fishing, she listened politely to all our lies – or, as we tended to call them, true angling tales.

I decided to set about changing her mind. One of my missions in life is to persuade people at least to try fly-fishing because I am convinced that it will greatly enrich their existence; introducing them not only to a wonderful pastime, but also engendering in them a fuller appreciation of our countryside and environment.

Eventually, with some trepidation, and I suspect much against her better judgement, Mavis agreed to join us for an evening expedition to our loch. Ann and Jean took Peter and, in consequence, had the large, fifteen-foot, fibre-glass boat. I agreed to take personal charge of Mavis – in the little Shetland monster.

I got Mavis into the boat at the mooring-bay, smothered in wet-weather gear. Then, pretending that everything was quite normal, heaved her and the boat over the shallows into deeper water.

'Do you always have to do this when you go fishing, Bruce?' Mavis inquired, surprised.

'All part of the adventure, Mavis,' I replied, emptying out a soaking wader. 'I'll row up to the top, out of the wind. We'll soon have you casting and catching trout with the best of them.'

I am convinced that the moment beginners catch their first fish, they are hooked for life, and our loch was absolutely full of free-rising trout. I thought warmly of Peter's delight when I returned with Mavis, an enthusiastic angler and convert to the gentle art.

I noticed Mavis gripping the sides of the boat tightly as we lurched and pitched northwards through the ever-strengthening wind, and I chattered away reassuringly about the pleasures of angling. It started to rain, lightly at first. Then heavily. An unremitting, Highland downpour. The skies darkened ominously, but I was determined that Mavis should at least have the opportunity of seeing a fish caught, if not actually catching one herself.

What had begun as a moderate breeze, quickly grew into a full-scale gale; and, as luck would have it, half a mile up the loch, the elongated keel of the boat got stuck between two rocks. I tried to keep up a brave face, in spite of the imminent danger of capsizing.

'Soon have it free, Mavis. Just you sit still,' I said calmly, instantly followed by a sharp bark of alarm as Mavis tried to stand up and help: 'Sit down, Mavis! For God's sake, don't move!'

As I poled the boat round out of the rock-trap, it turned sideways on to the wind. Water began lapping over the sides.

'Nothing to worry about, Mavis, just keep still.' I could see by the look on her face that she was not convinced and had decided that she was in the hands of a complete lunatic. She glanced down the loch, searching anxiously for Peter and the other boat, which had vanished in the darkness of the storm.

'Do you think they will be all right, Bruce?' she asked nervously. Knowing Ann, I was pretty certain that she would have headed straight for the shore immediately the wind rose. By now, they would be ensconced in the boathouse clutching mugs of steaming coffee. I cursed my stupidity.

Eventually, I forced the boat free and the wind instantly grabbed us like a giant hand, and hurled us down the loch, back towards the boathouse at a tremendous rate. Mavis was white as a sheet. So was I.

'I think we'll finish now,' I said, trying to sound non-committal, in control, at ease. 'Too windy really. We'll make for the shore. Please, keep still.'

With all thought of fishing or casting lessons abandoned, I concentrated upon keeping the boat afloat and directly in line with the wind. Even so, water splashed in by the bucketful over the sides.

As we approached the mooring-bay, I realised that I would have to make one final, dangerous dash, across the wind, to get to safety. There was no way in which I could ask Mavis to step out and wade ashore. It was all or nothing time.

I judged my moment, then turned suddenly shorewards. Using all my strength, mightily assisted by the wind, I virtually levered the boat over the bottom and into the mooring-bay, breaking one oar in the process.

Without waiting for a second invitation, Mavis leapt out. Showing remarkable restraint, she collected herself bravely and smiled down at me:

'Bruce, did I happen to see you with a hip-flask?' She had, and it was, for some unknown reason, filled with Green Chartreuse. I handed it to her and she disappeared behind the boathouse. A moment or two later, Mavis reappeared and gave me back the flask. It was considerably lighter.

'Now,' she announced brightly, 'I think that I would like a cigarette.' Mavis hadn't smoked for three years. 'Thank you, Bruce,' she said. 'That was one of the most interesting evenings of my life. An experience that I will never forget.'

101

The blood-vessel-bursting struggle

The very next day, I placed an advert in our local paper, the *John O'Groat Journal*: 'Loch-style boat for sale. Excellent condition. May be viewed, on trailer, at Ruther House, Watten.' But I'm sure, in retrospect, Mavis laughs at her experience and probably frequently dines out on the story of her Highland fishing expedition.

Mavis Greaves is not the only person I know who is nervous in boats. Jean, our youngest daughter, used to be terrified and, although you may not be aware of the fact, I have to tell you that back-seat drivers function equally as well in boats as they do in cars. This was apparent from her very first outing, when she was very little:

'Mind that rock!' she yelled, as we drifted quietly down the shoreline of a small Highland loch.

At one time or another, we have all proffered advice upon where to place the boat in relationship to a particular drift – or, indeed, where to place an oar, when we lose a trout because our companion has forgotten to 'ship' them. But perpetual, professional, back-seat bleating is something else.

I have been driving a car for more than thirty years but, even today, my mother, a rigorous lady well into her eighth decade, still directs me round Edinburgh as though I were a learner. Even when fishing, Mother finds it difficult to restrain her natural tendency to offer gratuitous advice and directions, and my most recent experience with her combined the worst of both worlds.

Having managed to drive her safely to the loch, much to her alleged astonishment, I then had to fight to persuade her to put on wet-weather gear.

'I'll look ridiculous. No,' she complained. 'I'm perfectly all right as I am.'

'You're not. Do as I say.'

'Don't speak to me like that.'

'Mother,' I explained, 'have I more experience than you when it comes to fishing?' Grudgingly, she agreed. 'Well do me a favour, please. Stop arguing and get into these waterproof trousers.'

Grudgingly, she did, and with my blood pressure hovering dangerously near heart-attack level, I eventually managed to get her, and all the gear, into the boat. I waded out, through the shallows, prior to starting the outboard:

'For goodness sake, Bruce, what on earth are you doing? You'll get soaked. Get in the boat immediately.'

I clambered aboard, started the engine and motored up the loch, directed all the way by the figure in the stern:

'That looks a likely spot. What about over there? Let's try behind that island.'

I cut the motor and turned the boat into the first drift, chucked out the drouge and reached round to hand Mother her fishing-rod. No rod. In the mad scramble to sort Mother out and load the boat, I had forgotten them. They were still lying by the side of the car.

Without saying a word, I pulled in the drouge, restarted the motor and headed shorewards:

'Where are we going? I thought you said that was the best drift on the loch?'

I remained stonily silent. Mother realised that we were going back to the mooring-bay:

'I know what's wrong!' she exclaimed in anger, 'You've forgotten your cigarettes. My God, can't you even last ten minutes without a cigarette? If your father were alive, he'd soon put a stop to your nonsense.' I held my tongue. 'If I've told you once, I've told you a dozen times to give it up. For all the good it does. Just like when you were a little boy. You never did what you were . . .'

I leapt ashore. Sure enough, both rods were lying on the bank. Grabbing them, I returned to the boat and began the process of getting afloat all over again, this time, however, without the chorus of complaints from Mother. She was laughing too hard to speak.

Apart from Mrs Sandison senior, I have never been unduly troubled by this particular form of torture, and assume that my

passengers are either completely relaxed or too stunned to voice
any complaints. Blair, my eldest son, tends to do a sort of clog-
dance from time to time but, being a good-natured soul, he
rarely breaks out into actual wild screams. Like most men,
erroneously, I fondly imagine that my standard of driving is not
too bad – touch wood.

But I do know how to handle small boats, for which I have
to thank Her Majesty The Queen. During military service as an
'other rank', I had the good sense to join the Water Transport
Regiment of The Royal Army Service Corps, then based on the
Isle of Wight.

The Isle of Wight was a magical place and I enjoyed every
moment I spent there, in spite of the fact that none of them
included game fishing. On warm summer evenings I would take
the *Snoddy*'s dinghy and scull up the River Yar as far as I could
go, by tall rushes loud with bird song, whispering in the wind.
Carefully mooring the boat, I would settle down to read, dis-
turbed only by the occasional flash of a kingfisher, red, blue and
silver, a sparkling gem, supper-time busy, the twilight call of
blackbird, or, sculling back down the river in the gathering
darkness, the dream-like notes of nightingale.

I spent nearly two years with the company, staying at Golden-
hill Fort Headquarters, then Fort Victoria, a damp, red-brick
structure on the shores of the Solent, and finally as a crew
member on one of our boats in Yarmouth Harbour. For a year
I lived on the *Snodgrass*, a general service vessel, plying the
Solent and Sound as part of our daily routine in all kinds of
weather. With typical military thoroughness, I was taught the
basic principles of seamanship and small-boat handling, eventually reaching the giddy heights of Seaman B4.

Once safely berthed in Yarmouth Harbour, our only means
of communication with the outside world was by way of the
Snoddy's dinghy, a ten-foot, brown, clinker-built boat which we
used in the same way as landlubbers use their cars. As a test
of small-boatmanship, try transporting three, large, drunken,
singing seamen, fresh from the delights of the Wheatsheaf or
George, home across a choppy harbour and getting them safely
on board, into their bunks.

The ultimate test consisted of doing the same for yourself,
when you were in a similar state, having missed the duty boat.
The only way back, apart from walking upon water – a feat only
once ever mastered, and not by me – was to tramp a mile up
the road to the Depot Barge and pinch their dinghy. The trouble

was that the Depot dinghy was about eighteen feet long and had to be propelled with a single oar over the stern. The boat was laboriously manoeuvred out to the *Snoddy*, where our own small dinghy had to be unhitched and roped astern. Then both boats were sculled back to base; hitch the eighteen-footer, scull back in the *Snoddy*'s dinghy. Sounds easy? Try it, four sheets to the wind, in a crowded, boat-bobbing harbour at 3 a.m., in a force six January gale.

So I understand the vagaries of small boats, which made it all the more galling for me to have to submit to the constant stream of gratuitous advice and insults emanating from Jean, perched in the stern like some infant Captain Bligh.

'Now look here, Jean,' I explained patiently, 'it's all right. Daddy will look after you. There is nothing to worry about.'

Ann smirked. She doesn't understand small boats either.

'It's too far out! Oh, oh, oh, help!' Jean screamed. I rowed closer to the shore. 'We're going to hit the side. Watch out! Ann, tell him to stop!' I rowed back out. 'You are going too far! Not so fast! Tell him, Ann. Make him stop!'

We had walked out from Melvich, in Sutherland, that morning, intent upon attacking the Eaglaises. There are two lochs, separated by about half a mile. My sons, Blair and Charles, had cleverly managed to get me to agree to them walking on and fishing Eaglaise Mor – leaving Ann and me to fish Eaglaise Beg, and cope with Jean. It wasn't as if it were rough or windy, the reverse was true. Conditions were perfect: a light, gentle breeze, ruffling the surface; warm sunlight, not too bright; flies dancing above the water; fish rising constantly.

'Look Ann, unless you do something about your daughter, I am going to spend the whole day rowing in and out like a yo-yo, catching nothing. Explain to her that she is perfectly safe and there is nothing to worry about.'

'You explain. She's your daughter too,' responded Ann, neatly hooking, playing and landing a 1lb trout.

'It's all right for you,' I yelled in exasperation, 'You're catching fish. I'm just a glorified marine taxi-driver.'

'Yes, dear,' she said, hooking another.

'Oh, oh, oh! Daddy, the boat's bent!' howled Jean. We had moved to one side, to land Ann's trout, and the boat had tilted slightly.

'Jean, stop it! The boat's fine.'

'Put the handles in the water. I want to go and see Blair and

Charles. Can I play on the bank? Stop the boat, I want to get off!'

I was losing patience as fast as Ann was catching fish.

'All right, Jean,' I said, exasperated, 'we'll fish down to the bottom and then stop.'

Jean screeched in horror, clutching her mother: 'I don't want to go under the water. No, no, no!'

'It's all right, Jean,' Ann explained, giving me a dangerous look, 'Daddy didn't mean *under* the water. He means down to the *far end* of the loch.' She quietly but firmly loosened Jean's grip on her casting arm and proceeded to catch her sixth trout of the morning. I was still fishless, and the explanation only made matters worse:

'When will we be there, Daddy? Will it take a long time? Can you row quickly?'

I realised that if I were to get any peace, let alone catch any trout, then desperate measures were called for. Ignoring the continuing volley of complaints, I concentrated upon the job in hand and eventually managed to hook a small fish.

Nonchalantly, carefully keeping the trout below the surface, I turned to the red-faced figure in the middle and said: 'Would you like to have a go, Jean?'

Jean paused in mid-flow and considered the suggestion. Making her decision, she got down on the bottom of the boat and, crawling under the thwarts, came and sat beside me, her fingers digging deeply into my arm. I handed my daughter the rod and told her to reel in. Immediately, the small fish jumped and splashed on the surface. Jean squealed in excitement and delight, her fear forgotten.

'Well done, Jean! You have caught a trout!' I exclaimed encouragingly. I carefully removed the hook from the trout's mouth and prepared to return it to the water.

'Ann!' Jean roared. 'He's putting my fish back! Tell him! I want it for Horace!' Horace was our large, grey cat. After a short discussion about babies, however, Jean reluctantly agreed to have the fish returned to the water. I sorted out the flies and handed her the rod:

'Now then, let's see if you can catch a bigger one.'

She thrust the rod forward and the flies leap-frogged over the surface, landing with a crash a couple of feet from the boat. As if by royal command a 12oz trout rose and greedily grabbed the tail fly. After several moments of complete confusion, the fish was landed and despatched.

'Well done, Jean! You are a clever girl! Well done,' I said proudly.

Satisfied that I had done my parental duty, and quelled a near mutiny, I picked up my rod and settled down to some serious fishing. Another problem solved, or so I fondly imagined. The back-seat driving had stopped, but it had been replaced by an even greater menace. From directly next to my right ear came an incessant plea:

'Is it my turn now, Daddy? When will it be my turn? Can I have a shot now, please? Would you like me to catch another fish for you, Daddy? I haven't had a shot for a long time, have I? Ann, tell him to let me have a shot. Oh, look, Daddy, you missed one! Do you want me to catch it?'

I turned to Ann in despair. She was busy looking the other way, playing yet another fish. I glanced down at Jean's earnest little face, aglow with pleasure, and handed her the rod:

'Come on, darling, you have a go. You catch lots of fish. Daddy will row the boat and land them. After all, what else are fathers for?'

'Couldn't agree more,' muttered Ann from the bow.

In my experience, the further north you go, the worse they become: boats, that is, not back-seat drivers, and weather conditions have a lot to do with this state of affairs. The constant buffeting of Highland gales plays havoc with planks, and there are some inconsiderate anglers about who merely abandon their craft at the end of the day, failing to secure them properly. If you are in any doubt about handling a boat, you should never set out, and one of the unwritten rules of fishing in the Highlands is that you always, no matter what the conditions, return the boat to the place where you got it. I have spent many a hard hour returning boats to their rightful place, in spite of prior words of wisdom advising caution to supposedly experienced anglers.

We once had an acquaintance staying with us who was possessed by angling. One windy evening, regardless of our warnings, he insisted upon going fishing. Reluctantly, we sent him off to St John's Loch, complete with drouge and excellent outboard motor. He returned late that night, complaining about appalling weather conditions and a complete lack of fish. Eventually, he mentioned casually that he had been unable to get the boat back to the mooring-bay, because of high winds.

'What did you do with the boat?' I asked, with a sinking feeling.

'What did you expect me to do with it?' he answered. 'I just had to leave it where I was blown ashore.'

'What about the outboard?' – which had cost me £300.

'Oh, it's still there. I couldn't carry it all the way back to the car, could I?'

Fortunately, Charlie was home, so we set off for the loch. The boat was bouncing up and down by the shore, half-filled with water, outboard propeller playing a tune on the bank-side rocks. Without too much effort, we returned the boat to the mooring-bay and recovered the motor. Fortunately, that night, the only thing we lost was an acquaintance.

Abandoning boats is an all too frequent occurrence, and the first the unfortunate owner knows about it is when lumps of broken timber come flying down the hill on the wings of the next storm. This tends to discourage them from replacing boats too often – and, in case you haven't inquired recently, like everything else, the cost of new boats has risen almost as fast as newly stocked rainbow trout rise to grab your first cast. When I checked a few years ago, it was possible to purchase a serviceable twelve-foot loch boat for around £500. Today, you would not get much change out of nearly treble that sum.

Nevertheless, in spite of the occasional stupidity and thoughtlessness of some anglers, I feel that Highland owners should get their acts together and maintain their boats properly. The most common form of maintenance carried out in much of the North seems to involve several hundred gallons of black bitumastic, applied liberally over the boat, oars, boathouse, nearby rocks, heather, and anything else that happens to get in the way. This glutinous coating manages to remain tacky all season, ruining trousers, jackets, fishing-bags and anything else that comes in contact with it.

There used to be such a boat on one of our favourite Caithness waters, Loch Ruard, a loch which has escaped the ungentle, market economy administrations that have destroyed the surrounding Flow Country, being safe in the hands of more enlightened owners. It is an excellent trout fishery. The east side, where the boat is moored, is shallow. Consequently, getting afloat requires much grunting, heaving and shoving.

After doing so, one morning a few years ago, Ann and I discovered to our horror that most of our clothes and fishing-tackle were liberally smeared with black bitumastic. The boat had been 'maintained' and we were suffering the consequences. We did discover some good, however, and proved yet again the truth of that old adage about ill winds. Not only were jackets, trousers and fishing-bags daubed, but so were any flies that touched the bottom of the boat. I was wondering why my flies were landing on the surface like a ton of bricks and had pulled my cast in to examine it. The 'bob' fly and middle fly were untouched, but the tail fly, a Silver Butcher, was barely recognisable due to a thick coating of tar. Being inherently lazy, I fished on regardless, eventually taking half-a-dozen nice trout – all on the tail fly, which I rechristened a 'Butcher & Tar.'

The Ruard boat was a sort of surplus to requirements speed boat: heavy, difficult to row and uncomfortable to fish from. It did the job, adequately, for many years and has now been replaced, but I confess that I miss my old, flat-bottomed friend, tar and all.

Boat design is a highly developed skill and in the hands of an expert, an art form. The user should have total confidence and feel safe and secure in all conditions. The next boats that I purchased, on behalf of friends, I tested thoroughly. Remembering past experiences, I launched one of them in the Firth of Forth in a strong wind and spent a happy hour fault-finding: standing on the thwarts; jumping about; flinging myself wildly from side to side. There were none. So we bought five.

Which is more than I can say about a boat I fished from at Altnaharra, in north-west Sutherland, in 1987. This – in my opinion – disastrous vessel, had obviously been designed by an engineer rather than an angler, and was reputed to be state of the art boat-building. It was about twelve feet in length and pointed at both ends so that one could row either backwards or forwards at will. There were lockers fore and aft, joined by a bow-to-stern seat, thus allowing the angler to sit sideways, facing the direction of casting without having to twist into contortions in order to do so – as is normally the case. The top of the bench-seat opened to reveal a space for storing oars and there was a multitude of other 'neat' features, all designed to suit the maker's perception of what fishermen required.

As far as I was concerned, and as far as my fishing companion was concerned, the damned thing didn't work. It was too deep to haul afloat easily and too narrow in the beam. Anyone other than a midget had to sit astride the bench, feet at ninety degrees, in order to cast. And, worst of all, it instantly brought back memories of the Shetland fiend: the slightest movement had it rocking to and fro like an out-of-control see-saw.

Very rapidly, we were devising excuses to avoid being sent to the loch with the 'designer' boat. Failure to do so meant an agonising, bum-aching, back-wracking day, generally rounded off with two wet legs for the unfortunate condemned to drag it ashore:

'We'll toss for it, David.'

'Toss nothing. I did it at lunch-time. Get on with it, Bruce.'

'What if I promise not to tell about that foul-hooked fish?'

'Get on with it!'

I was astonished to read a glowing review of this vessel, which the writer claimed to have tested on one of Scotland's largest, most dangerous and windy lochs. Everyone is entitled to his own opinion, but I would rather set out to fish in a bread-bin, than set foot in that awful, misbegotten craft.

Southern fisheries and reservoirs are generally well managed with excellent, well-found boats. More often than not one can step almost straight from the car into the boat. Indeed, willing hands will sometimes be available to assist you, cheerily waving you off. Up here, in the north, all too often it's more like waving you goodbye, leading to frayed nerves and touch-paper tempers.

Ann and I rarely argue, other than when we are afloat. You see, I have an absolute conviction that I know far more about handling boats in difficult conditions than she does. She does not agree. When storms rage, in our case it is not a question of a 'danger shared' but rather of a 'danger doubled', as we shout and argue about what to do.

Having been swept mercilessly on to some rocky shore, we clamber out, furious, and continue the fight with renewed vigour in the shelter of the nearest rock.

'I told you that would happen. You should never have launched that boat in the first place. It's leaking like a sieve,' she will complain.

'It would have been perfectly safe if you hadn't got fankled round the oar!' I explode.

'You should have taken the wretched things in. Then I wouldn't have got fankled, would I?'

'In that storm? Are you out of your mind? If you had given me a hand instead of fishing on as though it were mill-pond calm, it would have been far more useful.'

'I was bailing all the time, with one hand.'

110

'Didn't stop you fishing though, did it.'

'Just because I caught fish and you didn't!'

'Good grief! How childish can you get? What chance did I have to fish with you lashing away like a mad thing in the stern?'

'Don't you call me childish.'

'I'm expected to control the boat, land your stupid fish, unfankle your casts, light your cigarettes, *and* keep us upright, all in a howling gale. What do you take me for?'

'Don't tempt me, Bruce. Now be quiet and stand still. Look the other way. I'll get the hook out.'

'Ouch! You did that on purpose!'

It is generally at this point that we notice the boat drifting off round the headland and the fight flares anew over who should have secured it and why it wasn't done.

Even the famed Loch Lomond boats worry me. Lomond can be an extraordinarily dangerous, windy loch, and when I first visited it, I was confident that the boat we hired would be well tried and tested against prevailing weather conditions. Until motoring back from Inchmurrin Island to Balmaha one afternoon. There was a persistent, heavy swell and, in spite of the fact that I was zig-zagging across the waves, water still tended to splash in alarmingly over the sides, much to Jean's consternation – and mine. This was not a happy experience.

I was even more horrified, a few years ago, to read that the 'super-deluxe-designer' boat that David Aird and I had had the misfortune to use at Altnaharra, had been tested on Loch Lomond – and the reviewer had nothing but the highest praise for its performance!

Our worst moment came in 1987 when we had been fishing in Ross-shire, and proved that even in a well-found, sturdy boat, built for the job, it never pays to take risks. Loch na h-Oidhche, the 'Loch of the Night', is enclosed east and west by two mountains, the 'Wizard's Mountain', and the 'Mountain of the Birds', which form a tunnel through which the wind blows fearsomely. Ann and I were sailing north up the loch to the boat mooring-bay. Fortunately, the outboard engine, a 5hp Seagull, was excellent and I managed to keep the wind directly behind us as we cascaded down the loch.

The problem came when we approached the boat bay. The engine had to be cut, outboard shaft lifted clear of underwater boulders, and the boat manoeuvred into the narrow entrance of the harbour. All in the unlikely space of a few seconds. Cutting the outboard too soon would risk being swamped; too late and the boat would most certainly be badly damaged against the jagged rocks guarding the shore.

I stopped the outboard too early and realised that disaster was approaching. Heaving on the oars, I managed to get the bow of the boat pointing in the direction of the mooring-bay. At the last moment, I leapt out, waist-deep, and dragged the boat to safety. Exhausted, I slumped to the ground.

'Well done, dear. That was a close-run thing. Heathcliffe was quite upset,' Ann announced, stroking her Yorkshire terrier's sopping head. 'Will you manage the three-mile walk back to the road?' I squelched all the way.

Passing years have brought us caution when it comes to bobbing about in boats in storms. Nowadays, if in doubt, we don't. When the wind roars down the loch, churning the water to foam, you will find Ann and me tucked away in a small quiet corner, and it's surprising just how often we catch more than anglers who risk life and limb afloat. We fish contentedly and serenely from the bank, separated by several, mishap-free yards, calling occasional, endearing words of good-humoured advice and encouragement to each other across the wind. And never argue at all. Well, hardly ever.

The Annual General Meeting

LIBRA
24 SEPTEMBER TO 24 OCTOBER

There is a lot going on this month and life in general is getting better. The in-laws move four hundred miles south and will be unable to spend their customary four-week holiday with you until further, indeterminate notice. Try to be sad.

Many important changes are indicated, including a better and more understanding relationship within the family circle. This will not last, but make the most of this unaccustomed truce as long as you can. Encourage the full and frank discussion of issues which are causing concern, emphasising ways and means of obtaining more fishing time.

Later on there will be opportunities to broaden your horizon, possibly from a mountain-top close to an outstanding, and as yet undiscovered, trout loch full of 4lb fish; and in spite of the hard work involved getting there, you will recognise the advantages to be gained. Make sure that you have a young, fit companion, to carry the catch home.

Opposition of some kind could alter your current arrangements with regards to fishing plans – business commitments, a family wedding, divorce proceedings, or a minor heart attack, brought about by too much climbing to your newly discovered loch – and your obsession with secrecy could prove to be disastrous.

You also will have to exercise good judgement in the course of the next few weeks if you are to retain your spring salmon fishing. Therefore, keep doing the pools – and carefully reconsider your plan for robbing the local bank. There is too much at stake to countenance avoidable error.

In spite of present strain and stress, it should not be too difficult to continue to enjoy social outings with amusing companions, provided that the amusing companions are fishery owners, and that the outings are to famous salmon streams. It is probably an opportune time to seek favours and you should practise bowing and scraping, sycophantic smiles and landing other people's fish.

Although you are enjoying a good relationship with your family, you will have to be careful not to overreact to some minor problem, probably on a Saturday night during November. Boys will be boys, and a car is only a car, even if it is a Porsche. Nor should the fact that expensive fishing-tackle is destroyed in the blaze concern you. You are insured. Aren't you? Rise above mere pettiness and shouting. You have more rewarding things to do, such as robbing banks.

You may find yourself in a rather confused state early next year, particularly during the third phase of the February moon, but there is a great deal that you can do to help yourself, by concentrating upon future plans – secretly selling up and disappearing into the hills one dark night and damning them all.

Events in March will allow you to proceed with these plans, although possibly not in the way you anticipated due to the efficiency of the local constabulary. Have a false beard ready and plane tickets for the Argentine. There is excellent fishing to be found throughout the country, so you have nothing to fear.

You are using up a lot of energy just now, so make sure that you leave enough time for relaxation; otherwise your fishing technique could suffer. It is a good year for buying waders and thermal underwear.

DEMOCRACY should be more than just a remote, philosophical concept, even in fishing. To be credible, it must be seen to work, particularly when every member of the family is an angler. Otherwise, it would be too easy for one person to impose their will upon the others. At least, that's what Lewis-Ann said.

'When have I ever been able to impose my will on any of you?' I complained. 'You all do exactly as you please, regardless of what I say.'

Lewis-Ann ignored this statement of fact.

'My Social Studies teacher says that parents should listen to their children,' she continued, 'but as far as fishing is concerned, we always have to do what he says.'

'Who says? Your Social Studies teacher?' I asked. 'I didn't even know he fished.'

'Your Social Studies teacher doesn't have children,' noted Ann.

'*He* knows what I mean,' pronounced Lewis-Ann, glaring at me threateningly.

'By "he", I presume you are referring to me? Provider of rods, reels, flies, waders, baskets, landing-nets, outboard-motors, transport and sustenance?'

'My Social Studies teacher says that it is important that everyone has their say. Parents should discuss things with their children,' Lewis-Ann went on, pressing home her point. 'We should all sit down and talk about things – democratically.'

'What's democratically?' asked Charles, interested.

Blair, sensing that they had me on the run, joined in.

'Well, Charles, it means that if you want something – say a new fishing-rod, for instance – then we all discuss it. Rather than Dad just saying no.'

'That seems fair,' announced Charles. 'Can we start being democratically now?'

'Be quiet, Charlie,' I snapped, cornered.

My unruly brood glowered in unison, daring me to try and deny the logic of their argument. Ann hovered, concerned. Clearly, a nasty situation was developing. I kicked one of the cats, playing for time.

'That's not very democratic,' Blair pointed out.

I capitulated. In order to avoid my ultimate elevation to the status of Dictator, it was agreed to formalise our angling activities through the establishment of a family fishing association – where decisions could be taken in a democratic fashion, after full and frank discussion – and ever since we have had regular meetings.

THE ANNUAL GENERAL MEETING

The Annual General Meeting of the Sandison Family Fishing Association was held in the Dining-Room, Louisburgh Street, Wick, Caithness, at 8.00 p.m. on 23 October 1977.

Members Present: Mr Bruce Sandison (Chairman and President), Mrs Ann Sandison (Secretary and Treasurer), Mr Blair Sandison (Maintenance and Repairs Officer), Ms Lewis-Ann Sandison (Social Affairs Officer), Mr Charles Sandison (Catering Clerk), and Miss Jean Sandison.

Associate Member: Horace Cat.

The minutes of the last meeting having been read, the Chairman welcomed the members, including our newest, Miss Jean Sandison, aged two-and-a-half. He hoped Miss Sandison would enjoy her association with the Association and asked the Secretary to restrain the new member from eating agenda papers.

The Chairman reported that the catch for the year showed a satisfactory increase on previous years, due largely to his personal skill and untiring efforts on behalf of the Association. He commented that perhaps, in future, other members of the Association should try harder.

Ms Lewis-Ann Sandison said that if other members fished as often as the Chairman did, then the figure would have been considerably higher – but someone had to wash dishes, cut lawns, do the ironing, cook meals, baby-sit and generally look after the house.

The Secretary thanked Ms Lewis-Ann Sandison for her kind remarks. She said that she felt it was her duty to ensure that all the members had as much opportunity as possible to go fishing and that she did not really mind, as long as everyone else enjoyed themselves.

Ms Lewis-Ann Sandison replied that she was talking about herself, not the Secretary, who had been out fishing far more often than certain other members of the Association.

The Chairman called the meeting to order and thanked Ms Lewis-Ann Sandison for her work on behalf of the Association. He assured Ms Lewis-Ann Sandison that her remarks would be noted and appropriate action taken to ensure that other members shared her heavy burden.

Mr Charles Sandison pointed out that although he would be delighted to play a greater role in such matters, members should be aware that his time was strictly limited, due to the pressure of work at school.

Mr Blair Sandison said that he would like to raise the question of missed fish, and asked the Chairman what action he proposed to take, if any, to improve his casting technique.

The Chairman replied that he was far more concerned by the apparent difficulty some members had when trying to use a landing-net, particularly when landing the Chairman's trout.

Mr Blair Sandison commented that if members were expected to work with second-rate, worn-out equipment, accidents were bound to happen. Whilst he regretted losing the Chairman's 1lb trout, he felt bound to add that it was unreasonable to expect members to hang out of boats for hours in force-five gales whilst the Chairman allowed a small fish to run rings round him.

The Chairman said that the trout in question had weighed at least 4lb and that Mr Blair Sandison's failure to land the fish was, to say the least, suspicious. It was agreed that the Secretary investigate the purchase of yet another landing-net for next season.

Miss Jean Sandison said that she wanted to go fishing. The Secretary explained that it was too dark and that all the fish had gone to their beds. Miss Jean Sandison began to cry and said that it was not democratic.

Mr Charles Sandison proposed a short adjournment for warm, sweet tea, chocolate biscuits, lemonade, or anything else that happened to be going.

The Chairman said that he would prefer a large whisky with a little water and Mr Blair Sandison said that he would too.

The meeting adjourned to the kitchen for refreshments.

Due to the rising cost of electricity and the expense of keeping the dining-room fire going, the Chairman proposed that the meeting be continued in the kitchen. Ms Lewis-Ann Sandison said that it was only because some people wanted to be nearer the drinks cupboard.

Upon being put to the vote, the motion was carried and the meeting continued in the kitchen.

Mr Charles Sandison reminded the meeting that there were only fifty-one shopping days left until Christmas and please could he have a fishing-rod of his own. Miss Jean Sandison said that she wanted one too.

The Secretary was instructed to raise the matter with Mr Santa Claus, but the Chairman reminded the meeting that funds were limited and that his rod would require refurbishing after falling into Loch Watten.

Mr Blair Sandison said that whilst he sympathised with the Chairman's predicament, he felt that this expense should be borne by the Chairman, personally – since it had been due to the Chairman's own stupidity that the rod had been lost.

Whilst agreeing with Mr Blair Sandison, the Chairman pointed out that the cost of hiring a frogman for a day had not been light and that he had hoped that the Association might agree to help with these costs.

Ms Lewis-Ann Sandison said that she agreed with Mr Blair Sandison and that people should pay for their own silliness.

The Secretary reminded the members that it was customary to be polite to fellow members and asked Ms Lewis-Ann Sandison and Mr Blair Sandison to withdraw their remarks and apologise to the Chairman.

Ms Lewis-Ann Sandison and Mr Blair Sandison said that they were sorry. Mrs Ann Sandison said that the cost of recovering and repairing the Chairman's rod was far cheaper than the cost of buying a new rod, and that members should be glad that the Chairman's rod had been found.

Upon being put to the vote, it was agreed that the Association pay fifty per cent of the cost of having the Chairman's rod refurbished, provided that he promised not to do it again, and agreed to stop hiding his fly boxes from the other members.

At this point Horace Cat left the meeting to attend to urgent business in the garden.

The following year's holiday was discussed at length. Ms Lewis-Ann Sandison proposed that the 1978 venue should be the south-west of France, a Greek island, or at least somewhere where there was a beach and it was warm – like normal people had. Mr Blair Sandison sympathised with Ms Lewis-Ann Sandison but pointed out that baking beaches and Greek islands were not noted for the excellence of their trout fishing. Upon being put to the vote it was agreed that the 1978 holiday should be a fishing holiday in the wilds of Sutherland.

It was proposed by Ms Lewis-Ann Sandison and seconded by Mr Blair Sandison that the Chairman and Secretary curtail their smoking and drinking in order to defray anticipated holiday costs and provide better equipment for other members with the money thus saved.

The Chairman and Secretary suggested that a sub-committee be formed to investigate this possibility, reporting back to the Association at their next Annual General Meeting.

Ms Lewis-Ann Sandison commented that such a solution seemed to her to be nothing other than an undignified attempt to delay making a decision and demanded a named vote on the subject. Upon being put to the vote, three members, Mr Blair Sandison, Ms Lewis-Ann Sandison and Mr Charles Sandison, supported the motion. Mr Bruce Sandison, Mrs Ann Sandison and Miss Jean Sandison opposed the motion.

The Chairman then used his casting vote to decide the issue in favour of a sub-committee report, reminding Ms Lewis-Ann Sandison that this was simply another example of the democratic process in action.

The Sandison Cup for the heaviest trout of the season was then awarded to the Chairman, for a fish weighing 1lb 14oz from Loch Watten. There was some desultory clapping and Miss Jean Sandison said that she wanted one too.

Congratulating the Chairman, Mr Blair Sandison said that he had no doubt that he would win the Cup back next season, provided the Chairman stopped knocking his fish off while pretending to land them.

It was unanimously agreed that the Chairman and Secretary be reappointed for the following year.

In his closing remarks, the Chairman thanked the members of the Association for their continued support and said that he felt privileged to belong to one of the best angling clubs in the world.

Miss Jean Sandison having fallen asleep, and there being no further business, the meeting ended at 11.00 p.m.

Bruce Sandison (Chairman) SFFA

In spite of the formal tone of our deliberations, our competitions engender nothing other than good-natured family rivalry. They

are not really taken seriously. Provided that I always win. Most of the time.

My friend, David Aird from Edinburgh, is President and Secretary of a similar, exclusive association, which fishes for The Findhorn Trophy. They have very strict rules and regulations covering every eventuality of their fishing outings, from size and type of fly to starting and finishing times. They also have a complicated points system for assessing the value of the different species – so much for wild brown trout, less for a stocked fish, so much for spring salmon, less for autumn-caught fish – and each year the winner is awarded the Findhorn Quaich, a shallow, saucer-shaped, traditional Highland drinking vessel, which is immediately put to good use. There are only two members, David and his son Rory, and the name of the trophy was chosen simply because they happened to be crossing the Findhorn River on their way north to fish when they thought of the idea.

I abhor formal fishing competitions, international or otherwise, and I see great danger ahead for my favourite sport and for stocks of wild brown trout, if the present trend continues. Sponsorship, and the advertising value of commodities linked to clean, outdoor pursuits such as trout fishing, are, in my opinion, an evil we should all resist. I cannot understand how any group of supposedly sane men can get so worked up over which country catches the largest number of trout. There is far more to fishing than that. What possible satisfaction can it give to spend a day thrashing the water frenetically in order to achieve a few more ounces weight than several other similarly demented, so-called sportsmen?

If there must be competitions, I think they should be very private affairs, and for a number of years Ann, Blair and I have had the good fortune to be associated with one such event, known as the MacSob Log – the principal reason for which was the desire to escape for a few days' fishing and keep non-fishing wives happy.

The idea came to us a few years ago when Blair and I were fishing with my friend Harry Officer and his son, Alistair.

'What about a father-and-son versus father-and-son day out?' I suggested. Thus it was arranged, and soon afterwards we booked a Sutherland hill loch for our first meeting.

The party consisted of Harry and Alistair, other fishing friends, Adam Black and his son Stephen, and Blair and myself. In order to preserve peace and dignity, a senior, son-less friend, Donnie MacKay, was appointed President.

Donnie Mackay was a highly respected member of the community and hard-working church elder, and as we gathered that first morning, I couldn't help remarking that we were indeed biblical. A commemorative photograph was taken and entitled, *Father, Son, Father, Son, Father, Son and the Holy Ghost*, Donnie being good-humouredly dubbed the latter.

It was a super day out, full of light-hearted banter and laughter, and in the evening we all retired to a local hotel, complete with wives and girl friends, for a celebratory meal. Ann purchased a photograph album and each year a photographic and written account of our activities are written up by the father-and-son team which produces the best basket. The book is called the MacSob Log, after the initials of our names: MacKay, Sandison, Officer and Black. Another of Ann's ideas.

As with the minutes of our Sandison Family Fishing Association, whenever Blair and I are presented with the log we immediately pass it on to Ann – who is good at this sort of thing. Keeping records or accounts of any kind is beyond me. I have a fear of official-sounding functions or documents which stems from my school days when the very mention of examinations, or tests, used to bring me out in a sweat. Report cards were my nightmare – the culmination of months of blotched jotters, unconjugated verbs, forgotten dates and unsolved equations. Algebra was as clear to me as double Dutch, scientific experiments always ended up broken on the classroom floor and Latin left me cold. Apart, that is, from my hands. I went to school in the days of corporal punishment and my Latin master was convinced that he could motivate my latent Latin senses by beating my hands red with a thick, twin-thonged, leather strap every week.

At the end of each term, I would wait helplessly for my report card, the harbinger of certain doom, praying that perhaps by some miraculous mischance, officialdom had lost the evidence of my lack of endeavour – or that I had, amazingly, achieved at least average marks. But it was always to no avail. Our form master, the Latin fiend, would hand me my card with a cynical, all-knowing smile:

'Here you are, Sandison. And I wouldn't like to be in your shoes when your father reads this!'

A quick glance generally confirmed the worst. If I was not bottom of the class, then I had usually managed to capture second-bottom place. Red, heavily underlined comments highlighted my wrack, complaining bitterly about lack of ability and general uselessness. I would plod wearily homewards through the streets of Edinburgh, staring sightlessly into shop windows on Princes Street, purposely missing yet another No 9 tram-car until finally, taking courage in both hands, I would rush home to face the inevitable, unmitigated fury of outraged paternity.

Strange, how the mention of just a single word can suddenly conjure up images of things past and forgotten for decades. Trams, for instance. I had forgotten how important trams were in our young lives. After school I used to wait outside Elliot's bookshop at the east end of Princes Street to catch a tram home. They made a huge noise, particularly when the safety cage at the front accidentally fell. This structure was released should the driver encounter anything on the line in front of him. I vividly recall seeing one of my school friends fall in front of an approaching tram and being swept up, safely, into the cage.

Even worse was the nightmare of getting a wheel of a bicycle stuck in one of the rails. Apart from shame and terror, there was nothing one could do other than ignominiously stop and lift the bike out – whilst impatient tram drivers clanged their bells furiously.

Further back, I remember watching Italian prisoners of war arriving from the docks by tram at the foot of Leith Walk. There were hundreds of people watching and I was hoisted on to Mother's shoulders in order to get a better view. The good people of Edinburgh gave the poor souls a cheer and threw packets of cigarettes to the brown-clad soldiers as the trams rattled into the terminus. Buses were never quite the same. Impersonal, wayward vehicles. You could rely on trams. If you waited long enough another tram was always bound to come along. No other way it could go.

The auld grey city was crowded with tram stops and overhead wires, and the swaying, shining trams dominated our days. A trip to the zoo, on the No 26, was an adventure in itself, never mind the lions and tigers, and warm Sundays were spent on the beach at Portobello, or swimming in the vast, open-air pool, with its artificial wave-making machine.

But my fondest memory of trams was not so much where they were going, but rather who was in them. You see, trams were like present-day discos – where you met *girls*. They were focal points for discourse with the objects of our young desires, wonderfully trapped with us, at least for the duration of the journey.

A certain party of young ladies always used to travel home from school on the No 9, and they always sat, like warrior queens, in the upstairs-front, private compartment. We boys would stand outside Elliot's carefully watching every tram approaching until the tram of our dreams came in sight, red, square-shaped hats bobbing at the window. Then there was the mad dash through the traffic to the tram stop in the middle of the road. If you were unlucky, or held up by traffic, or even worse, if the tram was full, you would have to stand, utterly dejected as the smiling faces and waving hands disappeared down Leith Walk. I suppose it all seems a bit archaic these days, but then it was a threepenny ride to paradise.

Last night, as we were having our evening meal, I began to talk to the tribe about my young days in Edinburgh, the trams, and the games we used to play. One by one, the members of my computer-addicted, disco-loving bunch, sighed wearily and sidled from the room:

'Homework, Dad, have to go!' said Blair.

'Must get ready, party tonight,' said Lewis.

And Charlie just disappeared without anyone noticing. A trick he has perfected.

When they had all gone I looked to Ann for moral support: 'Surely I'm not as boring as that, am I?' I asked.

She smiled, and for a fleeting moment I imagined that funny square-shaped hat, perched jauntily on her head, and felt that same old feeling of excitement.

Fortunately, my elder brother Ian's academic achievements were exactly the opposite of mine, so after a cursory look at my disgusting report card, and a quick back-handed swipe, Father would turn with relief to examine Ian's. Latterly, when it became apparent that I was unlikely to improve academically, my parents stopped worrying and simply let me get on with it, or rather not. They stopped attending Parent/Teacher meetings and as far as school was concerned, I was considered to be a 'lost cause'.

When the going got rough, I escaped to my secret place, a small garden overlooking the Water of Leith near Canonmills, and sat on the banks of the river watching trout darting in the shadow of overhanging trees, listening to birds twittering in leafy branches. It seemed to me that there were literally thousands of creatures on planet Earth that I would rather be: golden eagle, black-throated diver, wild cat, badger, salmon, otter – particularly an otter. Marvellous life. Unlimited free fishing, moorland haunts, happy friends – and a protected species. What fate had condemned me to a life of unnatural, unrewarding study?

Fortunately, I have been blessed with offspring made of sterner stuff. Report cards are produced with untrembling hands. Results are discussed in a civilised, non-violent fashion. It is not that I was stupid, in spite of what my report cards seemed to suggest and so-called friends still frequently claim. It is just that I never managed to settle at school and the self-discipline required for sustained academic achievement simply passed me by. Perhaps it was the system. Or perhaps our examination system. I still remember the horror of facing the dreaded '11 Plus' exam. Which I failed. Blair was the last of our brood to go through that particular nightmare. He passed. His younger brother, Charles, was spared the experience, although Charlie declaimed bitterly that it was not fair and that he should have an '11 Bus' too, just like his big brother. But one thing is certain: when I saw my children sweating over some jumble of, to me, incomprehensible figures, or, with trembling hands, opening official, brown envelopes containing the results of 'O's or 'A's, then I thanked my lucky stars that it was them and not me going through such torment. All that is behind me, thank God.

A fishing friend, Bruce Cawthraw, who lives and works in Germany, tells me that in Bavaria I would not be so lucky. There, before being allowed to pick up a fishing-rod, I would have to pass an exam, testing my knowledge and ability of matters piscatorial. If successful, I would be awarded a Prufungszeugnias, Staatliche Fischerprufung (which sounds, to say the least, painful), giving me the legal right to fish. Bruce passed his exam in 1979, when preparing for it and sitting the test cost the equivalent of £60:

'The authorities organised the examination, the fishing associations, the tuition for it. I attended a course near my office. It was a serious business, three hours instruction each evening, two evenings a week during seven weeks.

'The questions set in the examination tested your knowledge of five different subjects: the knowledge and preservation of fish; the care of angling waters; fishing tackle and its use; angling practice and the care of fish caught; and finally, the law relating to angling. To pass the examination I had to answer correctly forty-five out of sixty questions.

'The examination took place in one of the halls of a huge beer-cellar, where some four hundred of us settled down at numbered places and waited for the examination paper to be handed out – a small booklet of seven pages, including five pages of questions. Three possible answers were given for each question, and the correct one had to be marked. The papers were then marked by computer.'

Bruce told me: 'The law is clear. If you are permanently resident in Bavaria and wish to fish with rod and line, you must first obtain a fishing licence. In order to do so, you have to pass a written examination held every year in March. I obtained this information from a friendly angler in Ammersee one morning in April. Therefore, I had to wait nearly a whole year before I could take the examination, or fish.'

The law introducing the Bavarian fishing examination was proposed by the Bavarian Government on 27 October 1960. The first examination took place on 3 March 1973 and since then it has been repeated every year. Bavaria was the first state to introduce such a law, and since then, other German states have followed suit.

The purpose of the law was to help to preserve stocks of fish by ensuring that all new anglers had a better knowledge of fish and fishing. Given the comments of German, Austrian and Swiss anglers whom I meet in Scotland, this law, like so many other well-meaning, half-baked, bureaucratic schemes, has failed miserably. Apart from a few, well-preserved locations, in my opinion Continental game fishing for wild fish is virtually non-existent and depends almost entirely upon put-and-take fisheries.

Bruce had also maliciously given me a note containing some of the questions asked during the examination – along with the correct answers. I scanned the list with mounting alarm:

Q *Which fish has two dorsal fins?*
A The bullhead

Q *How many feelers has the brown bullhead?*
A Eight

Q *Which fish have no stomach?*
A White fish

Q *Where is the heart of a fish?*
A Immediately behind the gills

Q *Why is it important to know where the forehead of a fish is?*
A To know how to kill it properly

Q *For which fish is sight unimportant when hunting its prey?*
A The sheet fish (wels), a night hunter

Q *Do fish have a sense of smell?*
A Yes

Q *How do you distinguish the orfe* (Nerfling) *from the churp* (Shied)?
A The orfe has a mouth with upper and lower jaws of equal length

Q *Which fish has a mouth like a duck's beak and a flat head?*
A The pike

Q *What influence has the water temperature on the oxygen content of the water?*
A Cold water can absorb more oxygen in solution

Q *Why is the musk rat harmful?*
A It damages dams and banks

Q What is the maximum strength of perlon-line for eel fishing?
A 4lb

Q Who is permitted to catch crabs?
A The duly authorised angler

Q What is the correct rule for choosing the appropriate strength of line and hook size?
A Line no stronger than necessary, hook no smaller than necessary

Q Who issues fishing permits as opposed to licences?
A The owner or tenant of the fishery

Well, how did you do? Is it back to the classroom, or off to the river? And that is only a small sample of the questions asked. Why is it that Germans appear to delight in making rules and regulations? And why is it that they seem to delight in following them implicitly? Last year, whilst on holiday in south-west Crete, Ann and I found a delightful little naturist cove where the majority of people were concentrating upon getting an all-over-tan. Prior to going swimming, most of the Germans present stood up and donned their swimming costumes. After returning to the beach, off they came again as their Teutonic owners settled down for more sun. A strange race. Swimming, you wear a costume – sunning, you do not. They must have a law.

I used to hanker after a spot of Teutonic angling, but Bruce Cawthraw's startling revelation instantly smothered any desire I had to fish in Germany. The prospect of having to pass an exam before wetting a line is bad enough: what about the consequences of failure? If I know my Aryan brothers, dunces like me would be instantly carted off to some desert island and incarcerated there until they had mastered the knack of tying blood knots, blindfolded, with one hand. I know that I would fail miserably. What I couldn't achieve as a boy, I am hardly likely to achieve years later as a staid, middle-aged man. Anyway, the amount of knowledge I have concerning angling could be quickly written down on one side of a sopping beer-mat.

I suspect that this is why I abhor the thought of any government tinkering with game fishing. From time to time the spectre of nationalisation looms and the old arguments about fair play and equal shares for all are dragged out from dusty cupboards. The advent of time-share fishing has exacerbated the situation, with operators and owners being variously accused of destroying once Sylvan streams and robbing local anglers of their ancient rights; of turning salmon fishing into the private preserve of the rich; of inventing cheque-book angling.

I disagree, strongly. Most time-share schemes are on rivers that have never been accessible to locals anyway – the Tay, Spey and Dee, for instance – and the best beats on these streams have always been strictly preserved. I believe that what is cheap is rarely valued. Generally it is abused. Time-share salmon fishing protects many of our finest rivers from overexploitation. Owners are highly organised and have but a single aim, unhindered by other financial considerations: to protect and enhance salmon stocks.

The prospect of officialdom organising angling is almost too horrifying to contemplate. There would have to be a Ministry of Angling, with expensive London headquarters and dozens of branch-offices scattered throughout the land, managed by Directors, Assistant Directors, Deputy-Assistant Directors, Regional Directors, their assistants, Area Managers and, of course, their staff – thousands of them. They would spring up like summer mushrooms after a warm night in a cow-pat-covered field, and at the end of the day, access to the best fishing would probably still follow that age-old dictum: 'It's not what you know, but who you know that counts.'

No doubt, sooner rather than later, following the shining example of our Common Market brethren, we would all be required to present ourselves for instruction and examination before being allowed to catch even the smallest minnow. It is easy to rationalise the thinking behind such a move: increasing numbers of anglers; diminishing resources; evidence of illegal fishing; raising standards; protecting our national heritage, and so on and on, all for our own good. Before I could mutter Peter Ross, I would find myself in some dank, brown-painted torture chamber, surrounded by hordes of ageing fishermen, all struggling to differentiate between caddis and chrysalis; trying to understand the scientific and practical implications of using ultrasonic aids in determining the course of gudgeon migration; describing the courtship dance of dace; outlining the incidence and effect of water-related and atmospheric, self-induced temperature disturbances on the balance of payments. There would be the practical examinations: techniques for paying officials (under the counter, plain brown envelope, free flies for life); effective forelock tugging for salmon anglers; advanced fence climbing; easy ways of filling in five thousand essential forms, in triplicate; and saluting senior fishery managers. My school-day nightmare would return to haunt me and I would quickly revert to type. Whilst the rest of the family would pass with flying colours, Father would let them all down: forget to take his fishing-rod to school; break his nylon during knot-tying classes; lose his waders; not learn the Latin names of insects and flies; and generally drive his teachers mad. There I would be, crouched, shaking in the Assembly Rooms, Wick, sucking my pencil, staring at my virgin, unmarked examination-paper, furiously trying to take the matter seriously, surreptitiously peeking at my neighbours' answers, watching the hands of the clock slowly ticking away my angling life, experiencing again the old feeling of helplessness and anger, mingled with grudging admiration for my compatriots, as pupil after pupil nonchalantly finished the exam and handed their completed paper to the invigilating officer. How many eggs does a 12lb female salmon lay? How many survive? Good Lord, I was looking at that only the other night. How could I have forgotten so quickly? Who is the present Minister for Angling? Who cares?

I see myself returning from the examination, head bent in shame, trudging the windswept streets of town, scared to go home and face the music, stopping on the bridge and staring into the dark waters – death before dishonour. Finally, I would drive back to Ruther House across desolate Bilbster Moss, my malignant end-of-term Angling Report Card on the seat beside me – offending, damning evidence of yet another examination failure:

MINISTRY OF ANGLING
HIGHLAND REGION/CAITHNESS DIVISION
End of Term Report and Assessment in Angling Studies

NAME:	Bruce MacGregor Sandison
AGE:	Old
CLASS:	Novice
NUMBER OF PUPILS IN CLASS:	87
POSITION IN CLASS:	87

SUBJECT

ENTOMOLOGY
Shows a complete inability to grasp any aspect of the subject. Sandison imagines that Butchers, Black Pennel and Dunkeld are natural flies that live under stones by the riverside. Has

129

an unhealthy fixation with exotic patterns, all unauthorised, and encourages other pupils to contravene regulations by fishing with them: Willie Ross, Charlie Maclean, Pubic & Claret, and Scrotum & Green.

In spite of repeated warnings, Sandison regularly fails to complete his Latin homework and becomes highly aggressive and abusive when asked to stand in the corner as punishment for his failure to do so. A disruptive influence on the other members of the class. Must try harder.

POSITION IN CLASS *87*

FLY-TYING

Forgets his feathers and tying-silk every day and shows little inclination to tie anything other than himself in knots. Has to be constantly restrained from jamming his own and his tutor's fingers in the vice. Spends most of his time attacking female students with old capes.

In my opinion, Sandison will never master the art of fly-tying. He has been given private, remedial, out-of-school instruction by Ms Lavinia Farringdon-Smythe, one of our most talented instructors, but she now refuses to be left alone in a room with this pupil.

POSITION IN CLASS *87*

ANGLING HISTORY

Sandison cannot seem to grasp the fact that G. E. M. Skues was in fact a famous angler, not a type of Arctic sea-bird. He also claims that Izaac Walton is a pub, because he once got drunk there. The implications of the historical-economic development of fishing are beyond him, as are recent developments in the use of high-technology materials.

This pupil claims that the only historical angling figures worthy of mention are James Hogg, the Ettrick Shepherd, who almost certainly used to worm fish illegally on St Mary's Loch in the Scottish Borders. Sandison also claims that Thomas Tod Stoddart, a Tweed Valley writer of doggerel, is the finest poet who ever lived. Sandison is a hopeless case.

POSITION IN CLASS *87*

CASTING TECHNIQUE

It would help if the student knew his left hand from his right, but teaching Sandison anything is beyond his tutor's ability. Sandison uses rods as though they were pokers, and has, on several occasions, almost blinded several promising students, as well as his instructors.

According to Sandison, the art of delicate casting is effeminate and a complete waste of time. He claims that the only reason people catch salmon is because they happen to be in the right place at the right time; or, as he so quaintly puts it, luck. Throws tackle into the river if anyone tries to question him, and often, teachers as well.

POSITION IN CLASS *87*

SOCIAL STUDIES

Shows some basic aptitude, often offering extra-mural instruction to other pupils, particularly young female students. Can talk reasonably intelligently about angling until after downing his second whisky; thereafter, Sandison rapidly degenerates into incomprehensible gibberish and slavers.

Sandison's views regarding Social Studies are narrow and subversive; entirely contrary to Section 3, Sub-Section XVII, Para ii of the *Ministry of Angling, Social Benefits for Under-Privileged Anglers (1990) Revised Manual*. Sandison claims that money paid to 'so-called' underprivileged anglers would be better used for, 'flushing the toilet for all the good it does'. Nor can he grasp the importance of non-means-tested subsidies for certain groups of anglers: nursing mothers, one-legged, one-eyed men over the age of seventy; children under the age of three; and all farmers, riparian owners, Members of the House of Commons and House of Lords, and all employees of the Ministry of Angling, as clearly noted in the appropriate section of the Manual.

POSITION IN CLASS *87*

DOCUMENTATION AND FORM-FILLING

This pupil is anti-social, dangerously aggressive and refuses to have anything to do with the prescribed, official forms required to be completed, prior to fishing, as described in the *Ministry of Angling Manual* (123rd Edition, 1990, Revised October 1990).

Sandison uses very short, extremely rude words to describe these forms and removes them illegally from the classroom. He takes them home, where he claims to have found a more suitable use for them in one of the smaller rooms of his house.

POSITION IN CLASS *87*

HEADMASTER'S REMARKS

Not only does Sandison show a complete lack of ability regarding the basic principles of angling, but he also seems to obtain perverse enjoyment and pleasure out of his lack of knowledge.

He is quite unfit to be a student at this angling school or, in my opinion, at any other angling school. Sandison should never be left alone with other pupils – otherwise he will

131

pervert them with his heretical, archaic, anachronistic views regarding game fishing.

Sandison is a serious danger to both himself and to any employee of the Ministry of Angling unfortunate enough to encounter him. I strongly recommend that Sandison is subjected to a concentrated, remedial course of psychoanalysis in an attempt to alter his attitudes – preferably as far away from this school as possible.

Signed: Oscar Willerton-Pyfil
BSc (Wading)., Dip.Cast., F. Inst.Oars.

You may well smile and claim that my fears are unfounded, that it could never happen here. What about post–1992? All these people, busily engaged under the English Channel. They are not there for the good of their health. Sooner, rather than later, an army of anglers is going to break through and descend upon our rivers and lochs, clutching their diplomas in Angling Studies. I can see it all now, far too clearly. Remember Bavaria. You can't say that you haven't been warned.

At that point Horace Cat . . .

132

The Loneliness of a Long-Distance Salmon Fisher

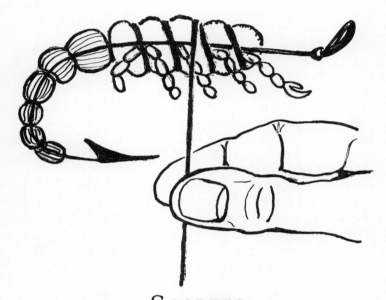

SCORPIO
24 OCTOBER TO 22 NOVEMBER

Domestic commitments are liable to prove very time-consuming but, with careful planning, you should be able to cope with the demands – gardening, painting and decorating, weekends with the in-laws, taking the children for walks – and still leave plenty of time for fishing. It would be wise, however, to remain diplomatic.

It is favourable to encourage group activity now, rather than to work alone, and there are a number of opportunities still available for good fishing. You should set up a regular telephone roster so that members of your family can search for autumn salmon fishing in Scotland, whilst you continue, uninterrupted, with your personal fishing activities. It seems unlikely that you will experience any set-backs but, should you come under any criticism, tell them that it is their duty to support their father and that doing so is far more important than exams, girl friends, boy friends, or wasting time at discos.

Your partner may insinuate that her predecessors, your four previous wives and their children, must have been saints to live with you, but this should not be allowed to deter you from the pursuit of your proper function in life: the removal of fish from their natural habitat. She knows the way to the front door, and you will have locked the cheque books securely away. Ignore any unwarranted, female whining.

Those close to you at work will listen to all you have to say regarding the availability of good salmon fishing. Make sure that you charge them for your advice, in order to defray the costs of your own fishing expeditions, and always remember to get their money before giving the advice. Preferably cash, rather than a cheque.

Be assertive if they bleat about the high price of salmon fishing and their personal financial problems. Salmon fishing is a seller's market and, if you react positively, you should be able to clear several thousands pounds' profit.

Do not worry that your friends and colleagues will be unlikely to catch any fish. Remind them that salmon fishing is very much a question of being in the right place at the right time – and of skill.

This year will see you enjoying a run of extraordinary skill and feeling very pleased with life. It is almost certain that you may hook the British Record, rod-caught salmon, beating Miss Balantine's record of 62lb; and with careful attention to detail, you could even land it. But be patient.

Towards the end of the season, salmon figure largely in your stars. So stay on good terms with those in authority at work since you will need plenty of time off for fishing.

In conversation with your superiors, it is important that you use every available opportunity to comment upon the frailty of life in general and of your nearest and dearest in particular. Sow the seeds for securing compassionate leave of absence from work early. Cultivate them assiduously.

It is vital that you allow time for fun, especially around your Solar Return, the astrological term for your birthday. October is an excellent month for fun, particularly on the Junction Pool on the Tweed. Why not treat yourself and burn off some Scorpio energy? You will also burn off most of the profit you have made.

The social scene is also rewarding and friends are unusually kind and flattering towards you and all the lovely salmon and trout that you will catch. Given the price of fresh, wild salmon and trout, be suspicious of their motives. Suggest that they catch their own, offer to arrange fishing on their behalf, and then charge them accordingly.

ON COLD, wet, windy days my spirits slumped and I wondered how it all began. As I struggled to keep the rod rings ice-free in knife-like February gales, the torrents beckoned suicidally and I doubted my sanity. During midge-ridden sultry afternoons, as I larded insect repellent on to my bite-blistered face, I sensed madness very near. In the long still watches of the night, I knew that I should search no further, try no harder, hope no more.

And yet, in spite of everything, despair, disappointment and disillusionment vanished at the prospect of another chance – instantly being replaced by absolute certainty, positive conviction and frenzied endeavour. After years of abject failure, 'salmon fever' still gripped me, as strong as ever. I was neither sadder nor wiser, simply older and more determined. I knew, you see, that the longer I tried, the nearer the day approached when I would hold aloft *my first salmon* for all the world to see.

I suppose it started when I was a boy, when days were endless and an 8oz trout a monster catch. I was born and brought up in 'Auld Reekie', Edinburgh, the Athens of the North, an unlikely place to begin a fishing career, but in the 1940s, whilst our parents were attending to Mr Hitler, we boys used to roam wild round town: parks, ponds, rivers, streams, woodlands and sea-shore. Few capital cities match Edinburgh's acres of open space and gardens. There are twenty-nine golf courses within the city limits, wildlife abounds, even in the centre of town, and it is possible to catch brown trout in the Water of Leith, almost within a stone's throw from Princes Street, one of the world's busiest thoroughfares.

Sea fishing was our most accessible angling and Newhaven the favoured venue. Dozens of boys used to jostle for the best position on either side of the twin piers that guard the narrow harbour entrance. Brown cord line, wrapped around rectangular wooden frames, vicious, shining hooks and a lot of patience was all that was required. Casting was dangerous, swinging the weighted line round and round, close to several other boys doing the same thing. Accidents were frequent, but we all survived, and, from time to time, even caught fish, carried proudly home to our long-suffering mothers who never failed to congratulate their off-spring on their success.

For summer holidays we travelled north across the Firth of Forth to the Kingdom of Fife. Four glorious weeks at the little seaside town of Kinghorn. The journey started at Waverley Station, black-taxi busy, sharp with the acrid smell of steam, loud with the hiss and puff of arrival and departure. Elegant, streamline locomotives, their sleek, polished bodies gleaming, waited impatiently to rocket travellers south to places with strange-sounding names: Newcastle, York, Doncaster, Grantham, and mighty London, where the King lived. I envied passengers as they crowded aboard. People had to be important to go to London.

Crossing the Forth Bridge was the highlight of our trip: expectation, as the smoke-belching train chugged out over the Firth past Dalmeny and Queensferry; below, the bustle of cars and match-stick people, waiting for the ferry; mysterious green islands, decked with grim, grey concrete gun emplacements; silver ribbon wakes trailing behind dark ships heading out to sea; red-painted girders flashing by.

Kinghorn was made for small boys: a wide sweep of yellow sand, fringing shallow warm waters. Round-the-bay boat trips, ice-cream and fishing. In calm weather we fished from a rowing boat towards Pettycur, catching flounders. When the wind blew we fished from rocks behind the harbour, tempting dabs from sheltered pools.

Inland, a few minutes' walk from town, was Kinghorn Loch, where I began to take a serious interest in bird life: white-nebbed coot and moorhen, like clockwork toys, bobbing and dipping across the loch; heron and mallard. I saw my first great crested grebe there, and puzzled over what kind of fish made these alluring rings on the calm surface.

Reading sharpened my interest. I discovered *Tarka* and *Salar*, but best of all, Mrs Johnson, a neighbour, gave me free rein in her library: Dickie's *Hunters of the Wild*; *Krark* and *Heron Garth* by W. K. Richmond; Robert's *Kindred of the Wild*; *String Lug*, by David Stephen; and many more.

Other friends encouraged fly-fishing. Mr and Mrs Tom Kelly, both expert anglers, had a newsagent's shop at the foot of Annandale Street and they supplied Collin Willock's books, *Come Fly-Fishing With Me* and *Game Fishing With Me*. I found Moray Maclaren and a wonderful book, Maunsell's *The Fisherman's Vade Mecum*, packed with practical angling information. The Kellys, with endless patience, answered all my questions, regardless of how busy their shop was. Tom often abandoned the counter completely in order to show me the most successful flies, or demonstrate how to tie up casts. I owe them a great debt, which I try to repay by showing similar courtesy to anglers who ask me for advice today.

My parents did not fish. Father was a keen golfer and found it hard to appreciate the passion I had developed for angling; but, when it became apparent that I was 'hooked', he came home one night with a fishing-rod and a small brass reel. The rod was a magnificent greenheart, eleven feet long and about fifty years old. Within minutes I was in the back garden, practising furiously. The rod became my most treasured possession – a trusted friend, although over the years, as I grew in height, it diminished in length, through accident and hard usage.

The opposite sex did not figure much in my general scheme of things. Weekends were for angling or Scout camps, invariably linked with fishing, and, as Patrol Leader of the 'Otters', I made sure that these outings and adventures took place close to rivers or lochs.

Our favourite site was a few miles west from Edinburgh, in the grounds of Hopetoun Estate. We made the ten-mile journey on foot, pulling a trek-cart piled high with camping gear and food for the weekend. We camped in a magnificent wood bordered by a narrow stream which met the Firth midway between Hopetoun House and the old castle at Blackness. To me, after labouring all week amongst unconjugated verbs, quadratic equations and occasional corn laws, the freedom of the woodlands and shores around Hopetoun was like another, far more friendly planet. Small trout splashed at flies in the burn, finch and wren flitted amongst russet-red autumn leaves, pigeons billed and cooed in the old dovecote near Midhope. Days seemed endless.

My years in the Scouts were amongst the happiest of my life – mostly because so many of them were spent out of doors. I felt absolutely secure in the hills and woods, confident, yet at the same time, constantly aware of all that I had to learn, and could learn. I discovered the Tay, camping at Inver Park, near Dunkeld, and hooked and lost my first salmon in the pool where the bridge crosses the A9, two miles north from town; swam in the pool below Hermitage, on the River Braan, where golden trout dart from dark shadows. Lyne Water, a tributary of the River Tweed, was another campsite, in a loop of the river near Romannobridge, where green plover nests and hunting owls hoot on long June nights, and brightly speckled trout hide from the midday sun in the shade of cool, weed-fringed boulders. Of Latin, English, science, mathematics, geography and history, I knew little and cared even less. The real world was sunlight slanting through beech woods and the sweet smell of dawn; woodsmoke round an evening camp fire and the happy sound of rising trout.

It took me decades to recover from the sudden shock of leaving school and having to earn a living. My only qualifications were an ability to cast a trout fly twenty yards and recognise a wide range of birds and trees – neither of which mightily impressed prospective employers.

I found work as a junior salesman and office boy with Smith & Wellstood Ltd, the Esse Cooker Company, in their Greenside Place showroom next to the Playhouse cinema, selling cookers and fireplaces, licking stamps and running errands. I was packed off to night-school to learn about salesmanship and ironmongery. Company Head Office was at Bonnybridge, a drab, dark town of factories and smoking chimneys. New employees were given an induction course which included classroom work and endless visits to the foundry. Not a tree, hill or river to be seen, other than the notoriously fishless, stagnant waters of the Forth/Clyde canal. It seemed like hell to me. A place where no birds sang.

But worse was to follow when the company sent me to Glasgow to attend a course conducted by the Coal Utilisation Council in their offices at Hope Street. A week in a basement learning about anthracite, coke and British Thermal Units. It was hard to be enthusiastic. None of my fellow sufferers had the slightest interest in fishing and few could tell the difference between a robin and a crow. Nor wished to.

Having failed academically at one school, I was hardly likely to succeed dramatically at another, regardless of parental prompting, and I was as miserable as sin. Reality was Hopetoun, or Lyne Water, to which I fled every other Saturday, on my half days off from work.

The little Lyne rises in the Pentland Hills from Muckle Knock and flows southwards through West Linton to Romannobridge. The bus stopped at the village inn and, after hanging over the bridge for a few moments to see what I could see, I would set off upstream, full of hope, the light of battle glinting in my eyes, determined that this would be the day when I caught my first trout.

Downstream was just as inviting, by the old church near Bordlands. The river was the perfect size for a beginner, easy to cast across, never too deep to be intimidating, but deep enough to fill Wellington boots taking an ill-considered step too far. I spent most of my time wet and, after two seasons, had caught nothing.

With remarkable patience for one so young, I taught myself the essentials of angling: catching trees, retrieving casts from underwater obstructions, falling in, tying casts by match-light in the dark, catching everything other than trout. But the moment of truth came when I was fishing near Paulswell and I remember the sudden thrill, the sheer excitement of that first fish. It was only about four inches in length but to me it was a prize beyond compare. At last I really could call myself an angler.

My fishing day was limited by bus times, to and from St Andrew Square, Edinburgh. Proper buses. None of this modern-day piped-muzak nonsense. Dressed for action, packed lunch in an old gas-mask bag, fishing-rod firmly clutched, I bumped expectantly south down the A702.

'Going fishing, then?' fellow travellers would inquire. Very observant, bus passengers. On the way home, it was generally, 'Been fishing have you? Catch anything? My, you aren't half wet.' More often than not I was soaked – soaked, but supremely happy.

One evening, just as I was facing up to the sad fact that I would have to pack up and run for the bus, Father's car appeared. Apparently, his golf match had been cancelled and, in a fit of good humour, he had decided to come down and collect me. I was fishing at Flemington, where a tiny burn tumbles down to greet the Lyne – a gentle glen, surrounded by majestic Border hills: Wide Hope Shank, Stevenson Hill, Hag Law, Drum Maw,

Father was an avid angler

White Knowe and Green Knowe. Even today, this valley remains almost exactly as I remember it, so many years ago.

Father, never noted for his mad pursuit of physical fitness, sat in the car and watched. I fished happily on, pleased at the prospect of another hour's sport. Light was fading and the first bats flicked overhead. Sensing that I would have to be dragged to the car, Father eventually came down to the river. He stood watching. Rising trout stippled the surface of the pool. Flies danced above the water. A sudden surge and splash. The sweet, evening smell of running water. Stillness and silence.

'Here, son,' he said. 'Give me a shot of that.' I handed father the rod and stood back. In such ways, fishermen are born.

For the rest of his life, Father was an avid angler, never happier than when he was up to his thighs in water. I don't think he played golf again and, not long afterwards, he gave his clubs to my cousin, Bruce Reynolds. Fishing became his whole life, which, as far as I was concerned, was very good news. No more buses and more time fishing.

Lyne Water joins the Tweed at Lyne Station, where there is a Queen Victoria post-box set into a cottage wall. It is still there and, as Father and I worked our way downstream, ever closer to the Tweed, we discovered salmon.

Darkness had fallen in the midst of an all-enveloping October night stillness. Lapwing called as I struggled to remove a Grouse & Claret from the back of my jumper. I think it was a Grouse & Claret, but by then the matches were running low.

As I knelt in the long grass by the river there was a sudden explosion. Water shattered and sparkled as a great shape hurled itself clear. Moonlight flashed and shone pure silver along mighty flanks. As though in slow motion, the salmon hit the surface and the sound of its landing rang through the quiet night. Waves from its spectacular leap rushed over the surface, sweeping into the bank at my feet. Birds rose, startled from sleep and scattered through the trees. I had never seen anything so magnificent. I had never felt such heart-stopping excitement. It was as though the world stood still, as though a great secret had been revealed, a sacred trust shared.

I remained motionless, hardly daring to breathe, as the river smoothed and silence returned; but, in that single instant, I knew that life would never be the same again. I had to catch a salmon.

Father had also seen a salmon and we instantly decided that the time had come for us to graduate to fishing the River Tweed. Father bought annual permits and for the next few years we stalked the banks, from Lyne Footbridge to Walkerburn Cauld, haunting the pools like demented spirits. From the moment the season opened, regardless of snow, hail, rain or sleet, until the stroke of midnight on 30 November when the season closed, Father and I thrashed the waters: the Red Yetts, Long Pool, Cadrona, Manor Water. I began to know every stone, ripple and eddy . . . but we caught nothing.

As season after fishless season progressed, Father became more and more determined, watching the locals with envious eyes as they played and landed mighty fish, and I frequently had to restrain him from taking ill-considered, illegal action in order to achieve his aim.

The most common fishing method used by local anglers was 'sniggering'. I didn't know it then but, even as a youth, it was

141

quite clear to me that such tactics were a highly suspicious fishing technique. A large, almost featherless hook was cast out over a holding pool, allowed to sink, and then jerked through the water with savage tugs in the hope that it would embed itself into the flanks of resting salmon, which it often did.

One member of the gang would stand on the old iron bridge across the Tweed at Innerleithen, locating the fish and directing operations: 'Hud on, Jimmy, yer too far downstream. Come up a bit. Aboot halfway o're the pool. There, ya almost had him! Give it another go.'

One morning, as I was fishing a little downstream, I heard a man on the bridge shouting directions. In horror, I realised that it was Father, bawling away encouragingly to one of the locals, who was wielding a seventeen-foot salmon-rod. I dropped my rod and dashed up to the bridge: 'What are you doing, Dad?" I complained. 'Do you want to get us banned from the river? For goodness sake, come away.'

The local leered up at me and cast again. His 'fly' caught in the branches of a tree and he tugged furiously. I scrambled down to the river-bank and climbed the tree, retrieved the huge hook, and handed it to him.

'What sort of a fly do you call this, then?' I asked.

'A bloody Scott Jock. Now get the hell out of here before I throw you in the river.'

Happily, Father realised the error of his ways, but thereafter I always worried when he was out of sight. He 'had aye a poachin' whim' and had to be watched like a hawk, for his own good.

On my sixteenth birthday my parents gave me a beautiful cane trout-rod made by Alexander Martin of Frederick Street, Edinburgh. The rod, a 'Scottie', is still hale and hearty today, unlike its makers who were eventually bought over by John Dickson's, their gun-making neighbours across the street.

From time to time my elder brother, Ian, joined us, but he was far more interested in more mature pursuits, such as girls, and studying furiously for final school exams (in those days known as 'Highers' in Scotland). A couple of weeks before Ian's exams it was decided that he should be given undisturbed peace and quiet, to complete preparations for meeting his Nemesis, so our parents rented us a small flat in the town of Innerleithen, close to the banks of the Tweed. It was on the north side of the main street, through a narrow passage at the top of a flight of stone stairs. Ian was to study, I was to keep out of his way, fishing.

This was no hardship, and every morning I set off, light of step, with a basic packed lunch, almost running to the river. I fished all day and every day, returning, usually fishless, in the evening for supper. My brother was an excellent cook. He could acquire fish and chips from the local shop quicker than anyone I knew. We were never hungry.

An old iron bridge crosses the Tweed south of Innerleithen, carrying the B7062 road over Deuchar Law into Ettrick and St Mary's Loch. Upstream from the bridge, past Traquair House, were the New Water, Cow Ford and the Long Pool, where salmon lay. New Water is anything but new, because the long, straight stretch was artificially constructed in the mid-seventeenth century by the 1st Earl of Traquair. The old river course was undermining the foundations of Traquair House, and the Earl had the stream moved further north, to where it runs today. A ribbon of woodland extends westwards from the bridge, and the track through the trees ends at the tail of Long Pool.

One warm, calm, windless morning I began fishing there. I always started from the shallow, shingle bank above it, working slowly downstream, carefully exploring the fast water on the far bank, where railway sleepers had been set to preserve the sides from erosion. I knew that salmon often lay close in to these timbers, but small trees overhanging the run made casting difficult. I kept catching the branches and, several lost flies later, eventually came to the main body of the 'kirk', where the river opens out into a deep, clear pool.

Once again my flies became stuck, this time on some underwater obstruction. I gave one or two tentative tugs, wondering if I should have to beg money to buy more flies (my small stock had taken a considerable hammering during the week). The obstacle came free and with the rod bent almost double I reeled in, wading out to retrieve my precious flies.

Suddenly, my whole body went numb with excitement. Lying about two yards distant, its great tail moving gently back and forth in the current, was a monster salmon. I could see every detail and I estimated the fish to weigh at least 20lb. Embedded in its lower jaw was my size 16 Silver Butcher; taut as a fiddle string was my 2lb 8oz breaking-strain nylon cast. The salmon seemed unaware of either and, in an agony of indecision, I wondered what to do. Should I try to grab the fish? Could I manoeuvre it into the shallows and 'boot' it ashore?

I looked round, desperately seeking help, but I was alone with my dilemma. I raised the point of the rod. The salmon shook its head in annoyance. I froze in terror least the slender cast should snap. The fish moved closer to where I stood, thigh-deep in the pool. We remained motionless, locked in time. I looked down at the salmon. The salmon looked back up at me. Every time I put pressure on the line, the salmon vigorously shook its mighty head. I couldn't move the brute. For what seemed like eternity, we stood there, joined together by a thread.

I decided to try and grab the salmon by the tail and bustle it to the bank. Cautiously, I moved forward until only inches separated us. I slid my hand slowly below the surface, feeling the cold water seeping through my jumper.

As soon as my fingers brushed its tail, the pool erupted in chaos. Stumbling backwards, fighting to retain my balance, I managed to stay upright, and the reel screamed in anger as the salmon set off upstream, ploughing through the narrows like an express train. The rod was almost wrenched from my grasp. I could only hang on grimly, hoping the fish would stop. Hold on, hold on, I prayed.

He leapt once, coming out of the water in a mighty rush, bursting into the summer afternoon like some Icelandic god, then struck the surface in a shower of sparkling silver. The flimsy cast snapped. The salmon surged onwards through the rapids and disappeared.

I was breathless, utterly broken, dejected. So near and yet so far. For a moment, I watched the pool as though I could will the salmon back. Then I let out an uncontrollable roar, a pure animal howl of absolute rage. I hurled the rod into the bushes and jumped up and down in anger, waving my arms and cursing furiously. Exhausted, I slumped to the ground, head between my knees.

I felt a hand on my shoulder: 'What on earth is the matter? Are you ill? Have you gone stark-staring mad? Should I call a doctor?' It was my brother and his eyes said it all. Clearly, I was having some sort of unidentifiable fit.

Gathering my courage, I restrained tears of rage.

'Ian, I have just lost a huge salmon,' I managed to gasp.

'You mean, that is why you were acting like a raving lunatic? There is nothing really wrong with you?'

'No – I mean yes. I lost a salmon. Don't you understand?'

There was a long pause as Ian thought this over.

'Oh, well, that's all right then. You had me worried for a moment. I thought that it was something serious. Come on, let's get home. I'm tired of maths and you must be tired of fishing.'

Bleakly, I retrieved my rod and followed him home. He couldn't understand. He wasn't an angler.

I lost my next salmon early the following year, in the pool below Manor Bridge, downstream from where Manor Water sweeps into the Tweed. The river charges through a narrow, rocky channel and then broadens into a long, wide, sweet pool. I was fishing for trout, from the north side of the river, when the salmon rose, as always, beyond my casting range, close to the far bank. Salmon fever gripped me and, in spite of near spate conditions, I hurried to the tail of the pool where it was usually possible to cross.

I arrived on the other side, soaked to the waist, frozen and barely alive, but none the less determined. Moving inland, I circled round an old hawthorn that used to guard the pool until I was well above where the fish had risen. As I hurried along I was tying on a size 8 Hairy Mary to a 5lb breaking-strain cast, the heaviest nylon in my fishing-bag. Crouching down, I approached the river on hands and knees. From a point well upstream, I cast out and let the fly swing round in the current, over where I estimated that the fish lay. Almost immediately the salmon took. There was an almighty tug, followed by a seemingly unending run before the fly sprang loose and flew back at me. Instinctively, I had struck as one does with brown trout, and the salmon had only been lightly hooked in the side of the mouth.

The more I fished the more discontented I became with Esse Cookers and balancing the stamp book, which I never managed to do. The more I read, the more certain I was that there was more to life than bottom-grates. I stuck it for two years and on my eighteenth birthday I joined the army. Anything to escape. I walked out to the recruiting office at Dean Park House on Queensferry Road and took the plunge. 'Please, sir, I want to join the army.' Within a couple of hours I had been interviewed, documented, medically examined and had taken the oath and the Queen's shilling.

I arrived home that evening, supposedly from work, to face the music. 'I have joined the army,' I announced. This statement was greeted with frank disbelief, and then astonishment, quickly followed by anger. It appeared that I had blighted my embryonic business career. I had better unjoin, pretty damn quick. Which was why I had said nothing in the first place. I knew that there would be opposition. Now, nothing could be done to reverse

Only Father could have got himself into such a fishing mess

my decision, even if I had wanted to. Which I most certainly did not. Three weeks later I was on the train heading for London. Feeling very important indeed.

For four and a half years I served Queen and Country; in Somerset, where I caught a splendid trout on lovely Sutton Bingham Reservoir, then for two years in troutless Southern Arabia, enlivened by a glorious holiday in Kenya, fishing the Rupengazi River. As for salmon, I vowed never again to waste my time trying to catch the brutes. I talked scathingly about the antics of the chuck-it-and-chance-it boys, sarcastically referring to them as the boredom brigade; but, deep down, I knew that I was fooling nobody other than myself.

Telephone calls home didn't help. Father was still thrashing away hopefully on the Tweed, and I was generally regaled with accounts of fish that got away: 'Bruce, I almost had him to the net, then the hook fell out and, damn it, he was away!' His letters, too, were always full of his fishing exploits: the 3½lb sea-trout that didn't get away, and, increasingly, his disenchantment with the Tweed: 'What have I got to do to catch a salmon?' he would complain bitterly.

He eventually managed to achieve his dream, but only after several expensive visits to the Tay, fishing at Stanley. A four-page letter gave me the details and I shook my head at the account. Only Father could have got himself into such a fishing mess. He was not fit to be let out alone on the river. On his third visit, one cold spring morning, he had been spinning away furiously from the bank, having abandoned the boat or, more probably I suspected, having been marooned for complaining about lack of fish, when his lure had stuck on the bottom – or so he thought. He had hooked a fish. The salmon ran wildly, tearing the line from Father's reel – which promptly fell from the rod – whilst at the same time, the top section of the rod which he had made himself, came off and started to follow the outraged fish.

Desperate, Father grabbed the line and wound it round his arm, protected by his fishing-jacket. There then ensued an almighty tug-of-war. There was no chance of the line snapping; Father never believed in taking chances and was fishing with a 25lb breaking-strain nylon.

After a furious struggle, the exhausted fish was dragged ashore by my equally exhausted father; whereupon he fell on the poor beast and battered it to death. He arrived home, bloody but triumphant.

'Jack, what on earth's happened?' exclaimed my distraught mother, 'you're covered in blood! Have you had an accident?'

'No, Mima, I've caught a salmon!' Father announced proudly.

By the time I returned to Edinburgh I had developed a protective, haughty disdain for salmon fishing, but my work involved frequent visits to Newcastle and very soon the bridge over the Tweed at Coldstream became a regular stopping place. There were times when, on looking down into the pool below the bridge, it was so packed with salmon that it seemed almost impossible not to catch one. Therefore, when my friend Tony Sykes suggested a day's salmon fishing on the Tweed at Lower Birgham, I threw caution to the winds, buried my pride and accepted with alacrity.

We arrived at the fishing-hut to be greeted by two disconsolate-looking gillies: 'Ah, you are wasting your time today, sir, the water is too high.'

Spirits crashed into our boots, but, maintaining stolid enthusiasm, we set about putting up our rods.

'Surely you don't intend to fish with that?' inquired one of the gillies. I inspected my fourteen-foot, built-cane rod and asked why not? The gillie disappeared behind the fishing-hut. A moment later the tip of an old greenheart rod emerged – followed seemingly hours later, by the gillie, clutching the butt. The rod was at least seventeen feet long.

'Here, you are, sir, this is what we fish with down here.' He handed me the rod. It weighed a ton. There then followed a similar discourse concerning flies. Nothing in any of our boxes would do: all too small. My gillie tied on an enormous fly, the size of a small herring, and, with ill-concealed displeasure, agreed to launch the boat.

As usual, the gillies were right. Salmon surged upstream, some even leaping over the oars in their desperate passage. Fish showed all day, but none would take, regardless of what they were offered. Eight hours hard endeavour later, during which time salmon were almost leaping into the boat by themselves, we drove home fishless, cursing, and I vowed, never again.

Other people seemed to catch salmon, like the time Tony nearly died of exposure. We were fishing below Manor Bridge on the Tweed on a very cold March morning. The rain was lashing down, with occasional gusts of snow. Hard, unrewarding work. We were trying to decide whether or not to pack up or stay and get pneumonia, when an angler on the opposite bank hooked a fish, in almost exactly the same position that I had lost my fish, five years previously. The salmon made several runs and it soon became apparent that the fish was far more experienced in these matters than the fisherman. Furthermore, he had no visible means of landing the salmon, should it ever get to that stage.

Sykes, a kind-hearted soul, responded instantly. With a determined glint in his eyes, he forded the barely fordable stream – collecting two icy bootfuls on the way – and was soon beside the struggling beginner, offering quiet, well-chosen words of encouragement and advice.

With devotion far and above the call of duty, he lowered himself into the river, standing waist-deep, directing operations. The excited angler eventually brought the fish between Sykes and the bank and, with one skilful swoop, the fish was landed. Cold, wet but triumphant, Sykes placed the fish into the eager hands of its rightful owner. I heard the novice exclaim: 'It's my first fish. What a beauty!' Still in the river, Sykes looked benignly on. The beginner opened his fishing-bag and, in one easy, practised gesture, poured and downed a large dram. He carefully replaced the bottle and, shouldering the salmon, marched off without so much as a thank you.

It had started to snow again. Sykes crossed the river again and sat down beside me. I heaved off his sopping waders. 'Bruce,' he asked, shivering, 'where is the nearest pub?'

I resisted further temptation until the mid 1970s, by which

time we had moved to Caithness, complete with four splendid children, all of whom we had introduced to fishing. My eldest son, Blair, in spite of my disparaging remarks about salmon fishing, was keen to try, so I arranged a day on the Thurso River, one of the finest salmon streams in the north. And as it seemed churlish not to join him, I booked two rods. On the appointed morning we set off, Blair full of hope, me resigned to yet further confirmation of my view that salmon fishing was 'for the birds'.

We were fishing Beat 8, below Westerdale, and, on my very first cast, the fly snagged on the bottom . . . then began to move slowly upstream. I stood speechless, watching in astonishment as the line tightened. At last. Fifteen minutes later, Blair landed my first salmon, a fish of 10lb 8oz.

I held it aloft, for all the world to see. 'Well done, Dad!' he exclaimed, 'I'll go back upstream and do likewise.' But he had hardly taken two steps, when I had hooked a second fish. Blair's face was bright with excitement as he landed another 10lb 8oz salmon.

He set off upstream but had barely gone a hundred yards when I hooked a third fish. Panting back, slightly crossly, he said: 'When do I get a chance to have a cast?' The salmon, weighing 8lb, was duly played and landed. 'Listen, dad, I think I will hang on a moment, just in case you do it again.' I did, ten minutes later: a beautiful fish weighing 11lb 4oz.

'Thanks, Blair, that is enough for me,' I said. 'As I told you, salmon fishing is simply a question of luck, being in the right place at the right time. You fish on and I will gillie for you.' We fished hard for the rest of the day – without seeing so much as another fin. The object of the exercise had been to catch Blair his first salmon but I found it hard to be too unhappy about the outcome of our day. After all, I reasoned, Blair was a lot younger than me. He still had plenty of time to catch fish. As far as I was concerned, time was running out, fast.

'Dad,' asked my despondent offspring, 'is it always like this, salmon fishing?' I sympathised.

'Never mind, Blair,' I replied, 'just give it time, I'm sure that you will go the distance. After all, I did.'

A few years later, living and working in the Outer Hebrides, Blair did. But I often remind him of our day together on the Thurso – particularly when he catches more than me.

Christmas is A-Coming . . . !

SAGITTARIUS
23 NOVEMBER TO 21 DECEMBER

Relationships are well starred and you will have a very enjoyable December being exceptionally happy, light-hearted and easy of mind as Christmas approaches. This is because a long-lost relative will leave you a small fortune, and at last the possibility of that fishing holiday in Chile will become a reality, rather than just a dream.

Difficulties which in the past have stopped you from fully realising your true fishing potential, such as lack of funds, will vanish; you will be able to tell your employer that you no longer require his services, and your wife will be only too happy to fall in with your plans, once your inheritance cheque has been cleared by the bank.

However, Sagittarians, being naturally kind, thoughtful and considerate people, could be in danger of losing fishing opportunities simply in order to bring pleasure to others. Their strongly developed sense of family loyalty might lead them astray and they should beware of begging letters from relatives suddenly expressing great interest in going fishing with them.

Angling Sagittarians also have difficulty in learning from past experiences and all too often give up excellent angling opportunities to their nearest and dearest, simply out of a misguided sense of duty: rowing the boat whilst others fish; sharing an autumn rod on an excellent salmon beat with a visiting son; looking after children whilst the rest of the party catch trout; always being the gillie, rather than the gentleman. Therefore, smoothing over family problems is likely to be one of your main concerns during the year. There are indications that a number of people in your immediate circle could create difficulties, given your financial good fortune, and a firm line must be taken. Fishing success depends largely upon your determination not to succumb to emotional blackmail under any circumstances.

Your ability to evaluate circumstances will be of paramount importance and there will be no time for complacency. Either immediately before, or immediately after, Easter a concentrated effort will be made to curtail your fullest enjoyment of your unexpected legacy.

Happily, travel is well aspected around this time and you should make sure that by then you are at an unspecified address and without a telephone, salmon fishing in the far north of Canada. Book your flight now. Do not delay or take chances.

Throughout the year, maximise upon your increased opportunities for socialising. Socialise on Tay, Tweed, Spey, Dee, Findhorn, Grimersta, Dionard, Thurso, North Harris and Shetland. Good communications are essential, and available – and you should use them to socialise in Montana, Alaska, New Brunswick, Nova Scotia, the Falklands, Norway, Iceland, Sweden and Finland.

Circumstances will be working in your favour and large catches of huge fish are absolutely guaranteed. Pack as much as possible into the year. You should also pack a friend – and I'm available.

A S A NATION, we tend to get the politicians we deserve. This also applies to relations. We have no personal choice in the matter and have to do the best we can with whatever bunch God in His infinite wisdom dishes out.

I am not suggesting, even for a moment, that my lot ever heap upon my head the load of ills and woes that the gang down at Westminster serve up; no, I am pleased to report that, by and large, over the years, my relatives have been supportive and considerate. Kind parents dragged me up, tolerating decades of Gargantuan tantrums; in-laws turned a blind eye to my manifold shortcomings when I absconded with their only daughter; brothers, aunts, uncles, cousins, sons and daughters, have been a source of constant joy. Most of the time.

I am never forgotten at Christmas. The festive season departs leaving me with a positive mound of presents: pyjamas, socks, underpants, handkerchiefs, jumpers, ties and after-shave. Nor am I ungrateful, as I am sometimes accused of being. I really appreciate their kind thoughts. But you see my problem. Of what possible use to a dedicated angler are yet another pair of large, comfortable, white knickers? Handkerchiefs can be used for staunching holes in mangled boats, but what can a fisherperson like me do with seven pairs of pyjamas? I am unlikely to be shipwrecked for decades on a desert island in the middle of a Scottish trout loch. Even if I were, pyjamas would hardly save my life. Or be run down by a double-decker bus by the banks of the River Borgie in Sutherland – requiring instant hospitalisation, decently attired in pristine drawers. Or need a quick shave, shampoo and set, halfway up Ben More Assynt.

'Gosh, thanks, Mum!' I say, admiring the sweater which is half a size too small. 'Just what I wanted.'

'I knew you needed a new jumper, son, and you will look lovely in bright yellow.'

'You really shouldn't have bothered, Mother-in-law. Yes, I know, socks are so useful . . . After-shave and talc, Blair! How very thoughtful . . . and that's super, Lewis-Ann, a sewing-kit for my fishing-bag. Now I can darn my socks when the fish are not rising.'

'Bruce!' The warning voice of reasonable wife.

We have three trees at Christmas: one outside, one in the lounge and one on the upstairs landing. They are put up on the Saturday, a week before Mr Claus arrives, complete with lights and tinsel – and they fall down the following Sunday morning. Because I am not very good at that sort of thing. Or the cats play with them, or the dogs knock them over.

The outside tree causes most problems, due to high winds. Up here in the far North, what the British Broadcasting Corporation describe as a gale, we refer to as a gentle breeze. From October until April we stuff our pockets with hundreds of stones, to weight us down. Otherwise, it's a quick whisk over the sea to Norway. Every Christmas, I find myself stumbling around on precarious step-ladders, fighting with the recalcitrant spruce – generally in the middle of either a blizzard or rainstorm. This provides endless amusement for the neighbours and I have become accustomed to their withering shafts of supposed humour.

'Great idea, Bruce, to have a horizontal Christmas tree. Clever, but I don't think it will catch on.'

My intention is to try and create a festive ambience. When aged parents arrive, having made the gruesome nightmare train journey from the south, I like to ensure that their first impression encourages them in the belief that their journey has been worth while.

Unless you have made the train journey from Inverness to Wick, you will find it hard to appreciate the significance of this statement. It can take up to five hours to travel the hundred miles involved – sometimes in an unheated carriage, with no restaurant, and often crowded with tired and emotional companions. Ann was once befriended by a pale-faced traveller, very much the worse for wear, who insisted on pouring out his woes into her unprotected ear. As the train pulled into Georgemas Station, where I was to meet her, he placed a hand on her arm and told Ann, confidentially:

'You know,' he said, 'you're a nice woman. Just like one of my f. . . . .g prison visitors.' He had been released earlier that morning from Inverness jail.

Miles Kington's smash-hit television programme *Great Railway Journeys of the World* was incomplete: Inverness to Wick should definitely have been included. I collect my Christmas visitors, stunned from the station, and drive them home to Ruther, where I hope that the tree will brighten their ailing spirits.

154

The outside tree causes most problems, due to high winds

'Oh, look, Bruce,' Mother will announce, 'what a lovely tree. Why is it lying on its side?'

All I really need to do is to design some sort of bracket/clamp, attached to the garden wall to make the thing secure, or perhaps sink a shaft in the ground, to hold the trunk in position, and every January, I pore over drawings and plans, promising myself that I will be better organised the following year. Come December, I am up at our local quarry, ordering yet another four-ton load of gravel chips, which I duly build into a pyramid round the barrel that contains the tree. Then the guy-ropes appear. But it never works, and to keep the tree upright over the festive period requires constant vigilance and constant, back-breaking shovelling.

Ann never complains. It is in her best interests not to encourage me to devise an alternative. The mountain of gravel chips left over each year have to be put somewhere, and her garden benefits. Come February, it's: 'Another barrow-load over here, Bruce, please. Perhaps one more? Then you can start on the drive and paths. Your back's not playing up is it? Good, then what about helping me re-cover the back yard as well?'

At times the wind blows so hard that it is impossible to stand upright. My son Blair once told me of a Christmas party he had when he lived in Balavanich on Benbecula in the Outer Hebrides

– or as he calls them, 'The Utter He Brides'. The local army padre was a guest, a man of slender physical stature although mighty of mind. When Blair showed him out, the wind was so strong that the poor man was simply blown away. Blair hustled after him and grabbed his legs. Together, they crawled on hands and knees to the padre's house and Blair saw him safely indoors.

'Staggering about legless, Blair. Are you sure that it was Christmas, and not New Year's night?' I asked unkindly.

Christmas tree lights are also difficult. No matter how carefully last year's bulbs are stowed away, twelve months later they never work. I spend much of the festive season crashing about in the dark, fighting unbalanced spruce and wayward electrical systems, cursing loudly. The only consolation is that this provides an excellent opportunity for surreptitiously inspecting the goodies piled below the branches – which I do every year, as long as no one is looking. I prod and poke, fingers crossed, which is difficult, but to no avail. My neatly wrapped parcels are invariably haberdashery-soft, or exude the unmistakable smell of astringent, undrinkable fluid.

Over the years we have had the usual crop of Christmas 'accidents', such as the time when Blair and Lewis-Ann beat us to it and had all their presents opened before we staggered from bed on Christmas morning. It took ages trying to match up who had sent what with the scattered mound of labels and goodies. But we have been lucky with our children, particularly Blair and Lewis-Ann, who both firmly believed in the existence of Father Christmas for years. Even when they were approaching double figures, I suspect that they still thought of Father Christmas as a real person. In fact, there are times when I think that Blair still does.

Charlie certainly does, but unfortunately he also knows for certain that it is Ann and me. Now a student at Glasgow School of Art, he telephones home regularly for moral and other kinds of support:

'Bit short this month, Dad.'

'What do you think I am!' I explode into the phone, 'Father Christmas?'

'Yes,' comes the clipped reply.

But my fondest Christmas memory of Charles happened when he was four years old. We had tucked him up in bed after dinner on Christmas Eve and then settled in front of the fire to watch television. An hour later, Charles wandered in, stark naked and

'Anyone heard any jingling yet?'

damp. He eyed us nonchalantly and inquired in a very grown-up voice: 'Any one heard any jingling yet?'

When I was a child we opened our Christmas presents at exactly one second past midnight on Christmas Eve. It seemed the natural thing to do, and, in retrospect, I suppose our long-suffering parents thought that it was the only way to get any peace and quiet out of three eternally squabbling boys. Ann is made of sterner stuff. It's hands off until at least after Christmas lunch. The children don't mind; after all, they have their well-packed stockings. Me? I have to maintain a semblance of sobriety and complacency for hours before being able to see what fate has brought. She calls it 'character forming'. I call it unfair.

On Christmas day, after lunch, we troop through to the tree and Jean hands round the presents:

'Here you are, Daddy, this one is for you.' A bag of biro pens, marked 'Happy Christmas, Dabby' from Charles. The family will have them away quicker than snow off a winter's dyke. 'And this.' Typing paper from Lewis-Ann. I see them all carefully noting where I stack it. 'And this is from your

157

mother-in-law.' Another pair of pyjamas. A shirt from Father, a long-handled shoe-horn from Blair, and, yes, knickers from Mother.

Thus it has gone on year after year. Come March and the beginning of the fishing season, I survey with dismay the previous year's ravages to my fly-box. I carefully finger my cracked fishing-line; wonder if the amateurish patch that took two hours to apply to my starboard wader will hold. In my heart of hearts I know that it will not. A cursory, confirmatory glance at last month's bank statement and the pile of unpaid Christmas/New year bills plunges me into even deeper despair. I envisage myself spending the season angling on one leg, fishing with a single, featherless hook attached to prehistoric nylon, tied on a rapidly disintegrating line.

My piscatorial friends do not seem to have the same problem. I try to be pleased for them, rather than simply envious, but, at the start of every season, I have to put up with streams of hurtful reminders of my impoverished angling state.

'Hello there, John, grand day. Look, there are fish rising. Let's get afloat. No point in wasting good fishing time,' I announce brightly, as I struggle into my still sopping left boot.

'Wait a moment, Bruce. Have you seen my new line? Look, isn't it a beauty. Double tapered and all. Cost a fortune. Got it for Christmas from dear old Mother-in-law.'

'Lucky you,' I manage to reply, surreptitiously tugging up my outsize, cardboard-stiff, thermal underpants.

Or, 'My goodness, Bruce, you should see the number of flies I got for Christmas. Dozens. Can't get them all into my boxes.' I note the use of the term 'boxes', indicating the possession of more than one. My single fly-box is so rusted and old that it has to be held together by elastic bands. 'Got them from my cousin. He is a real expert. Wonderful fly-tier. All I do is supply the materials. He does the rest and Bob's your uncle!'

'I thought you said that he was your cousin?'

'Stop being daft, you know what I mean.'

I do, and one thing is certain: I don't have an Uncle Robert.

Worse, though, is the 'new rod recipient'. My trout-rod is an old friend. Very old. Made for me twenty years ago by Mr Stott, who lived and worked in a small cottage astride the Roman wall in Northumberland. I am deeply attached to the rod, in spite of the fact that the top section is now badly warped. To avoid embarrassment, I twist the top round, slightly out of line with the other two sections; by so doing, the warp is less obvious.

Once out of sight of prying eyes, I realign the thing and get on with the job in hand. Nevertheless, when I see one of my friends proudly lashing away with a light-weight carbon-fibre wand, I have to admit to occasional pangs of envy.

'Got it from Santa Claus, it's terrific. Light as a feather. Look at the anodised reel fittings and Seymo rings.' Splash, lash, crash. 'Want to have a go?'

Adopting the superior air of one who has seen it all before, I reply grandly: 'No thanks, can't really use these new-fangled things. I prefer to stick to my cane-rod. Like a bit of weight behind the line. These modern jobs are not for me. Not really proper fishing-rods, more like high-tech toys,' I lie through gritted teeth.

Consequently, new developments in angling technology pass me by, and when talk turns to the relative merits of disc-drag for extra control, triangle taper-lines or fully-enclosed, hard, stainless-steel, sealed ball-races, my mind goes blank. What I never know, I will never worry about. But it does land me in embarrassing situations. Such as the time when, being gallant, I put up a rod for a visiting lady angler, Jo Kirk, from New Zealand. I had threaded the line through the rings of the rod and noticed that there was still nylon attached. Smugly observing that the previous outing's cast should always be discarded, I bit through the offending material close to the line, and tucked the nylon, complete with the little clear plastic object on the end, into my pocket.

'What have you done!' she exclaimed crossly.

'I'm going to make you up a cast,' I explained.

'You have just bitten off my butt-end and cast-connector. It took me ages to set that up.'

'What is a butt-end?' I inquired, sheepishly.

And one time I was in the carpark of the Scourie Hotel, in Sutherland, in 1983, when a guest invited me to try out his new cane rod. I reeled off some line, false casting furiously, thinking that the rod was nothing special and that my old stick was every bit as good.

'How much would a rod like this cost?' I asked.

'About £800. It is an American Thomas & Thomas.' I dropped the rod like a hot cake. It was his newly acquired pride and joy.

'Who are Thomas & Thomas?'

'The USA equivalent of Hardys. American Presidents give them as special gifts to important visitors who fish.' How was I to know that?

Over the years I have, from time to time, owned various items of superb tackle – Hardy reels, deluxe lines, New Zealand cedarwood fly-boxes, various, wand-like rods – but fitting out a family of four fishers takes its toll. Mostly on my prized possessions. They simply disappear.

When Blair, our eldest son, got married and moved to his first job in the Outer Hebrides, I was pleased for him; but after his departure, the pile of tackle in the rod-room looked as though it had been hit by a bolt of lightning.

Number two son, Charles, doesn't so much remove things, as break them.

'Sorry, Dad, but it was an accident. How was I to know your rod was lying there? You really should be more careful.' The fact that the rod was placed upright against the side of the boathouse makes no difference when Charlie's about. Landing-nets disintegrate the moment he touches them; reels fall apart; spools of nylon leap from his hands, straight into the loch, all by themselves.

Lewis-Ann, our oldest daughter, just grabs whatever is to hand and marches off, regardless of who the rightful owner is. New flies I have purchased and carefully hidden in the poacher's pocket of my jacket invariably go with her, never to return. And she invariably catches fish.

Jean, the youngest, is the great 'borrower' of the family. Anything that is not actually nailed down tends to disappear. Standing on some lonely hillside, shrouded in mist, I reach into my fishing-bag, groping for my compass in its accustomed place. No compass. Then I remember Jean's fit of geography:

'You get a map and I'll set it for you. It's quite easy, Dad, and I will show you how to do it. Now pay attention.' I should have, and should also have remembered to remind her to replace the compass she had borrowed. 'How was I to know that you would be going fishing on Saturday?' she will complain, hurt. 'It's not my fault that you got lost. You only have yourself to blame. You should have checked that you had it before setting out. That's what you tell me to do.'

As my career as a writer progressed, kind editors, knowing of my plight, have been most supportive, frequently sending me wonderful fishing books to review, but the moment the children arrive home, they descend upon them like locusts at a feast:

'That looks interesting, Father,' Blair will announce happily, 'do you mind if I borrow it?'

'Oh, Daddy, I have been meaning to buy that book for ages!' Lewis-Ann exclaims. I know that I will never see it again.

I suppose that it is but a small price to pay. Better by far that they should discover the joys and pleasures of the gentler art than that I should be well dressed, well equipped, well read, and safe in the hills; and I suppose the exercise did me good. I should be grateful to Jean for giving me an exciting, three-hour compassless hike in the mist; grateful to Blair and Lewis-Ann for clearing so much space on the bookshelves.

When we lived in County Durham, visits from angling friends and relatives were few and far between. Durham was not noted then as a centre of fishing excellence, Derwent Reservoir being the only really good still-water fishery. The Rivers Tees and Wear, other than in the upper reaches, were little other than open sewers. I know, because I used to be a member of the Tees Amateur Rowing Club, and anyone unfortunate enough to fall in had to be rushed to Middlesbrough General Hospital for an appointment with a stomach pump at lightning speed. On warm days, the smell from the river was disgustingly overpowering and some of the items that used to float by as we sculled the muddy waters had to be seen to be believed.

Today, happily, angling is much improved along the banks of the Tees and Wear, and Cow Green Reservoir, although flooding a once lovely valley, also provides reasonable sport for fishermen, without the danger of instant hospitalisation as a reward for falling in.

Now that we live in Caithness, surrounded by some of the finest game fishing in Scotland, they *all* come to stay, in droves, and I have to take them fishing. They know that I won't mind because I don't work. I am a writer. I have all the time in the world.

This is something I have learned to live with, but I often despair of ever achieving even a modicum of credibility as a worker. After ten years, people still stop my wife on the street in Wick and inquire solicitously:

'Mrs Sandison, has your man got a job yet, or is he still writing?'

Recently, I was sitting one morning at my word processor, weary and ill at ease, struggling hard to try and finish an article that should have been delivered the previous week, my mind a complete blank, when I heard the back door open and footsteps approaching. This is very much the country way, knock and

161

enter, and after a moment, one of my friends, a local builder, appeared at the door of my office.

'Good grief, Bruce!' he exclaimed. 'You certainly lead a life of luxury. Having another nice relaxing morning, are you?'

Billy was an urgent, large man, much given to clambering around on roofs, banging things, and he had arrived to give me an estimate for storm damage.

'I'm working, damn it! What do you mean, "relaxing"? Just because I'm not constantly bashing nails in or playing with building-blocks doesn't mean to say that I don't work.'

He ignored me completely: 'Must be a marvellous life. If you are not out fishing, then you just sit here tapping away at the keys.'

'Working!' I yelled, exasperated.

'Well if that's work, I wouldn't mind a few weeks of it. Any jobs going then, have you?'

Therefore, because I don't *work*, when guests arrive I have to abandon the purple prose and gillie. It is not so bad if they have never fished before. For them, I drag out my oldest reel, tie on a couple of nondescript flies and offer a lot of sage advice:

'Full of fish this loch. Any moment now. Keep casting. No, hold on, I will unfankle it.'

It is the so-called experienced anglers that present the major problems, the ones who claim to have: 'Done a bit now and then, but never seem to find enough time. Not like lucky old you, Bruce. Out fishing every day!' I grin weakly, thinking of the unfinished manuscript waiting in the office, the exasperated publisher roaring down the telephone.

Ann is up at crack of dawn, constructing the packed lunches. 'Let's get off really early. Mustn't waste a moment.'

I sort out the tackle and load the car. At the lochside, whilst they bumble around with boots and laces, I bail the boat, fit up the outboard motor, fill the fuel tank and secure the oars.

'What flies do you recommend, Bruce?' Which is another way of intimating that I should put up the rods and tie the casts. They then leap aboard and expect me too heave them afloat.

'Sure you can manage? Not too shallow is it? Wait a moment and I will give a shove with an oar. Oh, sorry, didn't see you there. Are you all right?'

Once afloat, I sit in the middle of the boat in a positive agony of despair, watching my precious trout-rods being used like horsewhips and tying on an endless succession of flies from the rapidly diminishing supply in my box in between pouring large drams down seemingly unquenchably thirsty throats. They are incapable of rowing. Boat management or holding a reasonable drift is beyond them. They offer, but, after half a minute, it is obvious that if there is to be even the remotest chance of sport, I will have to mind the oars.

'Jolly decent, Bruce. Sure you don't want a cast? Suppose with all the fishing you get, it's a nice change doing nothing.' I struggle in a force-eight gale.

By close of play, my guests are merry and bright and the fish sulking safely at the bottom of the loch. I am in a state of fishless, terminal decline: fly-boxes stripped bare; scarred and bleeding from half a dozen hook marks; the drouge somewhere at the bottom of the loch, having been chucked out before being tied on, 'Sorry about that, Bruce, was only trying to be helpful.' I wearily haul the boat ashore, taking off the outboard, stow the oars, collect rods and landing-net, the empty picnic basket and empty bottles, and carry everything up to the car – whilst they exchange pleasantries and admire the view.

'Super day, Bruce, thanks. Pity about the rod, but never mind. Just get it put together again and send me the bill. Lucky you had a spare one or it would have quite spoilt the day. What about another crack at them tomorrow? It is super being on holiday. I feel a new man already!'

Nephews and nieces are even nicer. We always have at least one day out, to a remote hill loch where little ones will be assured of catching fish whilst adults relax by the lochside, contemplating nature and a nicely chilled bottle of white wine.

Apart, that is, from me. I'm on duty from the moment of arrival at the water's edge until the last blink of evening.

'Uncle Bruce, I'm fankled!'

'Bruce, help! My flies are caught on the bottom!'

'Vicki is fishing in my place. Tell her to go away!'

'My fish is bigger than your fish, Becca.'

'No it's not, Jean. Mine is bigger than yours.'

'Can we go out in the boat, please?'

'It is awfully windy, Jean.'

'But it's too shallow here. We want to catch fish, don't we girls!'

'Yes, yes. Come on, Uncle Bruce, be a sport.'

Two hours hard labour. The day generally progresses through about five miles of nylon, four dozen flies and various minor and major accidents to both equipment and person. I never return dry. Invariably I have to carry them to the boat, or I wade out too far in order to retrieve irretrievably snagged casts.

Meanwhile, relaxing in the heather, brother Fergus, sister-in-law Liz and Ann look on benignly.

'Amazing patience, hasn't he?' I hear Fergus murmur. 'Never used to be like that with me when I was that age.'

Having finished the wine, they wait until I am in the midst of some catastrophe, such as wading out to catch a lost oar, and then announce brightly:

'I wouldn't mind a few casts. Could you sort out a rod for me, Bruce, please?'

Other urban, so-called friends, also add to my joy by sending their offspring north for a few days fishing.

'Are you sure Bruce won't mind, Ann?' they inquire solicitously. 'It's just that Phillip always reads his articles and would love to fish some of the lochs that Bruce writes about. Oh, and by the way, can he bring his fishing friend, David Smart. He's very keen.' Consequently, I have the pleasure of spending a great deal of my valuable time rowing young boys about distant lochs, acting as gillie and mentor; landing their fish, encouraging their efforts and tying up endless casts.

To be truthful, I wouldn't agree to do so unless I enjoyed it; and I do, very much indeed. In fact, during the past few years, the pleasure of playing host to these young angling guests has been a wonderful privilege. Particularly since they are all now old enough to take good care of me!

David Smart, now a medical student, recently asked me to find him a summer job as a gillie, and Paul Panchaud at the excellent Altnaharra Hotel in north-west Sutherland kindly agreed to employ him from May until the end of September. When I arrived during the second week of September for an annual holiday with a group of friends, David gillied for me on Loch Hope. Expertly. It was a super day out and, for me, a wonderful change to have someone else lugging the outboard and organising the drifts. This year, another young fishing friend, Jonathan Paterson from Berwick-upon-Tweed, now grown up and a student, will have the privilege of being my gillie at Altnaharra; and I am very much looking forward to the experience, having already warned him that I expect at least one sea-trout of over 6lbs. Or else.

A couple of years ago, during one of our family outings, I had a single moment of extreme, unadulterated, malignant pleasure. The previous Christmas, along with my usual load of

The boat was screaming across the loch

goodies, some kind soul sent me an umbrella. Just the very thing I wanted. Nobody uses brollies in Caithness. At least, given our furious winds, not for long. I still cringe with shame at the thought of one appalling umbrella incident which happened in 1988. Acquaintances were visiting us on a wet, windy September night, and had parked their car at the side of the house, entering by the front door, which we rarely use. The lady was beautifully dressed in an obviously expensive tan skirt and matching jacket. Her hair was pristine and she wore neat, high-heeled crocodile-skin shoes. Her husband was just as well turned out and their appearance was more in keeping with the Mayfair than with the wilds of Caithness. Their son, a tall, languid lad of about fourteen, uneasily matched his parents' sartorial elegance.

After coffee and talking about our northern lochs and suggesting various fishing venues, they got up to leave and, in a fit of polite concern, I ushered them to the front door, handing the lady an umbrella to protect her hair-do from the downpour.

As she stepped from the shelter of the front porch, the wind caught the brolly, and our visitor, clutching it firmly, went off down the slippery path like a rocket, shrieking. Within seconds she had tumbled over backwards ending up lying in an unseemly heap on the wet, moss-edged garden path.

Her husband shouted: 'Don't worry, dear, I'm coming,' and rushed to her aid. His foot slipped and he too fell, on top of his wife. Both of our dogs, concerned, hurried to their aid, licking wildly.

They struggled in the wind and rain, trying to regain both

balance and composure, whilst Ann and I stood absolutely horrified at their plight. I turned to see what their son was up to: the
young man was doubled up in laughter, holding on to the garden
wall, tears of mirth rolling down his face, unsuccessfully
attempting to conceal his delight.

Which is why when that brolly arrived for Christmas, I turfed
it into the back of the garage. But for some strange reason, prior
to setting off that day, one of my brother Fergus's daughters
decided that it should be carted along.

'What will we do if it rains, Uncle Bruce?' asked Becca. 'We
have to take it. I won't go otherwise.' In situations like these, I
have discovered that reason, logic and general bad temper never
work. I carried the umbrella.

This particular brolly was as bright as Joseph's multi-coloured
dream-coat. The last thing I wanted to be seen with on a Scottish
hill loch. Fortunately, it did not rain, so I was spared that
embarrassment. However, towards the end of the day, the wind
got up and we decided to head for home. Charles, who is enormously strong and absolutely fearless, courageously agreed to
ferry the ladies across the loch whilst Fergus and I tramped
wearily round the south shore. As much gear as possible was
loaded onboard, including the umbrella. Fergus and I, like
Tibetan sherpas, lugged the rest through the heather.

Halfway there, we stopped for a rest, slumping to the ground,
sweating profusely.

'Good grief, Bruce, why didn't you bring the kitchen sink as
well?' complained my panting brother.

'Don't blame me,' I snapped crossly. 'It was your daughters
who insisted on bringing the tape recorder.'

Through wet eyes, we looked up the loch to see how Captain
Bligh was faring with the girls. It was an amazing sight. Quite
unique. Ann sat in the stern, with two young ladies, sister-in-
law and Jean perched in the bow, and Charles bulked in the
middle, heaving mightily on the oars. Ann had put up the
umbrella, using it as a sail. The boat was screaming across the
loch at a vast rate of knots, children yelling with delight, like
some circus act, a blaze of colour, water cascading from the
bow, with barely two inches free board. Mr Plimsoll would be
revolving in his grave.

'Quick, Fergus,' I called, leaping to my feet and sprinting
off. 'There is no way they will be able to stop in time and that
shore is very rocky.'

Fergie grunted and lumbered after me. We need not have

worried. Ten yards from the mooring-bay, the umbrella blew inside-out, tearing the fabric to ribbons in the process, and the boat lurched to a wallow amongst the shallows. I waded out to help.

'It wasn't my fault, Dad, honestly,' complained Charles. 'It just seemed like a good idea at the time. You know, an accident?'

I smiled benignly, fingering the shattered brolly.

'That's all right, son, don't give it a moment's thought. Accidents do happen.' Exit at least one unwanted Christmas gift.

A few years ago I engineered a master stroke, which I thought would absolutely guarantee that all my Yuletide presents would be angling orientated: I persuaded them to move Christmas lunch from 25 December to 22 June, Ann's birthday, and the height of the fishing season. Surely, I reasoned, they must get the message.

I was aided and abetted in this by friends, John and Jill Henderson from Scrabster, who were blessed with a similarly warped sense of humour as Ann and me. We played bridge together regularly, for a pound a hundred points, with all the money either won or lost being deposited in a local building society as a holiday fund. As soon as enough was in the kitty, we would escape for a few days' hill-walking or general relaxation – or, if we had been particularly adventurous in our bidding, two weeks on a Greek island. It was after returning from one such jaunt that I had presented them with my master-plan.

What was the point, I suggested, of sitting indoors, huddled around a meagre fire, singing Christmas carols, when the whole thing could be done with much greater comfort and pleasure on Midsummer Night by the shores of some romantic loch.

'You wouldn't just happen to have a particular loch in mind, would you?' John asked me suspiciously.

'Toftingal,' I replied instantly, taking the plunge. At that time, Ann and I had the rental of the loch, which was only about ten minutes drive from home, the ideal place for a June Christmas lunch: a mile and a half from the main road and prying eyes; boathouse by the water's edge; table and chairs; an idyllic setting surrounded by wild moorlands; and, in June, loud with the sound of rising trout.

After a brief argument, we agreed, as an experiment, to have Christmas lunch there, provided that on the following Christmas, we should have a Midsummer Night supper, indoors. It was a small price to pay, and I readily complied with the plan.

We decorated the boathouse with paper-chains and bunting, and the Hendersons brought along a Christmas tree. A barrel-barbecue provided heat and kept the midges at bay whilst suitable music was provided from a tape recorder. The ladies produced a traditional Christmas lunch, complete with turkey and all the trimmings, Christmas pudding and mince pies, served up piping hot, and there were crackers, the inevitable bad jokes, streamers and paper hats. John and I organised the drinks.

In between courses, I excused myself and, taking my rod from the rack, had a few casts, even managing to hook and land a couple of nice trout, which, being *Christmas*, I released to fight another day.

During dinner, I cast anxious glances at the tree, and at the appropriate time, breath baited and with trembling fingers, I opened my parcels: films for my camera, the latest Dick Francis, a cigar, and yes, yet again, socks. It started to rain.

In spite of everything, I doubt if I would alter it, even if I could. Nevertheless, as yet another Christmas draws ever closer, it would be nice to think that, for a change, nearest and dearest were busily planning what item of fishing-tackle they were going to put under the tree for BMS. Anything will do: flies, nylon, waders, fishing-bag, another drogue, new line. Perhaps if they got their acts together and pooled their resources, who knows, even a new rod? But beggars can't be choosers. I will be grateful for whatever they come up with – as long as it is fishing orientated.

It shouldn't be too difficult for them. Lord knows, I leave enough glossy literature around to sink the *Queen Mary*. I suppose the answer lies in my own hands. I simply have to announce, in the nicest possible way, that all presents must be fishing-tackle; otherwise the money should be donated to a fund for distressed sock owners. Trouble is, it might seem ungrateful. Which I never am. In spite of what people say. If all else fails, I suppose I could simply apply direct:

'Dear Father Christmas . . .' Worth a try?'

Sandison on Resolution

CAPRICORN
22 DECEMBER TO 20 JANUARY

New Year is a time when steady progress can be made in spite of the fact that there may be some anxious moments. People you thought you could rely upon become difficult to contact, and you may discover that your so-called friend and fishing partner has topped your bid for that spring rod on the Dee, that you told him about in confidence.

169

The accent falls on leisure and, if you like to entertain your fishing friends, they will be impressed when you casually mention that you have taken the let of the River Laxford and Stack Lodge. Arrange to pay for it by inviting them to join you, plus fifteen per cent for your trouble in organising the week and to cover your personal costs.

Perhaps there is a neighbour, colleague or friend whom you would like to get to know better, such as the owner of that Lower Tweed beat who nodded to you from the other side of the river last autumn; invite him to the Laxford. Extend a friendly hand and broaden your circle – as long as your circle can offer you good fishing opportunities in return.

From January onwards, however, your affairs are likely to be complicated. This might be attributable to your own behaviour, which seems to be undergoing a drastic change as you frenetically devise means of spending more time fishing; in certain circumstances you need to be quick to recognise approaching danger before any real harm is done to your angling activities.

It will certainly be to your advantage to remain completely independent, otherwise your fishing could suffer. For instance, opportunities to climb the ladder of success and long-anticipated promotion are in the offing. Do not be tempted. The additional responsibility will only further interfere with the already limited time you have to go fishing.

Home life will be peaceful so take advantage of this by organising a family holiday that avoids being roasted alive on some crowded strand surrounded by regiments of barking Germans, miles from the nearest trout stream. This is the year when everyone will quietly agree to all you suggest and you should not waste a minute of it being boiled on a foreign beach.

It is essential that you organise your activities along sensible lines: book the South Uist fishing holiday now; plan a trip to the Shetland Isles; persuade the family to join you in north-west Sutherland. You will be surprised by how readily they agree to your every wish.

Invest in your future fishing comfort by making this the year when you teach every member of your family to fish. Eventually, they will thank you for it, and if they don't, you can always resell their rods and tackle; at least it should give you a few more trouble-free years and provide additional fishing opportunities.

Also find the time to visit ailing relatives, particularly those who own good fishing, or at least have regular access to it. Your schedules must be flexible, since angling invitations will keep you fishing all the best waters almost continuously. Tight Lines in all your efforts!

'**D**AD HOW do you start a revolution?' My small son stood before me, glasses awry, knees grazed from his latest scrap, smiling widely, shirt-tail hanging out, face creased in anticipation. Over the years, through bitter experience, I have learned to be wary of Charles, particularly when he approaches smiling, seeking advice or assistance. The most recent occasion cost me a pair of binoculars: 'I want to look at a strange bird down by the harbour, Dad,' he had muttered ingratiatingly, knowing my love of ornithology. The truth of the matter was entirely different and involved Charles and the rest of his gang in a James Bond-like adventure which ended in a flood of complaints from far and wide and my binoculars being returned in several mangled bits.

Charles has always been intimidating. Even before he could find proper words to express himself, he devised a means of putting people in their place. Glasses steaming in exasperation, he would raise his hands above his head, screwing his face into a hideous grin, and then point both index fingers in the direction of the object of his displeasure.

I used to show him conjuring tricks, complete with black-and-white magic wand, making various objects miraculously disappear. He waited until I was out of sight and then tried it on the nearest cat. Red with rage, he stamped through to the kitchen, clutching the wand:

'This bloody thing doesn't work!' he yelled. More worrying, however, was when I overheard him ask his mother, innocently:

'If I hit Dad with the magic wand, would he spin round and round three times and disappear?' Made me wonder.

As Charles grew older and began to 'build' things – gang-huts, sledges, carts and trailers – my suspicions were confirmed. Ann found him one day, deep in thought, scribbling furiously: 'How do you make a mantrap, Mummy?' he inquired nonchalantly.

Even his mother was not safe from his inquisitive mind. He once asked Ann if paint could act as a conductor for electricity. Ann was busy at the time, tidying his room – a major exercise, usually involving a barrow and bucket and spade. 'I suppose so, Charles,' she answered. The next time Ann pulled open one of

171

his clothes drawers, the moment she touched the handles she leapt back in alarm, having received a mild electric shock from yet another of Charles's devilish contraptions.

I put down my book and asked, suspiciously, 'Why, Charles?'

'Well, you see, Peter, Andrew and Duncan think that we should have one.'

I tried to keep calm. The gang had just concluded an important meeting in the garage. Hence the disappearance of half my scrap-paper, all my pencils, the card-table, two bottles of lemonade and a full packet of chocolate biscuits. The gang's parents suffered in turn. Peter's father provided the lighting at amateur theatrical productions, Andrew's dad was the local photographer, and Duncan's father, the minister of Wick Old Parish Church. The possibilities for 'borrowing' an astonishing variety of useful items for their various schemes was unending.

'Charlie,' I explained, as simply as I could, 'a revolution is when people get very angry with their government and rise up and overthrow it, by force of arms if necessary.' The eyes sparkled more brightly. I had his undivided attention.

'How?' asked Charles. I sensed myself getting into deeper, more dangerous uncharted waters and struggled to find safe words.

'Well, they try reason at first, of course, talking, you know, then . . .' Blair, our eldest, appeared on the scene at that moment and announced brightly:

'They collect an army together, get guns and sticks and stones, and rockets and tanks, then rampage through the streets building barricades.'

I exploded! 'What on earth do you think you are doing, Blair? Trying to start World War III?' But it was too late. By this time, Charles was completely engrossed. 'Now wait a moment, Charles, keep calm. Before you start burning down the High School or building barricades, why do you want to have a revolution? Has anyone been upsetting you?'

Charles pondered this for a moment and then, grudgingly admitted: 'No, it's just that everyone says that you should always have a revolution at New Year.'

Light dawned. 'It's not a *revolution* you want, Charles, it's a *resolution*: a New Year's Resolution.' I exclaimed, relieved.

'All right then, what is a New Year's Revolution?'

'Resolution, Charles, not revolution. Forget about revolutions. Do you understand?' In order to avoid a major civic disaster, it was important that Charles should understand that

172

revolution was a serious, dangerous business. The trouble was, I could see that he was by now only half-paying attention. His mind was clearly on other things – such as guns, sticks, stones, rockets and tanks.

'I think so, but, well, then, what's a *reso*lution?'

I counted up to ten, twice, but at that moment, our teenage daughter, Lewis-Ann, burst on the scene and grabbed Charles by the ear.

'I'll tell you,' she screamed. 'It means promising to keep out of my room, keeping your grubby hands off my records and to stop pinching my paper and pencils.' I managed to restrain myself from reminding Lewis-Ann that the paper and pencils in question were mine. She was not in the mood for reason. 'And whilst we are on the subject of resolutions, it also means not taking lemonade and chocolate biscuits without asking.' Obviously, Lewis-Ann had been entertaining her gang in her bedroom, without the aid of either music or refreshments. Lewis-Ann was at that stage of her life where her idea of a good afternoon was playing records at full blast whilst she and her chums took turn-about doing each other's hair and make-up; at the end of which they descended upon the town, mincing around looking like the 'Brides of Dracula'.

Charlie backed towards the door, his hand reaching behind him for the handle, ready to make a quick escape.

'Oh, if that is all resolutions are, then I don't think I'll bother.'

His face clearly showed his disappointment. Obviously, at the very least he had been anticipating organising a near riot. I could almost hear his mind working, planning what he would say to the gang about falsely raising his hopes. The memory of the last time this had happened was still fresh in my mind. There had been an enormous row which had taken the concerted efforts of all the gang's parents to sort out; and it had all been caused by a seemingly simple, inoffensive remark. Apparently, Duncan had suggested that they go to the church jumble sale his father had organised, except that Charles had misheard Duncan and thought that he was being invited to a *jungle* sale. Delighted at the prospect of an afternoon's fun with tigers, lions and elephants, at least, Charles had accepted with alacrity. Upon discovering the real nature of the event, murder had almost been committed and I was determined not to be party to a similar disaster.

'Just a moment, Charles,' I said, 'come and sit down. You really should try to make a New Year's Resolution. They are very good things and Peter, Andrew and Duncan are quite right, everyone should have them.'

Charles was not convinced, but realising Father was about to launch into a monologue, decided that he had better suffer in silence. At least for the time being.

Blair and Lewis-Ann hovered, ominously, mentally calculating how long Charles would put up with my ramblings. At various times, they had also suffered in silence as Father delivered himself of a homily – and then gone on and done exactly the opposite of what I suggested.

'What about you starting by resolving to buy me a salmon-rod for Christmas?' asked Blair, unkindly.

Given the anxious state of my bank balance, purchasing a salmon-fly, let alone a salmon-rod, was out of the question, as I had already explained to Blair on several occasions. I tried heavy handed humour:

'That wouldn't be a New Year's Resolution, it would be an *Old* Year's Resolution. Anyway, of what possible use would a salmon-rod be to you? You can hardly cast with a trout-rod.'

'I would have a much better chance of learning, though, if I had a salmon-rod, now wouldn't I?' Blair is always devastatingly logical.

Sensing that things were about to get out of hand, Ann appeared and announced brightly: 'Now then, what about a nice cup of tea, everyone?'

We trooped through to the kitchen and Lewis-Ann grudgingly put the kettle on the stove. Charles stared moodily at the empty lemonade bottle. Our youngest, three-year-old Jean, hovered expectantly. She instinctively knew something was up and was determined to get in on the act.

Refusing to be diverted from my purpose, I launched a second assault:

'All right then,' I demanded, 'who will begin? What about some meaningful resolutioning?' I crossed my fingers behind my back.

'What's "meaningful"?' asked Charlie.

'Be quiet, Charles.' I crossed the fingers of my other hand.

'I think Dad should resolve to stop boasting about all the fish he catches. I get sick of it,' said Lewis-Ann.

'Can I catch some fish, please?' asked Jean.

'That's only because you never catch any yourself,' commented Blair through a mouthful of biscuit.

'That's not true! I catch far more than you do.'

174

'Yes, with a worm, I bet,' quipped Blair.

'All right, all right. There is no need for bickering. I resolve to stop boasting about all the fish I catch – even though it's true,' I said. 'But,' I continued, 'I think that Blair should resolve to tie more flies. The idea of buying that kit last year was to save money. All the benefit we have had so far has been bent hooks scattered round the floor. My feet are permanently punctured.' Last Christmas, we had bought Blair a fly-tying outfit, in the fond hope that he would supply the family's needs during the coming season. To date, all that he had produced were a selection of Black Pennels, Ke-He and Butchers, all of which he used himself.

'I should have thought that a spade and bait-tin would be more in your line,' retorted Blair.

'That's not funny, Blair, and in any case, if anyone needs a bait-tin around here, it most certainly is not me.' Ann rose to the 'bait'. Ann is the 'complete angler' of the family, always ready to adapt her tactics to prevailing conditions. If a river is in spate, as soon as my back is turned she can be found, mole-like, searching for worms. I blame her father, a Yorkshireman, who believed that the only point in going fishing was to catch fish. When Charles Rhodes had returned from the army after World War II, he made himself a trout-rod out of an old tank aerial. This had been Ann's introduction to the gentle art, with a worm. A small stream ran behind their holiday cottage at Fala Dam, south from Edinburgh, and Ann and her father had great sport when water levels were right. 'Just because you lot are incapable of mastering the art of clear-water, upstream worming, there is no need to be so scathing. If you could see yourselves at times! It is ridiculous, fishing a boiled-tea spate with a size 16 Greenwell's Glory. I ask you!'

'There is never any need to resort to worming, Ann, and you know it,' I announced pompously. 'And I can assure you that a size 16 Greenwell's Glory can be most effective, even in spate conditions. It just depends upon how it is used.'

'Don't start on again about you and your Greenwell's Glory,' warned Ann. 'We have all heard that pack of lies at least a hundred times, and I still don't believe you.'

'I think that Blair should resolve to carry the outboard motor more often. Dad always has to do it.' I wondered what Charles was after. Blair glowered, Charles smirked.

'Listen, Charles, the only reason he carries the outboard motor is because I have to carry everything else – including the kitchen

'If anyone needs a bait-tin round here, it most certainly is not me . . .'

sink and the case of whisky he seems incapable of being without,' Blair snorted. 'And in any case, you monster, if you came with us to some of the hill lochs, instead of sulking in your steaming bed, you could help share the load – and get some of the weight off your idle frame.'

'What, with you map-reading!' snapped Charles. 'We would spend half the day trying to explain to you where north was, let alone find the loch.'

Blair, a precise and excellent map-reader, rose from his chair and grabbed his brother by the arm, neatly twisting it up behind his back:

'Apologise! Say you are sorry, now!'

'Blair!' said Ann. 'Stop it this minute. You're hurting him.' Not before time I thought, secretly. 'Now that is quite enough, all of you,' she said firmly. 'Stop fighting and get on resolving. To start with, you could all resolve to be a lot nicer to each other.'

'All year, nice to Lewis-Ann and Charles?' said Blair in disbelief.

'Considerate to Blair?' asked Lewis-Ann, as though she had been asked to swim the Atlantic.

'What's "considerate", Dad?' asked Charles.

'Be . . .' I stopped myself in time.

'Considerate means, well, like Blair taking a turn at rowing the boat for a change. That is being considerate, Charles.'

'That is a load of rubbish,' grunted Blair, starting on his tenth biscuit. 'I spend half my day rowing the boat as it is. In fact, if I didn't, we would never get anywhere. With him rowing all that happens is that we go round and round in ever-decreasing circles, and you know where that can end up . . .'

'Mummy, that's rude!' complained Lewis-Ann.

'It may be rude, but it's true.' Blair was adamant.

'I think you and Blair should take me out in the boat more often. I bet I could catch twice as many fish as either of you,' announced Charles, aggressively.

'The last time we took you out, Charles, you lay in the bottom of the boat complaining that you were freezing and wanted to go home,' I commented.

'It was snowing,' remarked Ann.

'That was after he had fankled his cast for the tenth time. Then mine,' complained Blair.

'And mine,' I added.

'Well, it wasn't my fault, and I didn't mean to drop the nylon in the loch. It was an accident. There was no need for Blair to lose his marbles.'

'It was my last spool. You had already destroyed the others,' said Blair.

The day had been a disaster, from start to finish: cold, wet, windy and fishless. In fact, although neither Blair nor I would admit it, we were delighted when Charles pleaded to be taken ashore. We were freezing to death.

'Anyway, Charles,' interjected Lewis-Ann, 'it wouldn't be too difficult to catch more fish than that pair. One would do.' Lewis-Ann never misses a chance, I thought.

'Jean, put the cat down. Cats don't like playing with dogs,' said Ann. Jean had been trying to organise a wrestling match between Horace, our large, haughty, grey cat and our boisterous ten-week-old golden retriever puppy.

'Really kind people don't have to make resolutions, do they?' said Lewis-Ann. 'They are considerate all the time, aren't they. So I don't think I need to make any, do I?'

Blair spluttered into his tea and I hid behind a newspaper. Charles was not so diplomatic.

'I've never noticed much of your consideration,' he grumbled.

'Well, of all the ungrateful little beasts! That's the last time I make up any casts for you.'

'The first time too, and it snapped the moment a fish grabbed,' muttered Charles.

'If she's not going to make any resolutions, I don't see why I should,' said Blair.

'Oh yes she will!' I threatened.

'Oh no she won't!' countered Lewis-Ann.

I tried logic. 'Lewis-Ann, are you seriously trying to suggest that you are kind and considerate all the time?'

'Yes.'

'But that is impossible. Nobody is perfect. We all make mistakes.'

'I don't.' I was becoming exasperated. 'God doesn't make mistakes,' Lewis-Ann smiled sweetly, sensing that she had me on the run.

'Don't start dragging the Lord into this argument. Just for once in your life, why can't you admit that you are wrong.'

'My science teacher says that God doesn't exist,' said Blair.

'What has that got to do with Lewis-Ann refusing to admit that she is fallible and human?' I asked desperately.

'I don't think that Lewis-Ann is human,' said Charles.

I turned to my wife. 'Ann, do something. Don't just sit there. Make them stop arguing and start resolving,' I pleaded.

'What's the use of trying to force people to make promises that they can't keep?' she answered, pouring herself some more tea.

'That's just great,' I exclaimed, hopelessly. 'I turn to you for help and support and what do I get? Stabbed in the back! Thanks a lot.'

'Yes, dear.'

'I blame you, you know. You let them all get away with blue murder.'

'Yes, dear.'

'And the telly. I should never have allowed it into the house. That is all they do, sit glued to the screen all day like dummies.'

'Yes, dear.'

'Or listening to their devil music.'

'Yes, dear.'

'And you can stop laughing, Blair, it's not funny, it's pathetic.'

'You mean like your casting technique, Dad?' he grinned wickedly.

'Right! That's it. I have had quite enough. I'm going to the study. Don't say you lot haven't been warned. Don't blame me . . .'

As I got up, the puppy made a playful lunge for my ankle and I felt its needle-sharp teeth sink in. I roared, hopping backwards on to the cat's tail. Horace screeched, shot straight up in the air and landed, claws slashing, upon Lewis-Ann's back. She screamed, dropped her tea-cup and clutched at me as I toppled over backwards.

As I fell, I was aware of Blair and Ann holding each other, shrieking with laughter, tears of mirth streaming down their faces. Jean was standing absolutely still, watching intently, a quiet, satisfied smile on her face.

As I lay on the floor, wondering where it was that I had gone wrong and what monstrous crime I had committed to deserve such punishment, a cheerful voice spoke directly into my left ear:

'Hi, Dad!' It was Charles. Completely oblivious to the pandemonium raging above him, he was lying full-length under the table, engrossed in a drawing.

I asked weakly, 'What are you doing, son? What's that you are drawing?'

'It's a street plan of Wick, Dad. I'm just working out the best places to build the barricades.' I closed my eyes in despair.

Charles is an attentive, studious-looking young man, with a dangerous sense of humour and a quick tongue. I have never won an argument with Charles, no matter what subject we happened to be discussing. Which is how I found myself, a few weeks later, in the garage, red-faced with embarrassment, wondering how Charles had got the better of me yet again.

At that time, Charles was much given to transporting his academic goods and chattels to and from school in a well-polished, leather brief-case. He never forgot it, and my wife and I smiled benignly as he set off, climbing the garden gate, the brief-case loudly proclaiming his serious intent.

I should explain that for several months the garden gate, the only entrance to Castle Sandison, was jammed tightly shut. Nor, this time, could I blame Charles. The new gate, purchased at great cost, simply swelled up after every night of rain. No matter how often our local joiner 'eased' it, the following morning the wretched thing was jammed solid. Every morning, we had to take ladders up and help the children over. Kindly neighbours soon got used to our plight and would help Ann manoeuvre the shopping up and over on Saturday mornings. After school, Jean would stand outside, shouting: 'Mummy, Mummy! Bring the ladders. I'm home.' One night, setting out for a formal dinner, Ann and I suffered the indignity of having to scale the gate, she clad in a full-length ball-gown, me in dinner-jacket and natty cummerbund.

Charles and his gang were delighted and spent hours charging at the gate, yelling their kung fu war-cries, trying to budge it, attacking it with saws and chisels. As far as they were concerned, it was the best thing that had happened for months. The noise was appalling.

In due course, several months in fact, the matter was resolved, and Ann and I would proudly watch our little boy marching off to do battle with the big, bold world of school. Our illusions were swiftly shattered one afternoon when I opened the briefcase.

I had been driven to this breach of privacy only after the direst provocation. My desk had been mysteriously cleared of pencils and all day long I had been struggling to scribe glowing words of deathless prose armed with a stub barely two inches in length. Every time I sharpened the point I endangered my ultimate emergence as the great undiscovered pianist of the twentieth century. I soldiered on, trying to write with the rapidly diminishing fragment but, by the time Charles arrived home from school, my patience had evaporated.

Nor was this a new system. Frequently, the light of historic verse gleaming in my eyes, I rush to my desk, or, as the rest of the family prefer to call it, 'our desk', only to find that it has been robbed of anything remotely resembling writing material: pens, pencils, felt-tips, all vanish. No matter how carefully I try to hide them, the result is always the same, and there are times when I am reduced to taking down urgent, important telephone messages with small bits of white chalk, scraped across my work-top.

The same fate overtakes the other tools of my trade: paper, envelopes, rubbers, rulers, not to mention reference books, cameras, films and fishing-gear. I am not suggesting for a moment that members of Clan Sandison maliciously misappropriate these items. Of course not. We all know that they get up off my desk by themselves and crawl away into obscurity with no help from any living soul. No one ever borrows them and fails to return them. I am sure of this because when I inquire, that's what I am told.

'Pencil? What pencil? I haven't touched it.'

'Your last black-and-white film? Isn't there? That's strange. Well, I haven't seen it.'

'Are you accusing me of pinching your writing-paper?'
'Yes!'

Now, I am a naturally trusting sort of person, but that day, after frantically searching through every likely hiding place, and quite a few highly unlikely ones – such as the microwave oven and under the carpet – my anger-maddened eyes lighted upon Charlie's brief-case and I fell upon it, tearing it open. But I should have known better. It was full of what can only be described as rubbish: old comics, crumpled up crisp bags, bits of paper, pencil shavings, crumbs, an apple-core, a broken watch, elastic bands, a shoe-horn, torn jotters and a five-pence piece.

Good grief, I thought, this is what Ann and I watch being ceremoniously carted off to school like the crown jewels each morning, and religiously humped home each evening: a heap of rubbish!

I cornered Charles in the kitchen where he was attacking a packet of crisps and a chocolate biscuit, washed down by warm, sweet tea. Charles likes tea. Adopting my most intimidating and superior tone of voice, I intoned:

'Now look here, son, your schoolbag is supposed to be for carrying school-books, not a portable rubbish bin.'

'It's a brief-case, Dad, not a schoolbag.' This had been a serious bone of contention when Charles started school. For some reason, best known to himself, Charlie had refused to wear a traditional schoolbag. He claimed that it was 'cissy' and refused to budge until an alternative had been produced. I now carried my papers in a plastic bag.

'All right, then, brief-case,' I conceded, 'but that makes no difference and it still does not mean that you should use it as a rubbish tip.'

'I use it for my school books. If you don't believe me, have a look for yourself.'

'I have looked and it is full of rubbish,' I argued.

'It may seem like rubbish to you, but it is not rubbish to me. I need every single thing in there.'

'Rubbish, Charles. Only an idiot would hump that lot around every day.'

'Listen, Dad,' Charles exclaimed wearily, as though trying to explain the obvious to an infantile imbecile, 'it's just like your fishing-bag. Now do you understand?'

'What has my fishing-bag got to do with you carrying a pile of rubbish to school every day? Stop changing the subject. We are talking about your school . . . brief-case, not my

181

fishing-bag. In any case, every item in my fishing bag is essential.
Do you think I would be so stupid as to carry unnecessary
weight over the hills?'

'All right, then, if you are so certain, let's go and see,' said
Charles smugly.

With a sinking feeling of impending doom I meekly followed
Charles out to the garage and watched him hunting among the
heap of fishing-tackle I had dumped there at the end of the
season. I had meant to tidy it up, honestly, but, well, you know,
I had been very busy and somehow just sort of forgot.

The fishing-bag was duly extracted from the pile and placed
intimidatingly on a bench. It was a very good fishing-bag – back
in 1963 when Ann had bought it for my birthday. Then it had
a proper wicker basket and a canvas hold-all, purchased from
Messrs Bagnall & Kirkwood, Newcastle, when they had their
shop at the foot of Westgate Hill, before moving to up-market
Grey Street. I was deeply attached to it, now mostly by binder-
twine. We had travelled all round Scotland together and even
as far afield as Finland. Yet, in the cold light of that bleak winter
afternoon, even I had to admit that the bag looked as they say,
done. The main section had rotted first, due to overexposure,
leaking Highland boats and black bitumastic. Then the pockets
had gone, until now all that remained was the covering flap, tied
to the lower buckle with binder twine. A few bits of wicker were
still seriously joined together, but I always had to cover the
bottom of the basket to stop things falling out. Clearly, the time
had come for a last farewell, a final parting with my old friend.

Under the hawk-like scrutiny of my smirking son, I carefully
undid the frayed flap and began to deposit the precious contents,
my treasured fishing-gear, on to the bench in front of him: half
a ham sandwich, still wrapped in cling-film; a dirty coffee-cup
and broken, leaking thermos flask; three trout reels, one of
which worked; six empty nylon spools; one semi-full nylon
spool; a bottle of Mucelin with a broken brush, *circa* 1969,
unused; anti-midge repellent, which didn't; mud-stained, smelly
over-trousers; rusty old pliers; rusty new pliers; a screwdriver
with a broken point; bone-handle all-purpose knife with no
blades; one empty fly-box which I can never open; one full fly-
box that never shuts; a tangle of old casts and flies; another fly-
box with eight featherless hooks; forty-seven loose, rusty flies
stuck to various bits of paper and a single right-hand glove; a
roll of unexposed ASA 400 black-and-white film; ten yards of
neatly wrapped binder-twine; one hundred yards of frayed

backing; a Hardy fly-wallet, purchased in George Street, Edinburgh, in 1955 and still empty; an extension butt for a trout-
rod which has never fitted ever since I fell into the South Tyne
with it in 1968; a crumbling, mouse-gnawed chocolate biscuit;
and my driving licence – I had been searching everywhere for
it for months.

'Well, what do you call that lot then, Dad? Essential equipment. Who wouldn't carry unnecessary weight over the hills?'
Charles was moving in for the kill. I stood speechless and
morose. 'Come on then, Dad,' he insisted, 'what do you call it
then?'

'Rubbish, Charles,' I whispered in shame.

'Pardon. I didn't quite hear that. Would you mind speaking
up?'

'Rubbish!' I yelled in fury.

'You can say that again. Now what about an apology for my
brief-case?'

That was too much, and I aimed a vicious swipe at my tormen-
tor's head, which he neatly side-stepped. My hand crashed into
the garage wall and I danced around hugging my throbbing
fingers whilst Charles made good his escape down the garden
path.

I stood surveying my wrack, wondering how Charles had,
once again, ruined me. I tried to contemplate life with a new
fishing-bag. Where did such things come from these days? How
much did they cost? I hadn't seen one I liked for, well, ages. A
day out in the hills wouldn't be the same without my old creel.

Slowly, light began to dawn. Carefully, I gathered together
the heap on the bench and packed everything carefully back into
the bag. Then, reverently tying down the stained flap, I retreated
to the drinks cupboard and poured myself a large, comforting
dram.

Safely ensconced before the fire, I smiled across at Ann, my
friend and fishing companion down the years.

'Had an accident, dear?' she inquired solicitously, indicating
my bruised hand.

Thinking of my fishing-bag, tucked happily beneath the heap
of waders, jackets and rods, I grinned back and replied, 'Not
really, Ann. Nearly, but it's all right now.'

You would imagine that the precise nature of fly-fishing would
indicate an equally precise attitude when it comes to accoutre-
ments. When you list the essential requirements for a day out

– rod, spare rod, reels, nylon, fly-boxes, basket, net and so on – it would seem sensible to ensure that they are easily accessible and regularly checked to ensure that nothing is left behind. If you have tramped four miles across a peat bog to get at the object of your desire and, upon arrival, find that you have forgotten your fly-box, then there is nothing much you can do about it other than curse. The wise angler, therefore, guards against this contingency by keeping his kit organised and in good order.

Blair is a meticulous man. All his work displays the attention to detail of a brilliant, well-organised mind. Or so he keeps telling me. However, I have lost count of the number of occasions when I have had to whisk large trout into the boat simply because he has forgotten to bring the landing-net.

'Oh, well done, Dad!' he will exclaim, as another 1lb trout comes flying onboard. 'Jolly good.'

'Blair,' I remark, with restraint, 'would you please be so kind as to pass me the priest?'

There follows a hurried scrabbling in the fishing-bag. He looks up: 'Didn't you bring it then?'

Nowadays, I do my own packing. It's safer. Struggling round a rock-strewn shore in two left waders is not my idea of fun, particularly when one is leaking; and another very good reason I have for caution is the ever-present danger of Charlie.

Teaching him to fish has been a costly nightmare. Rods seem to break as soon as he looks at them, spools of nylon always end up in a tangled heap, reels fall off the rod into the deepest part of the loch. A single moment's lost concentration generally means an hour paddling round the loch chasing the oar he *accidentally* allowed to slip overboard. A day in the boat with Charles – no, even a couple of hours – can knock up a bill for damages the size of which would make a whole barrack-room wince. In spite of everything he always seems to catch fish.

I am not a neatness nut but every year, at the end of the season, I promise myself that I will take better care of my tackle and Charlie's little exercise had reminded me of at least one useful New Year's Resolution I could make: instead of dumping everything in a heap at the end of the season, stow it away properly. My worst habit, I think – and anyone who has been stupid enough to borrow my fishing-jacket will confirm my opinion – is biting off flies at the end of a day's fishing and stuffing them into the first available pocket. By the end of the season my fly-boxes are empty and my pockets full. Pulling out a hankie can shower people for miles around with an astonishing assortment of killer patterns. Other than the dozen or so that stick into my fingers.

Charles is convinced that I only do it to annoy him. He is much given to grabbing the first available jacket in sight, prior to rushing out into the fields for a post-dinner walk: clambering round the quarry, climbing to the roof of neighbouring barns, hunting rabbits in the gorse bushes.

When New Year's Eve finally arrived, I watched Charles closely, ready for the first sign of evil intent, but he seemed to have forgotten about revolutions and, as far as I knew, Bridge Street was still clear of barricades. Ann was right. What's the point in trying to force people to do things against their will? Never worked with me, why should I expect it to work with Charles? Perhaps when he's older.

Pondering these weighty matters, and musing over the passage of time, I had suddenly realised that that New Year's Eve would mark my twenty-fifth year as an angler. I glanced anxiously at the clock: three hours to go. Should I announce this world-shattering fact to the assembled tribe, all eagerly awaiting midnight? After all, twenty-five years is a pretty large chunk of anyone's life. I could have expressed it as a percentage, but Charles had made off with my pocket calculator, and arithmetic, mental or otherwise, has never been my strong point. Nevertheless, it certainly represented millions of casts, several thousand missed fish, months of walking, wading and rowing, uncountable blood knots, thumb knots and turle knots, and endless days of endless hope. Perhaps, I thought, if I rushed to bed, it wouldn't seem quite so bad: in the morning, things rarely do. Cutting it a bit fine. I'll stay up and see it through.

'All right, dear?' asked Ann, looking up from her book and untangling a cat from her lap.

'Yes, thanks, just thinking,' I replied.

Outside, nothing could have been less like fishing weather. In the afternoon we had all packed into the car to visit our beloved desolate wastelands, the Flow Country of Caithness and East Sutherland. The wind was knife-like, force-eight and snow-filled, Loch More, a sheet of ice with the Thurso River rushing uncontrollably across the moor. Silhouetted in the late afternoon sunlight, Morven and the Scarabens looked supremely majestic, the 'D W's at their best: a solitary, hooded crow specked the incredible azure-pink sky; fine North Country sheep stared unblinkingly; a flight of mallard did a Marx Brothers' landing

185

on the frozen surface of the loch. Light was fading as we drove home, refreshed and happy.

Gathered round the fire, the family waited out the old year: Blair and Lewis-Ann played scrabble; Charles and Jean were bright-faced and expectant as though, at the stroke of midnight, a great secret would be revealed, that the world would never be the same again and that they would be awake to see it happen. Throughout the world, sober or not so sober, riotous or pensive, throats were tensing for a cheer: Parliamentarians planning new miracles of monetary juggling; industrialists wondering if anyone at all would bother coming back to work after the holidays; small traders worrying about diminishing margins. No doubt, in darkest Africa, dastardly coups were being planned, peanuts were doing a roaring trade in the good old US of A, and vodka glasses were clinking behind frost-encrusted Kremlin walls, heralding another year's increased ball-bearing production.

But I was thinking about fishing. Remembering . . . when Blair learned to cast, on Loch Boardhouse, in Orkney . . . Lewis-Ann, thrashing a Sutherland hill loch with an eight-foot greenheart rod whilst we tried to control our laughter – she caught the first fish . . . Charlie, eager and intent with stick and size 4 Hairy Mary, fishing in the sea . . . Jean, begging for a fishing-rod of her own . . . the day Ann and I almost drowned on Gladhouse Reservoir, near Edinburgh (should never have launched that boat, but she was insistent, in spite of being only three weeks from giving birth to Blair).

'Are you sure you're all right, Bruce?'

'Yes, fine. I told you, I was just thinking.'

'What about thinking of filling a few glasses, Dad?' announced Blair. 'It's almost midnight.'

Charlie brightened perceptibly. One minute left to go.

It's been a good *twenty-five years* and I regret nothing – not even losing that monster at Unthank on the South Tyne in May '69, or that huge trout on the Tweed on New Water, back in '55. All part and parcel of the joys of angling. I don't know, thank goodness, how many years fishing I have left, but, being older and, hopefully, wiser, I propose to enjoy their every second. Nor shall I have to worry about keeping up with trends. I am too set in my ways now ever to change. When the talk turns to the relative merits of WF5F long-belly floating forward-tapers as against DT7 floating and sinking, I shall ignore it all and continue with the same line that I have used for years. In my senior state, I will be able to climb trees for tangled casts without a single blush. What does it matter what people think? I should care. With the acceptance of my limitations will come the realisation that, more likely than not, I will probably continue to catch trout with the same old rod and the same old flies in the same old way. After the hard pull up the first twenty-five years, going back down will be like rowing with the wind perpetually behind me; and if I tend to go a bit too fast, then I can always chuck out a large drouge or two, to slow things down.

Well, there it is, midnight and welcome.

'Happy New Year!' everyone exclaimed in delight.

'Come on, Dad, out you go and then come in and first foot us,' pleaded Lewis-Ann, shoving a lump of coal into my hand. An old Scottish custom, bringing warmth to the hearth during the coming year.

Clutching the other old Scottish custom, a well-filled whisky glass, I allowed myself to be hustled into the cold night, velvet-black, pierced with a myriad stars. From the shores of the loch, wintering grey-lag geese chorused their welcome to the New Year. I knocked loudly on the front door, wondering if I should tell the family about having reached my quarter century as a fisherman. Seemed a good excuse for persuading them to lash out on the odd present and they were all in a good mood. I wouldn't mind it being late. Anything silver would do.

The Inner Man

AQUARIUS
21 JANUARY TO 19 FEBRUARY

There is a strong planetary focus on your mind, so you should use some of these lively influences to consider self-improvement; a week at the Arundel Arms Hotel, brushing up on your casting technique, or a salmon-fishing course at the Tweed Valley Hotel. This trend continues to give you a lot of support and your

189

involvement in these courses could boost your angling self-confidence and increase your catches. Practise beforehand, on the lawn, with your double-handed salmon-rod. Preferably at night, when the neighbours can't see. In order to avoid being frozen to death whilst improving your technique, make sure that you are properly dressed. At least six jumpers should be worn, along with the fifteen pairs of thermal drawers you received at Christmas.

Unsettling conditions will come to the fore during February when minor incidents could lead to an upset in your fishing plans. Be positive. Tell the family that you simply can't afford a continental holiday and carry on fishing.

Circumstances beyond your control will reshape your life and you and your family will have to adapt to these changes. At work you may be asked to transfer to a remote region, such as the Outer Hebrides, Sutherland or Caithness. Try to face up to these new challenges bravely and do not feel too depressed about having to leave an inner-city environment.

Relationships could become rather strained, but this may be avoided by careful planning and astute diplomacy. Do be prepared for violent opposition, however, when you announce the new plans to the family. Make sure that they fully understand that you are only obeying company instructions and that, much as you dislike the thought of living in the North of Scotland, you must go where your job takes you.

It is a time for strong, decisive action. Remind your children that they will soon make new friends and that they will look super in kilts. The promise of an increased weekly allowance should help to divert their suspicions.

You will not be able to rely upon your partner as much as you would like in these trying times, since the prospect of actually living in the desolate wastelands to which you drag her and the children, for their so-called holiday, may temporarily unhinge her mind. Don't worry, just carry on packing and encourage her to look on the bright side: the Woman's Rural Institute; Highland Games; county shows; church bazaars; unlimited haggis; bracing weather and quaint customs, such as drinking vast quantities of whisky, and the opportunity of learning Gaelic. She will soon come round, eventually, and start speaking again. Talk positively about shopping for new clothes and furniture, but upon no account mention the fact the North of Scotland has some of the finest fishing in the world. Should she raise the question, try to sound casually surprised.

As you will probably be feeling more unsettled of late, take extra care of your health during this period since your vitality is at a low ebb, due to three months without any fishing. Follow up recent introductions, since these could lead to useful fishing contacts.

COLD, CURRIED BEEF sandwiches are bad news in a packed lunch and should never happen to anyone, even in their wildest nightmares. But it happened to me one sharp, spring day, whilst fishing Loch Awe in Argyll. Now I always carefully investigate each picnic slice before the first bite, having learned the hard way that it pays to be cautious.

Ann and I, and the rest of the family, were staying with friends from Bridge of Weir, Tony and Isobel Sykes and their family, in a small hotel at the south end of the loch. Tony and I had met whilst in the army and, in due course, were 'best man' at each other's weddings.

During service for Queen and Country in the parched wastes of Southern Arabia, I had often talked to Sykes about the joys of angling, whiling away long, hot, sweat-drenched hours in the desert with tall tales of ones that got away and a few that didn't. I extolled the romantic virtues of fly-fishing and the delights of Scotland's rivers, lochs, mountains and glens, something which, I claimed, people from the Glasgow area, unlike those of us with the good fortune to have been born in Edinburgh, could never fully appreciate or understand – they were all inveterate 'townies', I suggested maliciously.

Sykes never failed to rise to the bait, defending West Coast people and their attitudes furiously:

'The best thing that ever came out of Edinburgh was the train to Glasgow. You lot wouldn't recognise a good joke if it hit you between the eyes. You're all so stuffy that you should be packed into glass cases and trundled off to Chambers Street museum. Edinburgh! The only city in the world where it is a capital offence to laugh in public.'

It helped pass the time and, when we returned to civilian life, I promised to teach him fly-fishing. Indeed, over the years he has become a skilful and keen angler, thanks to my patience, tact and not inconsiderable teaching abilities – a fact I remind him of constantly, particularly when he catches more fish than I do.

Our families are of similar age and the children all got on

191

well, as children seem to, in their own peculiar way. Blair and Paul, the eldest, fought furiously, Lewis-Ann and Emma giggled continuously and Charlie One and Charlie Two, both aged six, conducted their relationship with an air of armed neutrality.

In the evenings, once the children had been persuaded to go to their various rooms to carry on with their various ploys – out of sight at least, if not entirely out of mind – we adults played bridge, an all-consuming passion, or chatted with other guests until bedtime.

One of our fellow guests was Lew Gardner, then a well-known television presenter, much given to describing some of his younger colleagues as '£4,000-a-year baby Maoists'. Hearing Sykes and I arguing about who had taught whom what with regards to fly-fishing, Lew indicated that he would like to learn, and, since we were so obviously *experts*, would one of us teach him?

The Gardners had two children with them, both boisterous boys, and the following day I found myself on the shores of Loch Awe, with three eager pupils. Sykes, with typical consideration, had gone out by himself:

'Have a good morning, Bruce,' he called. 'See you at Portsonachan for lunch!'

After some rudimentary guidance from me, Lew entered the water and began lashing away. I retreated to a safe distance, calling words of advice and instruction. Like so much wasted breath. I was regaled with an endless stream of stories, gripping accounts of Biafra, Vietnam, what Moshe Dyan had said the last time they met, and so on, with hardly a pause for breath. My attention wandered, and I found a warm, sunny corner and was soon fast asleep.

I was rudely awakened an hour later by a cold, wet, tingling feeling on my face. Lew was standing over me, holding half a dozen nice half-pound trout:

'Come on Bruce, wake up. I've caught them all. Lunch-time. Did I ever tell you about the time I was ambushed . . . ?'

Give Lew his due, he was completely engrossed in his job and very good at it – as Humphrey Atkins MP, then the Northern Ireland Secretary, found out as soon as Lew spotted him in the bar one evening. I presume that Mr Atkins had been hoping for a few days respite from affairs of state. Within seconds, he was being heavily grilled by Gardner.

Our accommodation was comfortable, hot-water bottles were provided – and required – staff courteous and friendly, fellow guests pleasing companions. There were frequent, impromptu ceilidhs, generally involving fiddles, bag-pipes and piano accordions, and always very loud. In fact, everything one would expect in a remote Highland hotel. The picnic lunches were the only blot on an otherwise idyllic landscape.

My fishing partner had become a Loch Awe expert: at least, that's what he told me. So when Tony suggested a long boat journey north, to fish round Innis Stiuire Islands, who was I to complain? If he was prepared to motor six cold miles up the loch, then I, fondly, and as it later proved, erroneously, imagined there must be good fishing waiting.

We buffeted our way northwards, dipping and plunging into the waves, bailing the boat as we went, and eventually, frozen and battered, arrived at our destination. In the comparative shelter of the lee of the islands, we thrashed the water fruitlessly, without seeing so much as a snout showing above Awe's steel-grey surface. It started to rain. Heavily. So we decided to have lunch.

Tony, who casts a shadow almost as far as he casts a line, likes his food and brightened perceptibly at the prospect of sustenance, but after the first bite, a look of absolute horror appeared on his face.

'My God, this is last night's stew!' he exclaimed in disbelief.

With numb fingers, I unwrapped my sandwich and took a tentative munch:

'That may well be last night's stew, but *this* is even worse – it's last night's curry.'

We consigned our lunch to the bottom of the loch, where, no doubt, it pleased the fish far more mightily than it had pleased us. Freezing and hungry, we abandoned any further attempt to murder trout and decided to head homewards.

As is often the case in these situations, the moment we decided to go, the wind, which had been blowing strongly down the loch all morning, hearing Sykes start the outboard motor, immediately swung round and began blowing, gale-force, from the opposite direction. Before we had time to clear the shallows, the propeller of the outboard crashed into an unseen rock and the sheer-pin snapped. I grabbed the oars, shouting at Tony as I struggled to keep the boat off the rocks.

'You idiot! What have you done! Quick, replace the sheer-pin!'

'I can't find one!' Tony replied, hopelessly. No spare sheer-pin.

'Why didn't you check before we set out?' I yelled, 'I'm afloat with a lunatic.'

We took it in turns to row back into the wind, and, whether rowing, or sitting huddled in the stern, clutching the sides to avoid being catapulted into the loch, ice-cold spray lashed our faces. It started to snow. We inched our way slowly south through the blizzard, keeping close to the shore in case of accidents.

Several hours later, exhausted, soaked to the skin and starving, we reached the old wooden landing-stage in the comparative calm of the Lodon where, in days gone by, the steamers that played the loch had berthed. We returned the boat to its proper place, conscientiously bailing it out, yet again, and checking the mooring-ropes as we did so, to make sure that the vessel was secure.

We stepped unsteadily ashore and, dragging the useless outboard motor and fuel tank with us, staggered to the car where we turned the heater on full blast. Half an hour later, moderately thawed but with murder in our hearts, we drove back to the hotel. Our kilted host appeared at the door to greet us:

'Had a good day, boys? Any luck?'

He was only saved from certain death by the arrival of our wives and children:

'Gracious, you pair look cold. What on earth possessed you to go out on a day like this anyway? Only fools would go fishing in this weather. We had a super time at Crinan. There is an absolutely marvellous hotel with a blazing open fire. You really should have come. What a couple of idiots.'

I noticed the young ladies sniggering as I brushed snow from my hair. Blair and Paul looked smug, no doubt pleased with their earlier decision not to accept our invitation to go fishing. The Charlies were delighted at hearing their respective fathers being called idiots, confirming their own long-held, deeply rooted opinion of our real worth. I glanced at Tony and, without a word, we made for the bar.

The packed lunches were so bad in this hotel that we resorted to sneaking into the village shop, like ungrateful criminals, to buy an alternative; and, although I am sure that the hotelier must have heard of what we were doing, day after day, with seemingly malignant delight, the remains of the previous evening's meal were served up, cold, as our picnic. With typical British reticence, though, we did not complain – even when, at the end of our stay, the bill included the item: 'Loch Lunches,

We consigned our lunch to the bottom of the loch

£10'. We smiled weakly and paid up. But we have never been back.

That holiday also cost me a new fishing-line. The morning I had taken the Gardners fishing, Tony had asked to borrow a line for a friend of his who had appeared, Robin Whiteford, and I had given him a double-tapered line of mine, until then unused and still in its original box. Later in the week, fishing with the new line, I couldn't understand why my flies were landing with an almighty splash every time I cast, no matter how delicately I tried to place them. Watching me carefully, Sykes, who had insisted in putting up the rods and tying on the casts that morning, larded out gratuitous advice with malicious delight; but eventually he came clean and confessed. Apparently, Robin had got my line hopelessly entangled in the propeller of the outboard motor, and, in order to avoid wasting good fishing time, had simply cut off the tapered end. My leader was attached to the thickest part of the line which is why it hit the water like an ocean liner's hawser.

However, I had my revenge, which I enjoyed to the full. Soon afterwards, the three of us were sharing a boat on Loch Coille Bharr, a Forestry Commission water a few miles from Loch Awe. On the first drift, I was fishing the stern, Sykes at the bow, with Robin on the oars. As we passed a small inlet, a super trout rose. I cast over him and, after a great struggle, I managed to land the fish – to my companions' grudging congratulations. The next time we drifted past the inlet, with Robin fishing carefully from the stern and me in the bow, I rose and caught another fish. Robin caught nothing. And for the rest of the morning, fishing from either bow or stern, every time we passed the point I hooked a fish. By lunch-time, tempers were frayed. Not helped by my sarcastic comments about the general inefficiency of West Coast, pseudo fly-fishermen. Years later Whiteford still owes me a new line.

Memories of appalling loch lunches are all too vivid. Most hoteliers, in my opinion, seem to imagine that the average angler is so engrossed in his fishing that he never notices what is shoved between the inevitable slices of curled white bread – as welcome to the angler as is a 4oz perch on Loch Leven, and just about as exciting. The principle seems to be 'out of sight, out of mind'. If he catches anything, he will be too pleased to complain; if he catches nothing, he will be too embarrassed. So, in with the old apples, dry sandwiches, mouse-trap cheese and, if you are lucky, a single chocolate biscuit. Bring your own flask for the weak tea and tepid, powder-packet soup.

A few years ago, Ann and I were staying at a well-known fishing hotel, and we had walked out into the hills to a small group of lochs. The weather was appalling, but we worked hard and, after a long, hard climb up to the highest loch on our route, we stopped for lunch.

Crouched in the shelter of a huge sandstone boulder, dripping, cold and hungry, we were looking forward to reviving our flagging spirits and warming our insides. We should have been so lucky: two slices of wafer-thin crispbread, a small packet of processed cheese, an ancient, shrivelled orange, and the inevitable Penguin. One thermos flask was empty, the other contained only tepid water. We made it back, but only just, our consolation prize being the three beautiful trout that went with us – caught, as usual, by my fishing partner.

As we staggered into the hotel, feeling as though we had succeeded where Captain Scott had failed, we were greeted by the manager.

'Oh, you're back, are you?' This seemed to me to be an unnecessary statement of the obvious, given that we were standing there in front of him, dripping all over the floor of his fish room. 'I'm afraid you have missed dinner. We stop serving at nine and the chef has gone off duty.'

'But we are freezing and starving!' I begged. 'And it's only nine o'clock now.'

'I might be able to get you a sandwich?'

Choosing a fishing hotel from a brochure, without first-hand knowledge, is about as dangerous as walking over the Niagara Falls on a tight-rope. For many anglers, their two-week annual holiday is the only chance they really have to enjoy their sport but it is all too often marred by the lack of a little forethought and consideration on the part of their hotelier hosts. How often do we arrive at our selected destination to be greeted with the dreaded words:

'You should have been here last week. The river was full of fish. They've all moved upstream now. You're wasting your time,' quickly followed by a voice from the bar, declaiming: 'Och, you don't want to pay any attention to the likes o' him. He disnae ken a kelt frae a flounder. There's plenty o' fish in the river.'

It is only after you have plied this supposed paragon with several large drams that he announces: 'Aye, but you'll no catch them. The water's far too high.'

It never fails to amaze me how many hoteliers, who depend upon anglers for their livelihood, seem to show so little regard for the comfort and convenience of their guests. All too often, the glowing prose of their brochures fails miserably to live up to the reality of the service they offer. With unfailing regularity throughout Scotland, this bleak pattern repeats itself: the blank stares when you ask about fishing; the reluctance or inability to provide meaningful information; the insistence upon rigidly fixed meal-times; the same old miserable packed lunches.

Some of the best picnic lunches I have ever had were not in Scotland but in Kenya, when I fished the Rupengazi River. Being stationed in Aden, Kenya was the most convenient place for holidays and most of my colleagues travelled there for their precious two weeks annual leave; either on the beach at Mombasa, or in the game parks. Me, I went fishing.

My friend Sykes spent his time in Kenya on safari with his parents, who had flown out from the UK to join him. He enjoyed his holiday enormously, but I very much doubt if he will ever forget what happened to him when he returned.

Our Commanding Officer, known affectionately to his junior officers as 'Mad Mike Farmer', persuaded me to meet Tony at the airport, and place him under close arrest for undisclosed, serious crimes.

'But, sir, you know Sykes, he'll never fall for that,' I complained.

'Do it, Bruce. Stop arguing. Handcuff him and bring him along to the office. We'll have a mock trial. Don't worry, it will be great fun.'

I arrived at the airport, pristine in a fresh uniform, complete with highly polished Sam Browne, accompanied by a fellow officer, John Guthrie, who was distinctly uneasy about the whole affair. Suspecting that John might blow the scheme, I left him in the land-rover with Banyard, my driver, who was looking forward with unconcealed delight to Sykes's discomfort.

Tony strode towards me, hand out-stretched in greeting, smiling and relaxed. I kept him in conversation, encouraging him to recount tales of his enthralling encounters with elephants, lions and wild rhino, until the airport had cleared of passengers.

'Come on, Bruce, let's get moving, the bar's open,' exclaimed the unsuspecting Sykes.

Desperately trying to keep a straight face, I said: 'Look, Tony, I have some very bad news for you. I don't know what you have done, but I have been ordered to place you under close arrest the moment you arrive back.'

Sykes' face turned bright scarlet: 'You're joking!' he spluttered.

. I took the handcuffs from my pocket and held them out:

'Tony, I like this no more than you do. Please, be a good chap and don't make my job any harder. I haven't a clue what is going on. Only you know the real reason. Hold out your wrists.' I clamped the cuffs shut and covered Tony's manacled hands with his coat: 'The OC is waiting for you. Apparently you are to be charged.'

Tony shuffled along at my side, for once speechless, and I helped him into the land-rover. But when we arrived at camp, neither Mike Farmer, nor the OC were there, as promised.

'You had better sit down and wait,' I said, uncuffing one of Tony's wrists and attaching the steel band to his escort, John Guthrie. 'John,' I ordered, giving him the keys, 'if he tries to make a run for it, stop him. You're responsible for the prisoner.'

I dashed to the Mess and dragged Mike and Chris from the bar: 'For goodness sake, get a move on. If I know Sykes, he will have persuaded Guthrie to let him go in two seconds flat.'

As we entered the office, Guthrie and Sykes scrambled to refasten the cuffs. I had been right. Sykes was on the point of beating a hasty retreat.

Mike sat down, capped and solemn. Chris stood behind him. Guthrie and Sykes rose to their feet.

'46697, 2nd Lt. A. W. H. Sykes, is that your correct name, rank and number?' demanded Mike, slowly looking up from the fake charge sheet.

There was a long pause, and then, as though from the soles of his boots, Sykes croaked: 'Yes.'

'You are charged under the Queen's Regulations, with conduct prejudicial to the preservation of good order and military discipline, in that you did, whilst on holiday in Kenya, scurrilously and erroneously defame your Commanding Officer, to-wit, me, by failing to leave him the drink you promised when he signed your leave of absence papers. Have you anything to say?'

Sykes' whole body relaxed, tension flowing away.

'You rats!' he exploded in relief.

The sentence was that he should stay in the bar until otherwise ordered and consume anything that was placed before him. If my memory serves me right, during the course of that evening he did, to the tune of at least three bottles of champagne. For starters. But I still wonder why Sykes fell for it. What had he done, or thought that he had done, to have allowed himself to be handcuffed so meekly? Thirty years later, I still don't know the answer, and I probably never will.

My Kenyan safari was devoid of big game. The nearest I came to seeing wildlife in the raw was a fleeting glimpse of a large hare-like creature in the driving mirror, early one morning on the way to the river. I had planned my holiday with meticulous, military thoroughness, carefully searching through the accommodation lists until my eye stopped at an hotel called the Brown Trout. I booked, instantly.

The Rupengazi rises in the foothills of Mount Kenya and joins the mighty Tana River near the small town of Embu. The air is clear and sharp, the breeze an almost feminine hand on the brow, soothing away months of Arabia's searing, merciless blaze. The setting of the hotel was perfect, surrounded by green lawns,

trees covered in purple blossom, superb cooking, fresh vege-
tables, wonderful coffee, attentive hosts, and, from the garden,
a magnificent view of majestic, snow-capped Mount Kenya.

The river was narrow, fast flowing and deep. Throughout
much of its length, the banks were guarded by wild, prickly
thickets, enclosing long, swift runs and sweet pools where excellent trout lurked – circumspect fish, some of which grow to great
size. Hard to tempt. Local anglers have developed a technique to
cope with the undergrowth, fishing with a large hook, possibly
size 8, but heavily weighted round the shank. The momentum
gained is used to cast the fly, sideways, far upstream, between
the overhanging branches. As the fly is carried downstream it
sinks and the angler furiously hand-lines in the slack. As the fly
passes, the slack is let out. Thus, from one, often precarious
stance, a large area of water may be covered. It is an effective
fishing method which avoids a lot of tree climbing in pursuit of
snagged casts.

Inevitably, a small boy appears the moment you start fishing.
No matter when or where you arrive at the river, he is there,
ready and waiting. You have a gillie, whether you like it or not.
I chose not to adopt the local method, and fished in the traditional style, with traditional flies, and the small boy was a god-
send. He scaled trees quick as a flash, dived under to retrieve
snagged flies, untangled fankles in seconds, and was always
bright, cheerful and great company – which is volumes more
than I could truthfully say about some of the bad-tempered,
unwilling gillies I have had to work with back home in Scotland.

My most unnerving experience concerned a slightly larger
human: six feet eight inches tall, ebony black and unsmiling.
One moment I was alone, the next he was there, lean as a rake,
features gaunt, clad in loosely-fitting khaki denims, seeming to
have appeared out of thin air. On his head was a red, black-
tasselled fez: hanging from his bony wrist, a razor-sharp machete. He was swinging it to and fro, eyeing me suspiciously:

'Permit, Bwana?' he asked.

Keeping a watchful eye on the machete, I scrabbled furiously,
searching desperately for my permit, which, thank goodness, I
knew I had somewhere. I handed him the scrap of paper. He
took it and read intently. The document was upside down. I
stayed silent. After a few moments of intense concentration, he
marked the permit with the stub of a pencil and handed it back.
I turned sideways, in order to present the smallest possible

target. Fumbling, I replaced the permit, and when I looked up again he had gone.

My visit to Kenya took place in 1959, not long after the Mau-Mau uprising, and I vividly remembered that savage, sad fight; but during my stay I received nothing but courtesy from local people. The only time I was attacked was not by humans, but by hungry ants.

Because it is so hot waders are not worn, the norm being sand-shoes and bare legs. I was standing in long grass one morning, wondering how I was going to place my size 16 Greenwell over a large trout, when I felt my leg being bitten in about a dozen places. I yelped in fright and looked down. My leg was covered with ants, each nearly half an inch in length. I was in the middle of a small army that had just decided I was lunch. I jumped clear and began beating them off. Grinning from ear to ear, my gillie helped. Later, I was told that the natives use them as a surgeon uses sutures. The ants are allowed to bite the edges of a wound together and then their body is cut off, leaving the head and jaws firmly in place until the wound heals.

Lunch helped soothe my shattered nerves and, as always, it was magnificent, everything any angler could ever hope for: paw-paw slices, from a fruit similar in shape and size to a melon, except that the flesh is bright red, mouth-watering and refreshing, followed by lamb chops, salad, fresh strawberries and scalding Kenyan coffee. Neither the unprovoked ant attack, nor the machete-swinging river warden spoiled my Kenya holiday, and the memory of those days and the hard-fighting brown trout of the Rupengazi remains startlingly clear. Indeed, if anyone has a ticket for Nairobi going begging, I'd be back there, quick as a flash. However, the first thing that I would do upon arrival is get a permit. You never know when you might need it – fast.

I suppose that as far as picnics are concerned, it very much depends upon your attitude towards food. You may be the sort of angler who considers a break for lunch as only so much fishing time wasted; me, I like my food and have a healthy respect for the needs of the inner Bruce. Just because one is out in the hills or in the middle of a loch is no reason for lowering standards and it is perfectly easy to make lunch at least as interesting and exciting as the fishing.

Happily, my wife Ann applies the same care and attention to the preparation of lunch as she does to casting a neat fly, on a

201

short line, over the nose of a rising trout. She always succeeds, splendidly, in both. Lunch is something, fishless or otherwise, that I look forward to with great pleasure.

For a number of years we lived close to the River Tweed and, if non-fishing friends visited us, particularly those from south of Mr Hadrian's Wall, Ann would prepare a special picnic and we would take them to a favourite spot on the banks of the river to introduce them to the delights of nature, and to the pleasures of fly-fishing.

The site was in the midst of a proper wood, with beech, sycamore and majestic oak nodding gently over clear waters. To get there, you take the back road from Innerleithen and past Traquair House and Bonnie Prince Charlie's Bear Gates – closed when the Young Pretender left Traquair in 1745 and never opened since – but the way into the wood is very hard to find and it seems as though one is driving into a solid wall of haw-thorn before the track becomes obvious.

No matter when we visited our 'secret garden' it was always magical: April ushered in wood anemones; May and June were scattered with shy primroses, blushing from sunny corners; July and August carpeted the wood with nodding bluebells, the air heady with the sweet smell of the river; autumn shed burnished leaves around our feet as mighty salmon surged upstream; winter sparkled rhyme-crystal, sending moonlight slanting spear-silver across the eternal river. If you can lull guests into a false sense of security by treating them to dream-like lunches, before they know what has hit them, or they pluck up enough courage to complain, you can have them halfway up Foinaven, lugging most of the fishing-tackle whilst you amble along behind making *interesting* comments about the beauty of nature.

The trick is that first lunch, and Ann and I discovered that melon, game soup, cold chicken and Greek salad, strawberries and cream, washed down with large quantities of river-chilled Riesling, invariably did the trick.

Music helped too. Who could resist the charm of Elgar's *Cello Concerto*, played by the banks of a mighty river, with autumn leaves fluttering down in three/four time, or the sensuous warmth of Delius's *Song of Summer* on a hot, bare-chested July afternoon, loud with the hum of insects, lark and meadow pipit?

After lunch I would take them to the river, trance-like and content, place a rod in their hands and begin the indoctrination course. They followed my instructions without complaint, relaxed and happy – and invariably, without too much difficulty, they would catch trout:

'You know, Bruce, I really think I could get to like this. I had no idea that fly-fishing was so easy.'

When Ann and I were younger, not so very long ago, as we keep reminding ourselves, providing outdoor music was not as simple as it is today when the selection of a ninety-minute cassette does the trick. Then, thirty years back, we had to rely upon a battery-operated gramophone and traditional records. Fortunately, I had built up a large collection whilst in the army. Aden was a free port and records were very cheap. Much of my spare cash was spent upstairs in Bickashee Dinshaws, The Crescent, where, over a period of eighteen months, I bought some two hundred records, including all the Beethoven piano sonatas, symphonies, and string quartets. Sadly, now, many of these are museum pieces and the rest either worn out or badly scratched. Investigative little hands played havoc with our records over the years, but we smiled bravely and bore it: after all, we were introducing the children to good music, so it was a small price to pay.

As impecunious newly-weds, when it came to fitting out our lives, we quickly established our priorities, including spending far too much on a super little French, portable machine called, if I remember correctly, a 'Teppaz'. It gave excellent sound reproduction, worked off six torch batteries and provided us with some of the most memorable musical experiences of our lives: resting on a high crag, looking out over Bishopdale, listening to the strains of the *Introduction and Allegro for String Orchestra*; the haunting caress of Debussy preludes, echoing round the crags of a hidden cove.

Before we were married, we used to fish Portmore Loch, south from Edinburgh and always took friends there for a picnic, including Tony Sykes and his future wife, Bella. Portmore was very dour, with fish few and far between, but a good bottle of wine and huge, French-style sandwiches encouraged one mightily.

At that time, our source of all things excellent in food and wine was, and still is, an Edinburgh institution: Valvona & Crolla, in Elm Row. As a boy, on my way home from school, I used to stop and peer into the window, gazing at the Aladdin's cave of herbs, spices, cheese, hams, basket-bottled wines and bread in all shapes and sizes. The shop was always busy, bustling with customers loudly talking Italian. Even then, I knew it was a special place. In the early 1960s 15/6d (about 75p, in so-called new money), could buy a very acceptable bottle of wine and then, as now, nothing was ever too much trouble for the staff, regardless of the amount of money involved. Customers were treated with the utmost courtesy and consideration. To visit Edinburgh and not pay a call on Valvona & Crolla would be a serious mistake. Go there, even if it is only to look. You will be enchanted.

Producing an interesting packed lunch is a matter of pre-planning. Which is why Ann does it. I make grunting sounds when asked for advice, but have long since learned that the most useful contribution I can make is to keep well out of the way. I attend to other, just as important matters: the construction and transportation of drinks – which I am very good at.

One of my finest hours occurred a few years ago when we had taken two friends out for a day's trout fishing, their first ever. The loch we had chosen involved a stiff walk over the moors, and our northern moorlands are bog-filled, soggy and very wet. A hard, lung-expanding tramp. When we eventually arrived at the water's edge, our embryonic anglers were tired, hot and weary, and no doubt regretting that they had ever agreed to come fishing in the first place. The look on their faces made it quite clear that they thought Ann and I were quite mad.

As we settled, perspiring, on a grassy bank, a graceful black-throated diver, calling magically, swept by and landed in front of us. Curlew whistled down the hill; a large trout leapt spectacularly, like a silver sword rising from the loch. I delved into my fishing-bag and, like some rustic conjurer, produced their favourite tipples: one large Campari and soda, with ice and lemon, and a similarly adorned G and T. Good humour was restored, instantly.

After a splendid morning's sport we adjourned for lunch: avocado pears with lumpfish-roe, turtle soup, chicken legs, lamb cutlets, salad, cheese, celery and biscuits. The wines on offer were Batard-Montrachet and Côtes du Rhones, followed by piping-hot coffee, during which we listened to Dvořák's *Sonatina Op 100*, then Beethoven's last string quartet. Our fishing efforts produced twelve trout: the guests caught five, Ann seven, including a fish of over 2lb, and I caught the rest. It was an unforgettable day, thoroughly enjoyed by all, and the moorland miles back to the car slipped by almost unnoticed. In such ways are anglers born.

We do not eat like that every time we go fishing, couldn't

afford it, but we do try to avoid the standard recipe for afternoon indigestion beloved by many so-called fishing hotels: curled-edged, Spam-crammed sandwiches, chocolate biscuits and an apple. There are few sights more soul-destroying, after a fishless morning, lashing away in a rain-storm.

When our son Blair got married and finally flew the family nest, taking with him large quantities of my fishing-tackle or, as he preferred to call it, *our* fishing-tackle, I confess to wondering what his wife, Barbara, would produce for fishing picnics. Barbara was new to fishing but, under Blair's expert tuition, was progressing rapidly. Within an amazingly short space of time, she was handling rowing-boats like an expert, being capable of holding an excellent drift, regardless of the strength of the storm, whilst her husband fished. Would Barbara be just as expert when it came to the matter of lunch?

I need not have worried. On our first outing as Blair and Barbara's guests, to Loch Stilligarry on South Uist, lunch was absolutely outstanding. Neither too complicated nor too grand. Just right. The perfect end to a perfect morning during which I had caught the only trout. Blair, I am glad to say, also follows in his father's footsteps and always has one of the best-filled hip-flasks on the river. His selection of wine, when appropriate, is immaculate – even more so when it could be judged inappropriate, such as halfway up a mountainside.

With daughter Lewis-Ann, there was never any doubt. She was thoroughly brain-washed by her mother. A fishing lunch with Lewis-Ann is invariably an occasion to be remembered, particularly if her long-suffering husband, Mike, has made the terrible mistake of catching more fish than her. And our youngest daughter, Jean, now a student at a local catering college, shows all the signs of keeping up the female Sandison family tradition: bring them down to size by always catching more fish, then give them a lunch to remember. Keeps men in their proper place – well-fed, but subservient and fishless.

It doesn't require a quantum culinary leap to provide a decent lunch, nor is it very costly, yet few of our fishing establishments ever seem to get even to first base. Perhaps we anglers should be more ready to complain. After all, it is our health and well-being that are being put at risk, and we are paying the bill. Over the years it has given us just as much pleasure seeing our guests enjoying a good lunch, as it has given us seeing them catch their first trout. Producing that first fish can be difficult. Producing a decent lunch should be easy.

However, some of the most memorable meals that Ann and I have enjoyed out in the hills have been prepared from the simplest and most readily obtainable ingredients. What can compare with the delights of freshly caught trout, cooked in the embers of a lochside fire? Especially when the trout have been caught by yours truly.

Horsehair and History

PISCES
20 FEBRUARY TO 20 MARCH

Home life enters a peaceful phase. Some of your fledglings grow up and leave the nest. Late-night vigils become a thing of the past. Midnight telephone calls from errant daughters seeking transport home end. You can hear yourself speak, and gain reasonable access to the bathroom at most times. The house is tidy.

You are now free to leave your fishing-tackle in the open, rather than locked in the cupboard under the stairs. Stop counting the flies in your box and be confident that your prized 'killer' patterns will always be there when you want them. Unlock the drinks cabinet and stop marking bottle-levels with pencil lines. It never worked anyway.

It is a good year for making improvements and, with lower household expenses, you can afford it. With your new-found sense of security, turn the garage back into a fishing 'den' to which you can escape in times of stress: rod racks, wader hooks, storage cupboards, boot drier, comfortable armchair, log fire, bookcase for fishing volumes, back-numbers of angling magazines – and secret drinks store.

The emphasis this year will be very much upon outdoor activities. A four-wheeled drive vehicle will take much of the strain out of reaching the remote hill lochs you have always intended to fish: buy it now – also, the self-catering cottage in Sutherland and two time-share rods on the Tay in mid-September. After bringing up a family you deserve it and you will be surprised at how much more money you now have.

However, demands on your time and energy are likely to increase this year from domestic, non-angling sources, and, since you will want to respond to these suggestions, you may be tempted to take risks. Because there are fewer mouths to feed, shopping trips could get out of hand. Re-cover existing furniture, rather than buying new pieces; worn carpets can be revitalised by vigorous scrubbing and carefully placed mats. Take time to plan.

Concentrate available finances on fishing affairs and try to bring about a better understanding with those who are close to you. There is a grey area around the date of your wedding anniversary, when you should avoid money risks. Buy her a new fish cookbook and a bottle of wine and let her cook you a special anniversary dinner. Exciting romantic developments are indicated if you follow this course of action and this is the time to give your wife the money to purchase that expensive, carbon-fibre rod. She will be filled with delight at the pleasure you get when she presents it to you for your birthday.

And make a particular point of entertaining friends and acquaintances lavishly at expensive restaurants – providing that they have access to good fishing. Apart from that, during the rest of the year you can rely upon happier and more settled conditions, which should allow you far more time to fish.

FOR BRIEF moments I almost believe spring has come. The sun shines warmly, casting encouraging shadows across the room. Horace, our large, grey-haired cat, winks an approving eye and settles in the most inviting patch. Birds twitter at the window. Buds get ready to burst. But just as I decide to drag out the sandpaper and sharpen last season's rusty hooks, it starts to snow again. As though a blind has been drawn, the sky darkens and my hand fumbles for the poker to stir up the fire. Horace glowers and stalks off haughtily, as only a cat can, convinced that I am responsible for the change in the weather.

A few fool-hardy souls have been out salmon fishing, fingers crossed, but more as an act of defiance than as a serious attempt to catch fish: most of our trout lochs are still blue with cold, ice-fringed and frozen, winter's debris scattering their shores.

In the mornings we construct ourselves, rather than dress: vest, shirt, jumper, second jumper, scarf, coat and hat, pants, long stockings, thermal long-johns, socks, thick trousers, shoes. Any fool can be cold; but it takes ages to get ready in the morning and just as long at night to dismantle oneself, prior to leaping into bed. However, I suppose spring must come, eventually, up here in the far north. Trouble is that in Caithness we seem to have to wait a bit longer than most for that first, weak blink. Consequently, to me, March and April are the longest, darkest months of the year – and even May can leave you white and gasping in a sudden snow storm.

Ann and I were once caught out on Watten, towards the end of May, having been tempted afloat by unseasonably warm weather. Flies were hatching, the surface calm, and everything pointed towards a good basket. An hour later a merciless wind roared in from Sutherland, sending waves scudding down the loch, bringing huge flakes of snow in its wake. Within moments we were white from head to toe, gasping with cold and shivering. My fingers were so numb that it was agony starting the outboard engine.

'Quick, Ann, reel in! Let's get the blazes out of this before we die of exposure!'

'Wait a moment, Bruce, I'll just land this fish.' Ann always seems to catch fish, regardless of weather conditions. Where is there justice in fishing?

On another occasion, during an Easter break on Orkney, Ann did the same again, this time from the banks of Loch Swannay. A white blanket covered the moors, the temperature was minus something-or-other, and just getting there had involved plough-ing through several deep snow-drifts. When we arrived at the loch no one was breaking their necks to get into action.

'If anybody thinks they are getting me out into that storm, they must be daft,' announced Lewis-Ann firmly.

In the driving mirror I could see Blair, Charles and Jean nodding agreement, but Ann, made of much sterner fishing stuff, and as though to put us all to shame, grabbed her rod and strode off down the east bank. It had started to snow again, heavily, and within moments she was lost from view.

We waited for her to hurry back. And waited. And waited. Eventually, after about half an hour, Jean yelled: 'Look, there she is, see!'

We glimpsed a shadowy figure, fighting its way towards us through the blizzard, head bent against the storm, red hat bob-bing in the breeze. She looked like the front of a Christmas card. All it needed was a robin on her head to complete the picture. I got out of the car and took Ann's rod:

'Quick, dear, you must be frozen, get in the car.'

'Just put these trout in the boot for me, would you, dear. A little something for our supper.' She had caught two splendid fish, weighing in the order of 1lb 8oz each.

However, it pays to be cautious with Highland weather and one should never take chances, even on hot days. Sometimes things ain't what they seem to be. Ann and I were fishing at Scourie one spring and had climbed high into the hills to fish a remote loch – probably unfished for decades and, given the climb involved, unlikely to be fished again for several decades more.

The day was very warm, and we arrived at the loch covered in sweat from the long climb.

'Come on, Ann, let's have a quick swim,' I suggested.

As I stood on the bank, ready to plunge in, the sun warming my back, Ann tiptoed tentatively to the edge and dipped a foot into the water.

'Are you sure about this, Bruce?' she asked.

'Don't be silly, it'll be wonderful,' I scoffed.

'Try it.'

I did, and instantly realised that if I had plunged straight in, it could very well have been my last plunge ever. The water temperature was barely above freezing. Far better to be safe rather than sorry. After all, the trout won't run away, will they?

But each year, as the troutless months advance and the sense of anticipation mounts, I wonder: will the fish really still be there, waiting for my carefully presented flies? And I have to confess that it is not until that first trout is safely in my bag that I relax; it is surprising how often the first fish of the season is caught, each year, from the same place.

When I started fishing, the trout season on the River Tweed opened on 15 March. Regardless of the weather, Father and I were always there, the previous few days having been spent in careful preparation for this momentous event; as far as I was concerned, the most important day of the year.

Invariably, my first trout was taken from New Water, above Innerleithen, on a small Greenwell's Glory – with two bootfuls of water, collected whilst wading the river to fish from the south bank. We used to park the car just outside the town where the railway-line is pinched by both road and river, then stumble down the slope, crossing the track to the river bank. It was the quickest way but, unfortunately, not the best bank for casting. Consequently, I used to enter the river by the notice-board and wade across. In normal conditions, it was just possible to reach the other side dry. More often than not I ended up damp. Never seemed to feel the cold in those days.

That stretch of the Tweed was a trout fisherman's paradise then, back in the early 1950s. Some evenings the whole surface of the river, as far as the eye could see, would be alive with the dimple and splash of rising trout. I have had wonderful sport there, wading carefully down the long, slow pool, casting beneath the branches of the sentinel hazel trees that guarded the north bank.

I used to know every stone, bush, branch and twig along the river, intimately, from the railway crossing at Red Yetts Cottage, down to Innerleithen Bridge: where the best fish lay; when they were most likely to rise; what they were most likely to take; where you could cross the river safely; where you had to get wet. I always crossed, somehow, regardless – wet or dry.

The Tweed holds some of my dearest memories: days and nights fishing with Father; hearing the wild, devil-may-care screech of lapwing or the sudden plop! of a water-rat slipping into the river; the thin line of pines guarding the crest of Wallace's Hill; the kindness and encouragement of Mr Fraser, the Aberdonian river watcher.

Father loved the Tweed and fished it for years, generally unsuccessfully.

'I don't know what I have to do to catch fish, son. How do

211

you manage it? Are you sure you gave me the right flies?' he would complain. I always made up Father's casts.

'Keep trying, Dad, you'll get there some day.'

In fact, *getting* there was never one of Father's problems. The magic sound of the word 'fishing' brought a lightness to his step and a sparkle to his eye that had to be seen to be believed. Bodily and mental ailments disappeared in a flash and his fingers would twitch, anxious to be off. And once he had a fishing-rod in his hand, World War III would have passed unnoticed. He was never happier than when up to his waist in water. Freezing temperatures, horizontal sleet, driving snow or a force-eight gale meant nothing to him. Whether or not he actually caught anything neither deterred nor distracted him. Just being there seemed to be sufficient: as if there were only one fish left in the whole world and he had to catch it – before someone else did; as if each expedition, each cast, were to be his last.

Father's greatest problem was that he insisted upon fishing in the same place for far too long. If he had seen a fish rise, he would remain, rooted to the spot, casting endlessly in the hope that the fish would eventually take pity on him and grab. They rarely did, and no matter how hard I tried to persuade him to move on, he refused to listen:

'I'll just have another few casts here, Bruce,' he would call. 'You never can tell, and I know he's there.' At night, with first bats flicking by, I would wander back. Sure enough, there would be Dad, still lashing away where I had left him. Ever hopeful.

'Any luck, Dad?'

'Well, he rose again, but my cast was fankled at the time. Are you sure that you put on the right flies?'

I think Father missed me once I joined the army, but he soon persuaded Mother to accompany him on his fishing expeditions, and never seemed to mind too much when she caught more fish than he did. Something we men just have to learn to live with, I suppose.

Blair and I were there for Father's last expedition, on Loch Watten, shortly before the end. On a warm summer afternoon we carried him to the boat and set off to catch trout.

Father got tired very quickly in those days and soon gave up his rod and sat glowering in the middle, complaining loudly about the lack of fish:

'Are you sure you gave me the right flies, Bruce?' he asked.

In due course, as these things happen, Blair hooked a good

trout which set off towards the horizon, pulling yards of line out as it went. Blair handed his grandfather the rod.

'Here you are, Grandad,' he exclaimed, 'let's show Father how a real angler plays a fish!'

Father eventually brought the fish to the side of the boat and Blair netted it. Removing the hook he handed his grandad the trout:

'Well done, Grandad!' Blair exclaimed proudly. 'Played like an expert.'

When Father finally shuffled off to the great trout loch in the sky, he left his trout-rod, a lovely Alexander Martin, cane-built wand, to Charles, who has used it to good effect ever since. The rod was still in pristine condition, having hardly ever been bent in anger from one season to the next.

When we lived in Northumberland, at Hardriding near Bardon Mill, and fished the South Tyne, the first trout of the season always came on 23 April, across from the notice-board on the Willimotswyke side, to a March Brown and weighing about 10oz.

Our house was in a perfect setting, overlooking the South Tyne Valley, backed by wild Northumberland moorlands and crested by the Roman wall. There were wonderful walks: along the wall to Whin Sheils Crag, or Housesteads Fort; by the banks of the river, near Featherstone Castle; or simply sitting in the garden, surrounded by the sweet scent of honeysuckle, listening to the magic of Delius, or Vaughan Williams's *Sea Symphony*. Rods were kept up and ready on a rack in the garage – at first Ann's and mine, and then, as the children grew older, more: Blair's, Lewis-Ann's and, finally, a spare one, waiting for Charles. Jean was still some years off, but no doubt already twinkling, waiting to burst on an unsuspecting world and unsuspecting parents.

Blair often came to the river with me and generally managed to catch a few. He rapidly developed into a really skilful angler, tying up his own casts with no trouble at all, but I wondered if he was only trying to please me, rather than himself.

I need not have worried. One afternoon, when he arrived home from school, I saw him dump his books and wander out to the garage.

'Just going down for a few casts, Mum,' he called to Ann.

I watched proudly as the little figure disappeared down the hill, then saw him crossing the field to the river. The wind was perfect that day and he would have no trouble casting from the north bank. Two hours later, Blair returned and replaced his rod.

'Any luck, son?' I inquired, nonchalantly.

'Saw a few, Dad, but nothing took. I'll get them next time though.'

Lewis-Ann would come fishing, under duress, and seemed to enjoy it; but at that stage, she was far more interested in other pursuits, creating havoc all round the area with her arch-friend, Sarah. The pair of them, along with our farmer neighbour's children, were a force to be reckoned with and were never out of trouble.

Charles didn't start fishing until we came to Caithness but he has always been an incredibly lucky angler – although he claims that it is *skill*. I have never been surprised by his success though. Things always seem to happen when Charlie's around. He was born lucky – in Haltwhistle Hospital, on 23 April 1968. I went along to meet him and to congratulate Ann, and found my second son lying snugly in his mother's arms, grinning up at me. Somewhere deep inside of me I felt a strange, uneasy feeling. This child was different. On the way home a vast, bright flash lit up the sky. It was so stunning that I stopped the car to watch the phenomenon. The light travelled from north to south at great speed, then disappeared over the horizon. Charles has always been lucky.

The stretch of the Tyne we fished was club water, controlled by the Haltwhistle and District Angling Association, but it was sufficiently far from both Bardon Mill downstream, and Haltwhistle upstream to be almost like having ones own private beat. We lived at Hardriding for a period of six years and during that time I never once met another angler on the river. Not so many anglers then, I suppose, but I never complained. Too busy fishing.

The advantage of living so close to the river was that you could choose your fishing time to suit the best conditions: a falling spate; a suddenly warm, spring evening; or when the fishing urge became too strong to deny. A ten-minute walk satisfied all your needs.

Since we came to Caithness, first fish are caught on Loch Watten on a Ke-He – at about 9.30p.m. in mid-May, just off the entrance to Lynegar Bay. There is an old fence-post leading into the loch, and the fish lie fifty yards out from this. Magnificent trout, as silver as sea-trout and every bit as hard fighters.

This is one of my favourite spots on the loch and, when all else fails, at the end of the day I persuade Blair to row past while I fish 'the turning flee', a peculiarly Scottish method, guaranteed to succeed every time. Well, almost every time. The boat is rowed slowly along and the angler, sitting in the stern, casts out a longish line at right angles to the forward motion. The line is left lying on the water and the speed of the boat *turns* the flies. As the the line bellies out and the flies turn, the fish grab, generally hooking themselves. The rest, as we anglers say, is history.

It was whilst on Loch Watten that Blair and I developed our 'Theory of Thoughtless Fishing', a method absolutely guaranteed to catch fish. We were out one day when conditions were perfect: a south-west breeze gently ruffled the surface; a cloudless sky, not too bright after recent rain. With mounting hope we launched the boat and tied up our casts. Every fly had caught fish before: Ke-He, Black Pennel, Silver Butcher, Woodcock & Hare-lug, Invicta and Soldier Palmer. Fish were rising and obviously this was going to be a day to remember.

With consummate skill, Blair and I applied ourselves to our task. Lines shot out straight as arrows, flies settled gossamer-like on the waves and were worked expertly across the surface. Boat handling was of the highest order, each succeeding drift perfectly positioned. We fished the shallows, the deep, the island, the weeds, Shearer's Pool, Sandy Point, Lynegar Bay, Factors Bay, down the middle, round the sides, everywhere – but without so much as touching a trout. I fished on with the same flies, being too lazy and too dejected to change. Blair broke records changing casts, going through every pattern, in his box and mine. We resorted to well-tried clichés. What would be the point if you caught fish every time you went out? What fun would that be? Catching fish isn't all that important anyway; simply being out there, communing with nature, is sufficient, enjoying the beauty of the countryside. Try telling the cat that. Or the wife. When the cat's wrapping itself round your leg and the wife is sharpening the kitchen knife it still adds up to the same. The miaowing dies away to a reproachful croak and the expression on your wife's face turns from one of expectation to cynical tolerance.

Blair and I sat speechless. About the only thing we had not thrown at the fish were the remains of an egg and tomato sandwich. Like the Ancient Mariner, we drifted over the loch, flies trailing behind the boat, exhausted. We exchanged disconsolate looks and Blair grabbed the oars. Without a word, he began the long haul home.

It was somewhere between the island and the fence-post that it happened. My flies were trailing behind the boat and I thought that I saw the silver flash of a trout dash at them. Suddenly it came to me, 'The Theory of Thoughtless Fishing', the answer to our problem.

Have you ever asked yourself when most of the fish you catch *take*? The answer is simple. It's when you are looking the other way, when you are not concentrating. Nine times out of ten, in my experience, trout rise when you are watching a black-throated diver, lighting a cigarette, pouring a dram, changing a cast or, more often than not, when you are fankled. This indisputable fact is the corner-stone of my theory.

Blair must have sensed my excitement, but completely misjudged the cause:

'Come on, Dad, it's not as bad as that. No need to jump overboard yet.'

'Watch this, Blair,' I announced confidently. I yawned and, left-handed, flicked the flies out. They fell on the water in an undisciplined heap. 'What's on telly tonight, Blair?' I asked.

Almost instantly there was an almighty splash as a trout grabbed my tail fly. I dived for the rod and, three minutes later, had a splendid 1lb fish safely in the net. I removed the hook and half-cast again.

'You know,' I continued casually, 'I really think that we should make a start on digging over the garden when we get home. What do you think, Blair?'

Another fish grabbed, and was quickly landed and despatched.

'That was lucky, Dad,' exclaimed Blair.

'Luck be damned!' I replied. With breathless excitement, I explained my theory to Blair. A look of utter disbelief grew on his face, quickly followed by hysterical laughter.

'You expect me to believe that!' he roared. 'I knew it had to happen some day. You've finally gone off your trolley, Dad!'

As we were speaking, Blair had cast a long line out to starboard and had ignored it completely whilst wading into me. When the fish took he got such a fright that he toppled over backwards into the bow, his reel screaming in protest. He struggled upright and turned to face the action, his face aglow with pleasure.

'Perhaps you have something after all, Dad!' he cried joyfully.

For the rest of the afternoon we experimented: dipping the point of the rod under the water and leaving the flies to look after themselves; considering the play of sunlight on the water or the beauty of nature. We discussed politics, religion, literature, art, music and sport; the only interruption to our discourse was when we were otherwise engaged, landing trout.

In fact, the largest wild brown trout that I have ever caught, weighing 4lb 8oz, grabbed when my rod was lying across the boat, flies dangling inches from the side, whilst I unfankled my fishing partner's cast. And some of the largest fish that I have ever hooked have come to my flies when I was looking the other way – certainly on enough occasions to substantiate my theory. Try it. I guarantee that you will not be disappointed.

I know that there are anglers cleverer and more skilful than myself. Nearest and dearest remind me of this fact frequently, referring to my casting technique as 'Father's affliction'. Even with the irrefutable evidence of my skill lying before them they tend to talk scathingly about 'luck' and the stupidity of fish. However, given my 'Theory of Thoughtless Fishing', I think that it's the fish that are the cleverest and most skilful. I have heard biologists argue that if they possess a brain, then it must be rudimentary – the fish's brain, that is, not the biologist's – but I'm not so sure.

One evening I was fishing the Red Yetts on the Tweed, a few miles south from Peebles. The warm June twilight epitomised all the best conditions the Tweed could offer: water temperature, air temperature, height of the river, wind force and direction, hatching flies; and gentle, fading sunlight at the end of a warm day. I was fishing down towards a deepish pool which I knew held good trout, and the cast was horsehair, acquired at great personal risk from an unsuspecting Clydesdale, but, in spite of my best efforts, I caught nothing. Not even an offer.

A local had been watching, no doubt impressed by my cunning and artistry. Or so I thought. He gave me a cheery wave and marched straight into the river, false-casting as he went. Water flew in all directions as he tramped to the middle of the river and I heard the crash as his flies landed close to the far bank. As though by royal command, a fish rose and grabbed his tail fly. It was so big that he waded ashore, beaching the trout. I am not certain about the weight but, from where I stood, goggle-eyed and glowering, it seemed to be at least 3lb.

He waded back in and, from almost exactly the same spot,

217

hooked and landed another of about the same size. Basketing his catch he shouted goodbye:

'Tight lines, son!'

I often wonder if the fish I failed to catch that night were the clever ones? Were the two the local angler caught simply overgrown idiots? Does *artistry* really matter? Or is there, per-haps, down there under the water, some Aztec-like society that requires regular sacrifices to an omnipotent 'air-god'?

Years later, after a bad day on the loch when Blair had caught all the fish, I told this story to the gathered clan to regain some self-respect, not forgetting to mention the horsehair casts and asking aggressively: 'Tell me, Blair, did you catch the fish, or did the fish catch you?'

'What are you trying to say, Dad, that it was just luck?'

'Anything he catches is just luck,' commented Charles.

Blair gave me a grin:

'Look, Dad. You worry about the theory of fishing. I'll just keep catching them. Excuse me whilst I weigh *my* catch.'

Charles had been listening intently.

'Did you really fish with horsehair, Dad?' he inquired.

'The only hair he knows anything about is the one that leaps from his dog and bites him – the morning after the night before,' announced Blair, carefully examining the scales. 'Five fish, 7lb 9oz. How's that for skill, Father?'

But I had fished with horsehair on the Tweed, and discovered that it makes an excellent, practically invisible cast. Getting the horse to stand still long enough is a problem but, once one has a goodly bunch, it supplies enough material for several casts. At the cost of a carrot. Much cheaper than nylon. All you do is separate the strands out into single lengths and match them up. You will find some are thicker than others and it is possible to make up a perfectly tapered cast of about seven feet long. Several, careful blood knots are required, but the end product is well worth the effort involved and ideal for dry fly-fishing.

The first time I made one, being suspicious, I tested it out on mother's sweet-pea trellis. Attaching the fly to the wires, I reeled out some ten yards of line and then struck as though I was hooking a trout. The horsehair snapped. I tried again, but this time, instead of striking, I applied gentle pressure. The cast held. I simulated a fish charging off by running about the garden. So long as I did nothing rash or jerky, the horsehair held, even under considerable force, and I put a lot of strain on it – until mother appeared with a worried frown, muttering about what the neighbours would say.

On my next fishing expedition to the Tweed, I mounted a size 16 Greenwell and went into action. It was one of my finest hours; a supreme moment, the moment when I finally realised that I could really fish. At least for the time being.

The river was in spate, almost bank-high, and Father grumbled around, complaining that we were wasting our time. He stood chatting to a local and I instinctively knew that they were discussing whether or not they could get away with worming. As I tied up my cast, they broke into laughter:

'You're mad, son, you'll never catch a thing with that.'

Ignoring their sarcastic comments I crept to the river. As delicately as possible, I fished down stream, letting the fly drop just on the edge of the current so that it swam round into the slack water by the bank, covering enticing lies beneath overhanging branches.

The first trout rose and grabbed within a few moments. A fish of some 10oz. I played him carefully, my heart in my mouth least the cast should break. I played the second fish with greater confidence, and ended the afternoon with a basket of six nice trout; all taken on the Greenwell, in a brown spate, using a horsehair cast.

'Well, damn me!' said Father, 'I never would have believed it.' Neither he nor his companion had caught a single thing.

'Charles,' said Lewis-Ann, 'don't believe a word of it. He's just making it up.'

Stung to the quick, I responded instantly to the challenge: 'If I had some horsehair now, I'd soon show you who is making it up; and it wouldn't be you, my little precious. You couldn't tie a blood knot to save your life.'

'Here you are, Dad,' said a voice by my side.

Charles was standing, glasses awry, clutching a large clump of horsehair.

'My God, you haven't been attacking Flora's horses, have you?'

Our neighbour, Flora Gunn, was horse daft, and kept several, very expensive, highly groomed animals in the field next to our house.

'Just a little, Dad, and Flora will never know,' replied Charles.

Under the circumstances, I decided to let the matter rest. We trooped through to the kitchen, complete with horsehair, and I set to work; but I had forgotten just how fragile the material is, or perhaps my patience and eyesight had suffered in the intervening years. No sooner did I attempt to tighten my blood knots than they broke.

Then I remembered, and moistened the hairs before tying the knots. Within minutes, I presented them with a pristine, horsehair cast, complete with single fly.

'That's all very well,' said Blair, 'but will it work?'

With complete confidence, I hooked the fly to the end of the fire tongs and, with an even motion, tightened. The cast held.

'There you are! What have you to say now, you bunch of doubting Thomases?'

This was greeted with a satisfactory silence. For once they were speechless.

But I noticed Charles edging surreptitiously towards the door.

'Don't you dare!' I barked. 'If you so much as lay a finger on those beasts I'll flay you alive.'

'Ah, Dad, come on, be a sport?'

'No, Charles. And I really mean it!'

We seem to have spent most of our married life surrounded by animals, of all kinds, shapes and sizes, both inside the house and out, dead and alive. There have always been dogs and cats; generally two dogs, always at least three cats.

The present tally is one golden retriever, mine and called Breac; one Yorkshire terrier, not really a proper dog, but much loved by Ann; and three cats – Serendipity, often referred to as Horace, Milkwood, a crippled, one-eyed Siamese, and Boadicea, a kitten that appeared at the window one wet winter's night and quickly realised that he/she had discovered suckerville. Apart from them, there is Percy, the noisiest budgie north of Inverness, Ridley, a somnambulist hamster, and, until very recently, a geriatric, seven- or eight-year-old hen named Hicket.

There used to be two hens, given as a present to Ann by her darling daughter, Lewis-Ann. These hens ruled the roost for years. We called them Hinge and Bracket, after two of Ann's favourite comedians, and they strutted round Ruther keeping all the other animals in check, firmly at the top of the pecking order. Of eggs, we saw none. They either ate them or hid them.

Eventually one of the birds died, but we were not sure whether it was Hinge or Bracket who had gone to the chicken-run above, so as a compromise, in order not to hurt her feelings, the remaining hen was rechristened 'Hicket'.

Hicket seemed to be indestructible and lived absolutely free,

220

generally taking care of herself. An independent lady. Caithness foxes and wildcat must be a feeble bunch because, winter or summer, Hicket soldiered on, impervious to danger.

Earlier this year Hicket took to coming into the kitchen, greatly encouraged by Ann:

'Look, Bruce, it is Mothering Sunday. Surely I can do as I please for just one day of the year?'

'But Ann, look at the mess she's making,' I protested. Hicket was perched on the back of a chair in front of the fire, luxuriating in the warmth and making grateful low-pitched squawking sounds.

'She can't have long to live. Don't be so mean. Let me give her a little pleasure. Think of all the pleasure she has given us.'

'That's not what you say when she digs up the garden,' I grunted, capitulating, and settling down resignedly to read the Sunday papers. With Hicket.

When we were on holiday earlier this year, a friend looked after the menagerie and, on our return, Hicket was nowhere to be seen. I heard Ann and the Good Samaritan talking in low voices and, eventually, Ann came over and announced in sombre tones with tear-filled eyes.

'Bruce, Hicket has passed away. Isn't it sad.'

Sad be damned, I thought. One less mouth to feed.

When Lewis-Ann telephoned her mother that evening, Ann explained about our 'loss'. I listened to their conversation intently.

'That's very kind, dear, yes, that would be lovely. Thank you.'

I grabbed the phone.

'Don't you dare!' I roared. 'The first hen that I see within a mile of Ruther will be casseroled quicker than you can say Rhode Island Red. I'm warning you!'

I quickly passed the phone back to Ann. Long experience has taught me that discretion is always the better part of valour when it comes to an argument with Lewis-Ann. I never win.

Lewis-Ann was the first to rebel when it came to planning holidays. Daughters are always difficult. She simply announced that if we thought that she was going to spend yet another year of her precious life standing in the pouring rain in the middle of some desolate trout loch then we were living on another planet.

'That's only because you never catch any fish,' said Blair, not helping one bit.

'Mind your own business. I catch far more than you do and I don't have to resort to worms to do so.'

'That's a lie!' roared Blair. 'I've never fished with worms in my life.'

'Shut up, Blair, leave this to me,' I snapped.

Blair lapsed into sulky, hostile silence.

'Now listen, Lewis-Ann, you know that you always say the same thing, every year, but you enjoy it once you're there.'

'That's only because there is nothing else for it! What do you expect me to do? Bleat like a baby all day?'

'Tell me something I don't know,' said Blair.

'Please, Blair, give me a chance,' I pleaded. Then I lost my temper. 'Lewis-Ann, that's quite enough, you're coming and there will be no further argument.'

'No I won't,' screamed Lewis-Ann.

'How do you know that you won't enjoy it until you've been, darling?' interceded my reasonable wife.

'Because I'm not going, that's why. Why can't we be like normal people . . .'

'You wouldn't recognise normality if it was staring you in the face.'

'Blair, for the last time, be quiet. Do you want to start a war?'

'. . . and all my friends at school always go away to the sun. Think how I feel when I have to tell them that I went fishing? They just laugh at me.'

Lewis-Ann was in full flood and there was no stopping her. I looked for support from Ann and found none. Perhaps they were in league together? Perhaps the whole scene had been carefully planned in advance?

Blair and I spent the rest of the evening as miserable as sin, watching them poring over holiday brochures describing awful, troutless places. Where had these brochures suddenly appeared from? All part of the plot?

The following August found Ann and me stretched out on a deserted beach in south-west France, enjoying the feel of the hot sun beating down on our bodies; and I would be the first to admit that it was very nice indeed: reading, sleeping, swimming, drinking vast quantities of wine, eating super, crisp French bread and huge tomatoes. Happy days. Meanwhile, Lewis-Ann, with the logic only known to young ladies, complained from start to finish about the heat. She sat, hugely ill-humoured and fully attired under the shade of a large, multi-coloured umbrella

222

and refused to come out. Even nights on the town were regarded with disfavour; there was nothing to do, nowhere to go.

Then, halfway through our holiday, Lewis-Ann dropped her bomb-shell. From the hidden depths of her umbrella we heard her mutter: 'This is a complete waste of time. I might just as well have gone fishing. It would have been much more fun than roasting on this awful beach.'

Give me strength, I prayed.

Our youngest daughter, Jean, has benefited mightily from being the last of the brood. There were always strong shoulders ready to carry her over the worst parts of our fishing journeys into the hills, where she sat in splendour, surveying the view and giving urgent directions:

'Come on, Blair, hurry up!' she would shout. 'The fish will all be in their beds by the time we arrive unless you get a move on.'

Jean is now a young lady of sixteen and still loves fishing. On our first outing this season, to Loch Stemster, an easy thirty-minute drive from home, even the terrible weather did nothing to dampen her enthusiasm. We arrived at the lochside in a whirling, snow-white blizzard, with a cold east wind sweeping the surface into neatly combed, steel-grey ridges.

Almost before the car had stopped, Ann and Jean had disappeared into the storm, and moments later their shouts indicated that they were catching fish. I was still putting my rod up. We spent four hours fishing amidst a mixture of sunshine and showers, and ended the day with six trout: Ann caught four, Jean two, and me the rest.

Only Jean remains at home now. The others have long since left, hopefully to start their own fishing clubs. As it should be. But our greatest pleasure is having them all together for holidays. Then, as in days gone by, we head for the hills in a convoy now mustering a total of nine: Ann and me, Blair and Barbara, Lewis-Ann and Mike, Charles and his as yet unsuspecting fiancée, Eilidh, and Jean. Would there be, in future years, other members in the party?

Waiting for the first one is hard. Heart-stopping, sweet expectation mingled with doubt. But when he finally did arrive, he was worth waiting for – a beauty, weighing 8lb 8oz, perfectly formed, pink-fleshed and fighting fit: Brodie Telford MacGregor Sandison. Our first grandson. A wonderful gift and another angler born.

So now there will be ten, with Brodie perched on Blair's

strong shoulders as he strides across the moors. Brodie will hear the call of curlew whistling down the wind, the shrill piping of greenshank echoing round the hills; feel the cool, Highland breeze brushing his cheeks; hear the sound of loch water lapping the shore; notice the urgent splash of rising fish. And wonder.

For more accessible locations, Blair informs me that he has already formulated his plan of campaign. He has constructed an all-weather, four-wheel pram, complete with panniers for his fishing-tackle, rod clips and ring for landing-net.

'What about the other essentials?' I inquired.

'Optics on the hood, Dad. Easy to get at. One hand casting, one hand filling the glass that cheers,' came the quick reply. Blair has always been a highly organised man.

The happy days Ann and I spent teaching our own brood to fish have not ended. They are just about to begin, all over again. There is life after fifty, particularly for fishermen. Being fifty-three is even nicer. Say hello to Brodie's sister, Fearn Elizabeth Sandison. No doubt, like her grandmother and aunts, Fearn will keep the female flag flying. And, in due course, out-fish us all!

Keeping the female flag flying